Great Unsolved Mysteries of North America

Lionel Martinez

CHARTWELL
BOOKS, INC.

To Barbara,
who watched the clutter in my office build to knee-deep levels.
Many thanks for your patience and gentle chiding.

Photo Credits: *New York Historical Society, Library of Congress,*
Bettman Archive, Grumman Corporation, Trevor Wood,
North Carolina Division of Travel and Tourism, UFO Research Society,
Buff Research Library, Hastings Photo Collection

All Rights Reserved.
Manufactured in Hong Kong.
Printed by Leefung-Asco Printers Ltd.
Origination by Regent Publishing Services Ltd.
Design and Editorial Director: Tony Meisel

ISBN: 1-55521-302-2

Contents

American Nessies: Creatures of the Lakes   5

The Bermuda Triangle and Other Mysterious Places   13

Shoe Size 13+... The Search for Bigfoot   43

Mysteries in Color   49

Some Open Files on Murder   75

UFO's in Color   113

Going, Going, Gone   129

Profitable Mysteries   139

The UFO Debate   173

Index   191

American Nessies: Creatures of the Lakes

Lake creatures or, as some call them, "monsters," usually bring to mind the currently elusive inhabitant of Loch Ness, Scotland... Nessie. Hre is an animal not known for giving interviews, and only on rare occasions does it allow itself to be photographed. Even when pictures are taken it is usually under less than optimal conditions. With all of Nessie's reticence to be in the public eye, this Scottish lake dweller has received more than a fair share of worldwide press attention. In North America Nessie's cousins remain either unknown or the subject for ridicule. But the North American branch of the family may be very real and related by common ancestors across the millennia.

Before we examine the evidence for the lake creatures, let us examine the history of the lakes themselves. In almost every case where these animals have been reported in the northern hemisphere, the lakes were formed by the last great ice age. Nessie's current address is a remnant of the dynamic action of the last great ice age.

The last glacial ice sheet retreated from its most southward advance about 10,000 years ago. It had weighed heavily on the land for at least 5,000 years previously. On the North American continent it reached a height of 5,000 feet and on the European continent it was in places 10,000 feet tall. Ice is a funny form of water. We tend to think of it as being solid because it is hard. Actually since it is frozen water is still rather plastic much like super slow honey. In great ice sheets there is still a lot of movement even if the progress is slow. This glacial activity coupled with its colossal weight carved the fjords of Norway, the sea lochs of Scotland and many of the lakes of Canada and the United States.

While the glacial ice sheets dominated the land the, oceans of the world were at their lowest levels; almost a third of the earth's water was "locked up" in the form of ice. After the melting of the ice sheets the sea levels rose about 200 feet and the land began to rebound. For a period of 5,000 years the land and seas rose together and for a period 2,000 years the land continued to rise alone. This slow rising of land and water filled many lakes with water and, at much the same time, dammed many of these lakes which had had easy access to the sea. Later this access to the sea was made more difficult if not blocked altogether. Some of this blockage was due to the erosion and silting of the recently sculptured earth and some to the land rising by itself. Imagine what might life forms might have found themselves trapped in these newly formed habitats.

SETTING THE STAGE: SOME MINOR LAKE AND RIVER SIGHTINGS

Nestled in the sand hill country of Nebraska lies Alkalie Lake, twenty miles South due South of Hay Springs. Indian legend told of a creature which inhabited the lake and that this monster would venture forth hunting for food when the shore was swathed in a thick fog. The first white settlers heard the stories with interest but since they did not experience this beast themselves, they chalked it up as a myth. Soon it became part of the folklore of the area. There it remained, almost forgotten until the summer of 1923.

On July 24, 1923 the Omaha *World-Herald* broke the story of J.A. Johnson and his encounter with the fabled lake creature the night before. The story was picked up and carried by other newspapers, including the New York *Times,* the next day.

Mr. Johnson and two of his friends had come to the lake to camp and hunt. It was early in the morning when the three men were walking along the shore watching for a duck flight. They had quietly stepped around a tiny hill when they saw, twenty yards away, the creature of legend almost out of the water. "The animal was probably 40 feet long, including tail and head, when (it) raised in alarm when he saw us. In general appearance, the animal was not unlike an alligator, except that the head was stubbier, and there seemed to be a horn between the eyes and nostrils." The startled trio watched as this heavily built grey-brown monster slipped back into the lake leaving an unpleasant odor that lingered for several minutes.

They were stunned; all that they could do for the next few moments is peer across the lake in silence. Suddenly there erupted a great splashing about 100 yards from shore.

The creature broke the surface of the lake, floated for a minute, lashed the water with its tail and disappeared.

By 1939 sightings of the lake creature had ceased. In that same year scholars and writers from the Federal Writers Project discovered Alkalie Lake. In that time of social realism and searching for American roots, whatever thing it was that dwelled in the lake became part of the great American folklore; which is to say that the writers had a field day with the creature. The lake monster grew to 300 feet and at the same time so did its appetite; for these researchers claimed the beast swallowed a small island in the lake. If this were not enough, a fanfare of thundering earth was added to the creature's every appearance. Sighting of this animal would result in hair turning white or, even worse, permanent madness. Those rational collectors of folklore gave the monster a name....*Giganticus Brutervious*! With this ignoble act they consigned the Alkalie Lake creature to the realm of ridicule.

Indian legends are often based on something either real or perceived to be real, Lake Manitou in northern Indiana is a good example. Before the white man settled the area the Potawatomi Indians believed that the lake was inhabited by a huge monster. Their belief so governed everyday life that fishing, bathing or canoeing was the province of the very few and the very brave. Fearing for the safety of the tribe they never camped beside that lake. It has been claimed that the original Potawatomi name was roughly translated to mean Lake of the Devil's Bones.

When the white man encountered the natives of the Indiana Territory it was usually not on the best of terms. The first Europeans were unlicensed French fur trappers and therefore not eager to upset the Indians; least the authorities discover their secret and lucrative activities. Soon legitimate trappers followed and their claims to trap and hunt were backed by the armies of England and France. After the French and Indian wars the Indians found themselves in conflict with the victorious English, and soon after the Revolutionary War, with the victorious and expansionist Americans. For eighty years the Native Americans sought to keep their lands and their traditions. It was a losing battle, ending with the various tribes in the Indiana Territory leaving their ancestral hunting grounds.

In 1835, John Brown Dillon, the editor of the Logansville *Telegraph*, ran a series of stories on the Lake Manitou monster. The real purpose of those articles was to preserve the folklore of the Potawatomi Indians. To most of the frontier readers these news items were seen as either a hoax or a good source for humor. As the Indians drifted westward their legends faded into history; only their most outrageous tales lingered in places like overgrown cemeteries to remind anyone of their passing.

It would be nice to find a conclusion to these sightings and in a way there is one. In 1968 Stump Pond was partially drained and all the fish cleared out. The biggest "critters" found in the lake were several 30 pound bass. Yet, when questioned again, all the eyewitnesses still stuck to their stories about the creatures in the pond. Needless to say, there has been no more unusual pond activity since then. Were there any creatures in the pond? If there were creatues at one time, where did they go? And why did the sightings last for 90 years? If you are ever in southern Illinois, stop by Stump Pond and talk to the local people. You may find a clue that has been missed all these years.

SOME MAJOR SIGHTINGS: THE LARGER THEY ARE, THE HARDER THEY ARE TO FIND

In Canada, something has been slipping into Lake Utopia, New Brunswick every summer. Lake Utopia is located in the southeastern tip of New Brunswick, it has easy access to the Bay of Fundy, which opens on to the Atlantic Ocean. Early settlers in the region sighted strange churnings in the lake. Many of the reports of that time are sketchy, but there is a drawing in the New Brunswick Museum that shows two men in a boat being chased by the lake monster. Contemporary reports of odd tracks in the mud also existed. They were not the expected paw print tracks but rather a thick slimy trail, much like an odd mud slick. Several times claw marks were observed in the trail. The tracks always went toward the lake in the spring and toward the Bay of Fundy in the fall. This led the settlers of Lake Utopia to believe that the creature only inhabited the lake in the summer.

Almost 150 years later zoologist Roy P. Mackal published a possible answer to the legendary creature of Lake Manitou. He felt that persistence of many of the Indian myths meant that many of those tales have had some objective basis in reality. Working on the premise that what may be unfamiliar and frightening to some people may be the result of a scientifically familiar set of circumstances, Dr. Mackal investigated further.

That the original Potawatomi word for manitou meaning "devil's bones" intrigued Dr. Mackal. He reasoned that these bones were real in some sense and could have possibly formed an objective basis for the Lake Manitou monster. The area around the lake is rich in fossilized mastadon bones. Anyone finding such horrifyingly large remains would seek some logical explanation. If the Indians were unable to find an answer in the world that they were familiar with, then they would have to look to the unknown to fill the gap. It would seem logical that if you found bones, the former owners were probably still around somewhere. In this case the lake was the likely choice for the monster's residence. And so grew a legend and around the legend

Some places have more recent sightings in smaller bodies of water, Stump Pond in DuQuoin, Illinois is one odd example. From 1879 until 1968 there have been strange sightings in this mini-lake. It started with fishermen noticing something rushing through the water at night. Whatever it was it was big enough to rock rowboats with its wake. The first real sighting occurred in 1880 when two miners saw a green 12 foot serpent swimming toward their boat. Not given to adventurous spirits, they hastily retreated without so much as a second glance at their pursuer.

For over eighty years people reported: that something large struck the bottoms of their boats and swam away, that alligator-like creatures were dwelling in the algae covered shallows and that submerged large-bodied "critters" with their fins sticking out of the water could be seen at around dusk in the middle of the summer.

In 1967, some lumbermen working at a lakeside sawmill reported a 30 foot creature playing and splashing in the water. To some it looked like a moving black rock, except it had a head and body. For the rest of the summer the residents and workers around Lake Utopia tried to catch the monster with an assortment of hooks and food. The efforts were rewarded with more creature sightings, but the monster never took the bait. Intermittent observations have been reported since then. The last sighting was in 1982, by one Sherman Hatt. He compared the creature to "...a submarine coming out of the water with spray on both sides."

The Lake Utopia sightings have one distinct feature as compared to other lake observations reported so far. Many times the creature is seen by several people simultaneously from varying distances. The reports are remarkably uniform and the conclusions of the witnesses are rather similar. Whatever has been taking its summer vacation in Lake Utopia comes from the same class of unknown animal.

Ogopogo, a humorous name for the creature that inhabits Okanagan Lake, British Columbia, Canada. Lake Okanagan is a finger shaped lake. It is very much like Loch Ness in temperature, depth and abundance of food. The major difference with the famous Scottish lake is its size; Lake Okanagan is twice as large. The creatures of this region are well documented and their existence probably predates the arrival of man to this continent. The Indians called the lake dweller Naitaka. Although thought to be of Indian origin, Ogopogo comes from a popular 1924 British tune which impishly describes a baby sea monster and its parents.

Nonetheless, this is a species of creature which lacks a sense of humor. The local Indians held the Naitaka or Ogopogo in dread and regularly made offerings of food every time they ventured forth across the lake. Sometime in the 1600's a visiting chief, wishing to fish by a barren little island in the lake, ignored all warnings and rowed out on Lake Okanagan with his family. To the horror of his watching hosts, the canoe was overturned in a great rush of water. The guests attempted to swim to shore in the churning foam, but one by one some unseen force pulled them under the water. Not a shred of clothing nor a fragment of canoe was ever found. The Indians so feared and revered the Naitaka that they would make pictographs of the creatures on boulders surrounding the lake. Only three very worn rock drawings survive today. All of the stories and artifacts could be considered just another series of Indian legends; yet, in the 1700's, the European settlers to this far west land had encountered Ogopogo and the sketchy reports continued. And so too did the practice of offering food every time someone boated across the lake. But times change and so do traditions.

In the remote Canadian West horses were, until recently, the most efficient means of land transportation available. In order to deliver the horses where they were needed, great bodies of water had to be navigated with a team of horses led by a small boat or canoe. The handler would row the boat and the steeds would swim behind under loose rein. In 1854 and again in 1928 teams of horses were being towed across Lake Okanagan when Ogopogo struck. In each case the horses disappeared in a large splashing of water and their owners barely escaped with their lives. In each case the men involved did not leave a food offering for safe passage across Lake Okanagan.

Those who have seen Ogopogo usually described it as a big snake like creature, covered with scales and having a small bearded goat or horse like head, supported by a slender neck. Of those who have seen Ogopogo's head close enough to make out details, they describe him as having horns. Its size varies from 25 feet to over 60 feet in length. A few witnesses have told of small front flippers. Others have noticed both front and rear flippers. More than half the sightings tell of a split rear tail pushing the rest of the body through the water. When viewed in the lake it has the appearance of a black log or a series of snake like humps as it zips through the water. Ogopogo moves at times with great speed. In the 1920's a country doctor tried to pace the monster by car. In short order, Ogopogo outdistanced him.

The land evidence of Ogopogo consists mostly of foot or paw prints. None of the reported prints ever matched with previously found prints. The size and shape varied so much that these land traces are not reliable proof of Ogopogo or of any other creature. There was one strange land incident in 1914, when a torn and decayed carcass was found on the shore of Lake Okanagan. What was left of the animal was 5 feet long, with flippers, a tail and round head attached to a dark grey body. No one had ever seen anything like it and no one could venture a guess as to what it was. Finally an amateur naturalist found a close match in some of his books. His research identified the corpse as belonging to a sea cow. He had no idea how the sea cow, whose natural habitat was off the coast of South America, could have gotten into Lake Okanagan. Writer Peter Costello, in his book *In Search of Lake Monsters*, stated that the beached creature was probably an Ogopogo. The similarities of physical characteristics between the poor beached animal and the legendary creature of the lake are too close to ignore.

Although sightings of Ogopogo still continue, one of the most cited occurred on July 2, 1949. The Krays of South Kelowna, British Columbia and the Watsons of Montreal were spending an early summer's eve by the lake near Kelowna with their children. The

Lake creatures show a remarkable affinity for fjord-like surroundings. This 1890 picture of the Lake Champlain Palisades could easily be of and inlet in Norway or the cliffs of Loch Ness

Krays were on shore socializing with a few of their neighbors and the Watsons were boating nearby. Suddenly everyone noticed a black snake-like creature, about 30 feet long, slowly undulating about 100 feet away. All the witnesses counted five separate humps spaced about 2 feet apart. Occasionally a forked tail would appear above the water only to disappear again. In their excitement, Mr. Kray asked his friend Mr. Watson to row closer to the creature and Mrs. Kray ran to the house to get a pair of binoculars. With his whole family in his boat and fearing for their safety, Mr. Watson only inched closer to the strange aquatic beast. Mrs. Kray not only grabbed a pair of binoculars but called her friends the Underhills who lived nearby.

Up to now, the period of time that Ogopogo was observed was about 10 minutes. When the Underhills reached the shore, although somewhat further away, the creature was being viewed from at least four different vantage points. Through his binoculars Dr. Underhill thought that he was watching not one but two Ogopogos. He came to this conclusion by the way the humps were spaced; they were too far apart at times to belong to just one creature. The Ogopogos swam about Lake Okanagan for 5 more minutes and then dove under the water for the last time. The total time that the creature was closely observed was for 15 minutes, making this one of the longest group sightings of a nessi-like animal ever recorded.

In Lake Manitoba a similar creature has been often sighted and the residents have named it Manipogo After Lake Okanagan's Ogopogo. There are not as many reports of Manipogo as there are for Ogopogo but there exists a superb photograph of Lake Manitoba's monster. The photo matches Ogopogo's description very nicely indeed. If there are aquatic visitors to the Canadian lakes they seen to be from the same species.

North America has two landmarks in the continuing saga of lake creatures. The first concerns the small town of Kelowa on the shores of Lake Okanagan, the home of Ogopogo. The townspeople have erected a statue to Ogopogo. This is the first and perhaps the only statue in honor of a yet unidentified lake creature.The other landmark concerns the states of Vermont and New York. In 1982 both state legislatures passed a resolution protecting any possible lake monsters found in their respective jurisdictions "from any willful act resulting in death, injury or harassment." Why did they do this? Were these resolutions passed in jest? Or is there a very real and serious reason behind these legislative maneuvers? The answer can be found in Lake Champlain.

Nestled in the Champlain Valley, Lake Champlain is a fine example of a glacial lake. In the United States, with 435 square miles of water surface, only its ice age cousins The Great Lakes are larger. Unlike the larger relatives it is a finger shaped lake with a length of 125 miles running north/south and a maximum width of 13 miles. The normal depth varies between 100 and 335 feet, but at its deepest Lake Champlain is a little over 400 feet. One of the lake's major sport attractions is its abundance of fish; the catch may include trout, bass, salmon and pike perch. There are also the kinds of munchies that any lake monster might crave.

That we know anything factual at all about the Lake Champlain creatures is due to the almost tireless research of Gary Mangiacopra and Joseph Zarzynski. Working independently of each other, they have done much to record and lend credence to eyewitnesses' accounts of a lake monster. The inhabitants of the Champlain Valley have affectionately called their lake creature "Champ."

The first person to report seeing an unusual creature in the body of water named after him is explorer and cartographer Samuel de Champlain. In 1609 he noted in his journal sighting a 20 foot snake-like animal, with a horse-like head, swimming in the distance. He did not have the luxury to study this aquatic phenomenon; he was engaged in a struggle to insure the northern fur trade for his native country, France. With the aid of his newly found Indian allies, he won a victory over the Iroquois at the southern end of Lake Champlain. This began a century of warfare in the region with the French and Hurons on one side and the English and Iroquois on the other. While the combatants were busy with each other no one had time to notice the creature of the lake. In fact the Champlain Valley featured in quite a few conflicts; The French and Indian Wars, The Revolutionary War and The War of 1812. It wasn't until after 1816 that the region free of conflict and settlers moved into the Champlain Valley that sightings began to be reported once more.

In 1819 early settlers, near Bulwagga Bay, New York, were startled by the sudden appearance of a large monster with its neck and head out of the water. On July 30, 1878, a small yacht containing a party of six ob-

Samuel de Champlain, intrepid explorer and cartographer, was the first European to sight a snake-like animal in the lake which bears his name. He did nothing more than make a note in his journal about this creature since he was busy winning a battle over the English and their Indian allies at the time.

servd a 50 foot creature leisurely swimming by. Picknickers near East Charlotte, Vermont were enjoying a lazy summer afternoon in 1887, when they observed a snake-like creature in the lake. The monster seemed to notice them. It stopped its leisurely swim and began to churn toward the watchers with the speed of a steamboat. As it picked up momentum, people began screaming and several fainted. But there was no attack, no horror coming out of the lake devouring helpless humans. At the last moment the creature dove beneath the water and disappeared.

In the following decades, snake-like, eel-like, horse-headed, goat-headed, front flippered snake, forked tailed, grey, black. and green-black creatures were observed in Lake Champlain. In fact it was just one type of animal; it was also sounding very much like the description of Ogopogo; in fact both Ogopogo and Champ sound very much like Nessie. But no one was interested in such mysteries back then. At best these tales were the basis of humorous ridicule.

On August 18th, 1929 The New York *Times* ran an article that began..."In the course of the summer "silly" season, the sea-serpent is certain to make himself known. This year the report comes from Lake Champlain..." The article continues on by telling of a 1915 sighting and then adding a new set of observations by "Two maiden ladies who lived seventy five years at the end of Willsboro Point have told to other generations of how on summer evenings

they watched the esoteric performances of the huge serpent. He was harmless, they thought." The article ends the two ladies story by informing the readers that once the railroad was built on Willsboro Bay cliffs, "...the old serpent changed his haunts. Perhaps the rumbling trains frightened him off." The rest of the piece is about sea serpents in general and of course it ends with a joke, a rather bad one at that. This was the state of newsmedia coverage of Champ and all those quaint tales about him until very recently.

Sandra Mansi and her family were picnicking on the Vermont shore of Lake Champlain, north of St. Albans. July 5, 1977 was a fine sunny summer's day; it was just the kind of day that Lake Champlain is famous for. While her children were playing in the water, Sandra Mansi noticed something swimming in the middle of the lake. At first she thought it was a huge fish, but then she saw the snakelike head and neck. It was peacefully looking around the shoreline. Quickly she took a picture with her Instamatic, grabbed her children and took off away from the lake, without ever glancing back.

The incident became a family joke and for three years the photo remained hidden, lest it bring ridicule upon her and her family. But secrets of this magnitude do not stay hidden long. Her close frineds urged Ms. Mansi to show her unusual snapshot to a very serous investigator... Joseph Zarzynski.

Zarzynski had the photograph subjected to close expert scrutiny; the negative was misplaced. Dr. Roy Mackal was one of the authorities asked to give an opinion. In all cases the photo was found to be genuine and of an unknown energetic object. In July of 1981 Macleans and Time magazine ran stories on Champ; each magazine included Sandra Mansi's photo. This one incident has brought intelligent public discussion to the true nature of the Lake Champlain creatures. It ranks with the first photograph of Nessie taken in 1933. Since 1981 the sightings of Champ have continued.

SOMETHING IS STILL SPLASHING IN THE LAKES

We may be close to the day when the mystery of the lake creatures may be solved. Evidence is being collected on a serious and scientific basis. Each new expedition to Loch Ness brings new photographs, sonar scans and underwater video views. But for some reason, probably a hunch on my part, I believe that the first conclusive proof of lake creatures will occur in North America, maybe in Lake Champlain. We have seen the evidence for some of the lake monsters; now let us see what the current theories are to date.

HOW THE CREATURES GOT INTO THE LAKES

There are two main lines of thought on why creatures may dwell in some North American Lakes. The first idea holds that after the last ice age these creatures freely swam into and out of the lakes from the sea. The creatures swam into the lakes because they were searching for food or because they were compelled to the lakes by their spawning instinct or both. But at some point, either the land rose or there was a natural change in water flow, they were cut off from free passage back to the sea. This sounds like the Lake Utopia monster that still seems to have free access to the sea. Trapped in an environment the creatures were partially accustomed to, they found it easy to adapt fully to the fresh water. It is also possible that the salinity of some of the lakes was higher than it is presently so the monsters had thousands of years to adjust to fresh water living as the levels of dissolved salt dropped.

Another idea is that these creatures still have access to rivers and from the rivers to the seas. Dr. Roy Mackal is the leader of this school of thought. He has mapped sightings in all the major areas of North

America. Not only does his research show credible sightings in Okanagan Lake, British Columbia, but similar sightings on the rivers connecting to the lake. These and other reports are usually brief and infrequent at any one particular point on the waterways, but show a clear pattern when seen in light of an ongoing migratory process. The creatures may have been living in this fashion for thousands of years.

WHAT ARE THE LAKE CREATURES?

Two prehistoric creatures are spotlighted as possible candidates for mysterious lake dweller. The plesiosaur plods forward as our first candidate. It is a relic from the age of dinosaurs. Big, sleek and terribly romantic, it is every monster movie's favorite and every sea captain's sea monster. It lived in both fresh and salt water; it had a long neck and flippers; it, as now believed, could have been warm blooded. The problem with the plesiosaur is that it was not known to inhabit very cold waters and it rode high in the water, exposing more than just its head and neck. Perhaps the plesiosaur evolved into our lake dweller? The questions have yet to be answered.

Less known and perhaps more likely is the basilosaurus. Not a dinosaur but an early relative of the modern whale. It was certainly warm blooded; from the fossil records, basilosaurus fits the lake monster descriptions better than the plesiosaur; it did have the ability to live in both fresh and salt water. Dr Roy Mackal believes that this creature or an evolved branch of the species, will someday be found as the answer to the mysterious creatures that dwell in the lakes of North America.

THE LAST SPLASH

What we have are aquatic creatures that shun publicity, but are noticed as they periodically navigate the waterways. They probably followed the fish in from the sea after the last great ice age and decided they liked the life style the lakes had to offer. For many thousands of years the lake creatures had no natural enemies and so they thrived in their new homes. Now a curious and intelligent species has taken notice of the clues these aquatic creatures leave and has declared them to be one of the great unsolved mysteries of North America. The new species is also quite relentless when it comes to mysteries; it loves to solve them.

The BermudaTriangle and Other Mysterious Places

The region nicknamed "The Bermuda Triangle" is the largest in area of any of the mysterious locations in North America. It has also generated a vast amount of controversy; perhaps more angry consideration has been paid to this subject than all the UFO discussions of the 1950's. At the core of the controversy are the ships, airplanes and people that have vanished under unusual if not bizarre circumstances in this region of water and land. The explanations for these enigmas range from the commonsensical, like navigational and pilot error to UFO's, the fourth dimension and the second rising of Atlantis. Everyone has a possible answer; yet no one can neatly solve all the mysteries. Despite the continuing salvos fired in fierce debate, many of the mysteries of the Bermuda Triangle have not been solved to date.

HOW THE MYSTERY WAS DISCOVERED, SOME BACKGROUND

When is a triangle not a triangle? When the triangle is the Bermuda triangle. To understand why this is so we should first examine how the area of the East Coast of the United States became known as the Bermuda Triangle.

In 1964 journalist Vincent Gaddis wrote an article about disappearing ships for *Argosy* magazine titled "The Deadly Bermuda Triangle." This was the first article with this designation to appear in print. One year later Gaddis's *Invisible Horizons* was published; it was a book of non-fiction sea mysteries. In this book was a chapter devoted to the long list of ships and airplanes that had vanished without a trace in the "The Triangle of Death." The area that was defined as the triangle had as its three points Miami, the east most tip of Puerto Rico and of course Bermuda. If one drew three lines connecting those points one would have drawn a triangle.

It wasn't that both the book and article contained new facts, but that Gaddis had realized that all these known and seemingly unrelated incidents all occurred in one geographical location. It was his correlation of disappearances to the area off the East Coast of America that was the unique feature of his writings. The problem with his discovery was that Gaddis claimed that the earth coexisted within a "space-time continua" and occasionally this unseen phenomena would interact with our known world at scattered geographical locations like the Bermuda Triangle. In other words, all these missing ships and airplanes were sucked into the forth dimension. At the time, the mass cultural mind was more attuned to the advent of the Beatles and the American presidential elections than to articles and books on mysterious places. No one was ready for the idea that anything could traipse into the fourth dimension; North America generally and the United States specifically was beginning its psychedelic journey through the sixties. *Invisible Horizons* was not a best seller when it was published.

Enter Ivan T. Sanderson, a biologist and writer by vocation and a popular earth mystery researcher by avocation. A friend of Gaddis, he took the Bermuda Triangle concept one step further. He mapped areas of anomalous incidents over the entire planet. His criteria for acceptable data was any event that could be considered "paranormal"; this included reports such as strange sounds, odd lights, UFO sightings as well as disappearances. What he found was ten definite clusters of anomalous incidents that fit into ten evenly-spaced lozenge shaped areas, belting the globe. To be more precise, each of these lozenges was found to be spaced 72 degrees apart and–starting at either the North and South poles–found between 30 degrees and 40 degrees longitude. Included in these zones were places like the Mediterranean Sea, the Indian Ocean and of course the Bermuda Triangle. Now the Bermuda Triangle had grown in size and lost its sharp points; it became a blob. This blob now encompassed the Leyward Islands, a good part of southern Florida and the ocean about 100 miles off of New York City. Sanderson had a name for these regions; he

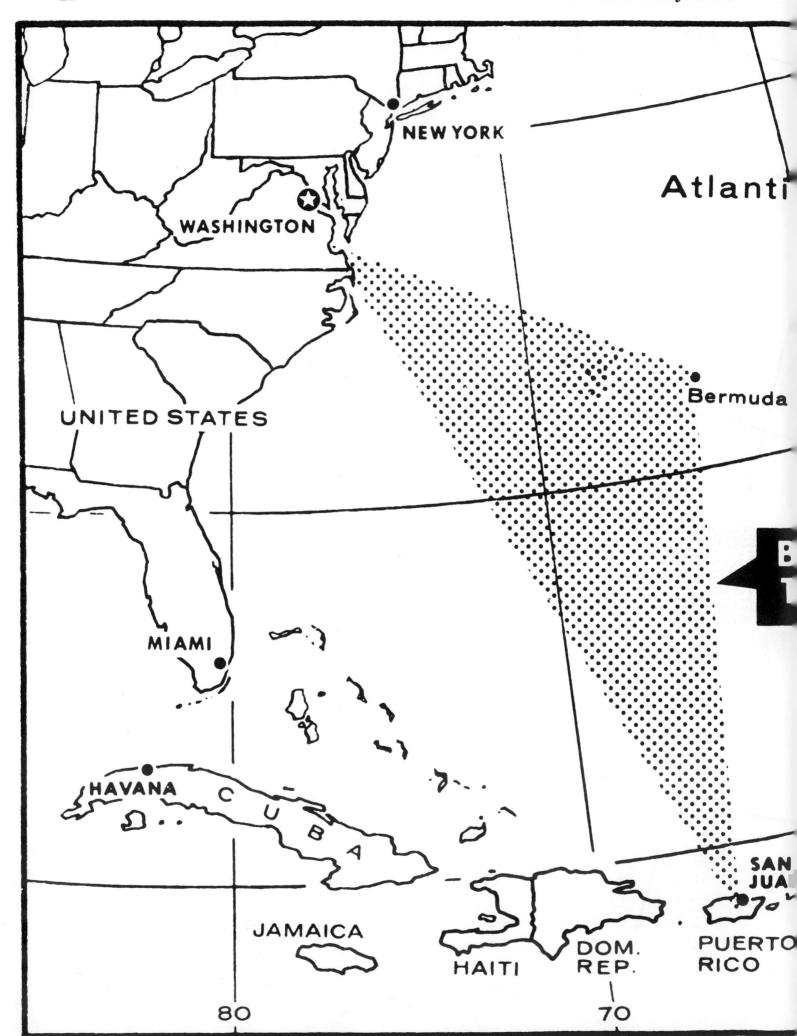

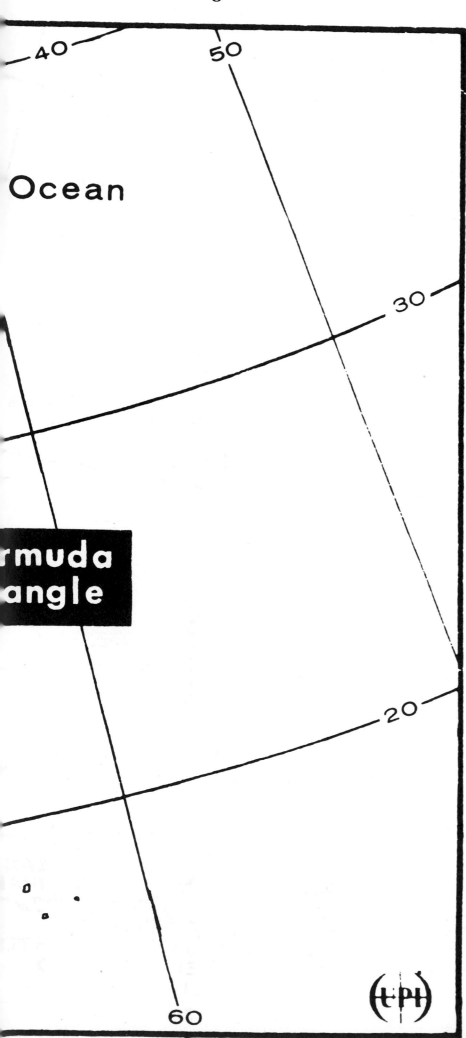

40 50

Ocean

30

rmuda
angle

20

60

The area known as the Bermuda Triangle
is clear from this map. Vincent Gaddis
placed the western point of the triangle at
Miami, Florida. This conception of the
Bermuda Triangle would leave out about
half of the myseries attributed to the area.

called them "Vile Vortices." In 1970 his book *Invisible Residents*, containing his theory on these mysterious regions, was published.

Another fellow with a theory was George Rouse, an earthquake specialist. He had speculated that there was either a physical or electromagnetic ditch that was etched into the molten core of the planet. It was this valley that determined the direction of seismic activity on the earth's crust. When Rouse compared Sanderson's map of the Vile Vortices with his own map of major and minor earthquakes he found that the areas on both maps neatly corresponded to each other. This led Sanderson to further speculate on the formation of whirlpools caused by erratic twitches of Rouse's ditch that might cause ships and even airplanes to vanish. Another theory that Sanderson was working on was the possibility that these ellipsoid regions might contain hidden UFO bases. But Ivan T. Sanderson never finished his work on the Vile Vortices, he died a few years after the publication of his book in 1973.

Something about the Bermuda Triangle mystery was arousing the interest of two writers. One of them Adi-Kent Thomas Jeffery wrote a book that was titled, rather plainly, *The Bermuda Triangle*. Some of the ideas of Ivan T. Sanderson were incorporated into the book, but Sanderson did not receive any credit for them. The book was published by a small publisher in Pennsylvania. It was meant to be popular reading matter for the mass market. Unfortunately, the publishing company did not have the large distribution and sales force that would have made Jeffery's book a best seller. But the time was right for something big to happen with this peculiar topic. More people were turning to alternative forms of thought; astrology, holistic medicine, encounter groups and other non-established points of view had made vast inroads into the mass culture. Enter Charles Berlitz, grandson of the founder of the famous language schools. His book also titled *The Bermuda Triangle* was published in 1974 by Doubleday. Here was a publishing company with marketing and distribution clout. The name Bermuda Triangle spread throughout the world as the book grew into an international best seller.

Even if the man on the street had never read any books about the mysterious area, he now knew of its existence. Berlitz's book had the kitchen sink approach to possible solutions to the disappearances. UFO's, At-lantean death rays, extraterrestrial kidnappings, space-time warps, Von Daniken, chariots of the gods, governmental coverups and electromagnetic phenomena were all used to full dramatic effect. If the popular mind found all this speculation exciting, critics of these ideas found it infuriating.

One very meticulous and precise critic quickly (in one year) fired off a tome in rebuttal. In his book *The Bermuda Triangle Mystery Solved* Lawrence Kusche, research librarian and pilot, dismissed the whole concept with a well-researched account of sixty cases. This work was so convincing that large numbers of Bermuda Triangle enthusiasts dropped the subject faster than a squirming jellyfish. His work is still the last word in the genre of Bermuda Triangle debunking. It is *not* the last word on the Bermuda Triangle.

The mystery remains. The latest generation of Bermuda Triangle writers is typified by David Group. His work *The Evidence for the Bermuda Triangle* is an even-handed approach to the subject. All possibilities are explored without the reactive stridency of some critics. Group does have a point of view, but he does not let it get in the way of serious exploration of the subject. Some of the debunked mysteries are reexamined and found to be inconclusively solved.

IT ALL BEGAN WITH COLUMBUS

The year was 1492 and everything west of the Azores was a mystery. When Christopher Columbus set sail from the Canary Islands on the morning of September 6th, little did he dream he would discover a new land, a new continent, a new source of wealth for his employers—the monarchs of Spain. He was searching for a sea route to the East, to the riches of the Orient and to Cipango: as Japan was known in the fifteenth century. For weeks they sailed on in an empty ocean with just sky and water for companions. Three brave ships whose crew came very close to mutiny by October 10th. By sheer force of personality and sound reasoning he persuaded the crew not to turn back. In actuality they could not, for their supplies were insufficient for a return trip. On October 11th branches and a wooden staff floated by the ships. Land was near, but not in sight. On the morning of the 12th the *Pinta's* lookout cried "Land! Land!" and the new world was found. This is the story as it is frequently told of Columbus's first voyage. But what is usually left out of this version is the discovery of the fabled Sargasso Sea.

Christopher Columbus settled the debate on the shape of the Earth, but he may have begun the dispute over the mysterious occurances in the Bermuda Triangle.

In the central North Atlantic lies a relatively still region of water choked with floating seaweed; this yellow and green seaweed is called sargussum, hence the name Sargasso. As an area it is quite large, almost the size of the continental United States. It is bounded by 20 and 35 degrees north latitude and 30 and 70 degrees west longitude. In addition to the ubiquitous seaweed there are tropical plants, branches of trees and wrecks of ships that have drifted into this area from South and Central America. Strange examples of marine animals that are found nowhere else dwell among the seaweed and plant debris. And it is through this eerie region that Columbus sailed on his first voyage to the western edge of the Atlantic.

Columbus noted in his logbook that on September 16th his three ships found themselves becalmed in the Sargasso Sea. It seemed as if the vegetation of this sea was snagging the ships, impeding their progress and threatening to imprison them in these bizarre waters. The sky and stars looked peculiarly different; the temperature of the air and water was warmer than one would expect. Strange, unknown creatures could be seen moving about in the seaweed. More unsettling than these still natural phenomena was the malfunction of the trusted compass.

A few days before the three ships became becalmed the compass began to shift away from the north star. In the following days the shift increased. Soon the pilots of the other ships noticed the variation with alarm; the crews hearing of this strange development were terrified. Unlike sailors in the twentieth century, in the fifteenth century it was believed that the compass pointed directly to the north star, not to the north magnetic pole. Columbus correctly reasoned that the compass must be pointing to something other than the north star, but he had no idea what that other something was. He kept track and adjusted for the variations from the north star and stayed on course. The crew was convinced by Columbus's reasoning and by his powers of leadership. Yet they still held this strange area in dread.

Columbus also observed paths, he assumed made by other ships, through the seaweed. As the ships progressed in this strange sea the sailors' terror grew. They were in an area where the laws of nature as they knew them did not work, just like their compasses. Seaweed, birds and plants, clear indication of land, in these God forsaken waters meant only more of the same with no land in sight. It did not help the crew's confidence when they observed a large bright light falling one evening, usually an omen of unhappy events to come.

Onward they sailed. After leaving the dread sea, signs of land were still observed. Everyone on the three valiant ships was anxious, waiting to make landfall. At approximately 10 o'clock on the evening of October 11th, Columbus sighted a light in the distance. Several of his crew members saw the same illumination. Before anyone else could see the light, it disappeared. Four hours later the New World was formally discovered.

The Sargasso Sea was to fill sailors with abject fear for centuries. It gained the nickname of the "horse latitudes." In the sixteenth century when Spain was sending ships as fast as she could build them to the Americas, those small vessels would find themselves often becalmed in the Sargasso. When drinking water became scarce, the sailors stopped giving water to the horses they were transporting. Driven mad from thirst, the horses would break free and throw themselves overboard. Many a fine steed found its end in the seaweed-choked waters.

What Columbus found in the Sargasso was strange but it did not warrant the terror in which it was later regarded. Of the unusual incidents encountered by Columbus only a few point the way to genuine mysteries. Seaweed and marine life in the Sargasso are manifestations of organisms finding an ecological niche where favorable conditions prevail. The huge falling light sighted by Columbus' crew was obviously a sizeable meteor. The strangeness of star and sky, as well as the warming of water and air has more to do with the warm Gulf stream feeding the Sargasso than with inexplicable supernatural happenings. Since the Sargasso is the garbage bin of the Atlantic, it is not surprising to find branches and other signs of land floating there.

But the paths of other ships through seaweed is yet unexplained. They could have been trails of other unknown explorers venturing across the Atlantic; or they could have been natural forces at work; or they could have been exaggerations of a man who was always matter of fact in his observations; or these paths might be some answers to yet unasked questions.

Many theories have been put forward to explain the phantom light before Colum-

Theodosia Burr, daughter of Aaron Burr, lived in an exciting time in American history, the early years of the republic. Her unsolved disappearance in the Bermuda Triangle all but broke her father's spirits.

bus's historic landfall. Some experts believe this was a small meteor falling on the horizon. This explanation is a little weak. Shooting stars were a familiar phenomenon to Columbus. He would not have found it notable if it were just another meteor. Besides there is no mention of the light moving in the sky, if anything it just hovered in place. Somewhat more plausible is the notion that it was a mass hallucination. Everyone was under stress and any hopeful sign, even if it was imagined, was welcome. This sounds likely, but Columbus was the most experienced sailor on the three ships. He was also a meticulous observer; he was also the first person to see the light. It is doubtful that such a man, however anxious, would panic in such a manner. An interesting idea comes from a marine biologist, L.R. Crawshaw, who in 1935 said that Columbus might have witnessed the fertility rite of the Atlantic fireworm. When these creatures mate they glow for a few brief moments just under the surface of the water. Historians believe Columbus saw the light from an Indian's torch out in a small boat. Of course there are those who believe it was a UFO, perhaps pointing the way to land. The source of that illumination still remains clouded in mystery.

Compasses do not point to the north star or the north pole; compasses point to the north magnetic pole. The earth's magnetic poles periodically shift and currently the north magnetic pole is located halfway between Hudson Bay and the north pole. Depending where in the world a reading is taken, it can vary from true north by as many as 28 degrees. Columbus was one of the first to notice this. He also may have been one of the first to compensate for this discrepancy. No matter how much debunkers try to down-play the significance of this geological force, magnetism, especially erratic magnetism and compasses that do not read true are a reoccurring theme in the Bermuda Triangle, as we will see later.

UNNOTICED DISAPPEARANCES

At first vessels disappeared in the Bermuda Triangle without anyone thinking that there was anything unusual. After all, it was the age of exploration and the ships were traveling to and from a largely unknown land. Occasionally they passed through the dreaded demon infested waters of the Sargasso Sea. Sometimes ships were never heard from again; what else could any rational sixteenth century person expect? Toward the end of the 1500's piracy became

another hazard to shipping. All that New World gold was a temptation that some poor seafarers could not ignore. In the next century the overwhelming European hostility toward the attempted Spanish monopoly of gold and the American seas brought about a new form of ship raiding, the buccaneers. English, French and Dutch adventurers, under license from their governments sent even more vessels into oblivion. So who missed a few unaccounted for ships under those conditions?

Ocean traffic in the Bermuda Triangle region increased throughout the 18th century; so did the small number of unexplained disappearances. Later in that century, the Revolutionary War was won by the colonists and a new nation was born. Freedom of the seas becomes an issue that brought the United States into the War of 1812 with England; it is also the setting for the first famous personage to vanish in the Bermuda Triangle.

A FAMOUS LADY VANISHES

Theodosia Burr Alston was an intelligent and beautiful woman whose short life was dogged with tragedy. She was the daughter of the scandal ridden former Vice President of the United States—Aaron Burr. Her mother died when Theodosia was quite young. At the age of seventeen she was married to a prominent southern aristocrat and had to leave the exciting world of New York for a quiet life on a South Carolinian plantation. Very devoted to her father, Theodosia anxiously watched from afar as he went from the height of his career, to standing trial as a traitor, to a self-imposed exile in shame, although acquitted of the charge of treason. She focused her energies on family life, doting on her son. In late May, 1812 Aaron Burr wrote to his daughter that he feared that war may soon break out, so he was leaving England and coming home to New York. Theodosia was overjoyed. But on June 30th her son died of malaria and her whole world crashed around her. The only person who could bring her out of her depression was her father, who now was living in New York. Her husband, now governor of South Carolina, arranged passage north for her on a packet ship. The departure date was New Year's Eve.

The *Patriot* was a small, speedy coastal vessel once used to haul mail and light freight. Since the outbreak of hostilities it was successfully employed in raiding British shipping. Part of the arrangements for this special journey included the disarming of the *Patriot* and stowing her guns below the deck. This was a concession to the English; who in turn would allow the nasty little ship, carrying the First Lady of South Carolina, through their blockade of New York Harbor.

In Charleston, South Carolina, the last day of the old year was warm and clear with a good breeze. Theodosia's family and many friends came down to the dock to wish her a safe voyage. After everyone said goodbye, the Captain was heard ordering "anchors aweigh." Those were the last words recorded from anyone aboard the *Patriot*. She sailed away, in a turbulent time, never to be seen again.

Theodosia Burr Alston had vanished and both husband and father were grief stricken. Governor Joseph Alston died three years later. Aaron Burr lived for another 21 years. In that time he tried to find the answer to the disappearance of the *Patriot*. He died learning nothing more about his beloved dauther's fate.

Some strange facts and incidents have come to light since then. Theories of war-time sabotage and sudden stormy weather have been ruled out as causes of the *Patriot's* disappearance. No one ever found or reported seeing the kind of wreckage that would have been generated from either of those types of disasters. Piracy is a definite possibility. In fact, for quite some time there was no end to the hoard of former pirates who confessed to the crime on their deathbeds.

In 1835 a tavern keeper lay dying in Mobile, Alabama. A doctor, attending the expiring man in his impoverished domicile, reported that his patient believed himself to be haunted by a ghost. After hearing the man babble about this female apparition for a few minutes, the doctor finally asked him the name of the ghost. "Theodosia Burr," he weakly replied. On his deathbed the man confessed that he crewed on the pirate ship that had captured the *Patriot*. The code of this particular band of cut throats was to leave no witnesses. It was left to him to make the pleading Theodosia walk the plank. When she understood that these pirates were not going to allow anyone from this ship to live,"...she walked the plank like a lady." This vision of Theodosia's last few steps haunted the tavern keeper for the rest of his days. With a last spark of life he whispered, "...She keeps comin' towards me, her white arms outstretched...Oh, Jesus save me..." And then he died.

A string of rumored confessions from buccaneers seeking contrition followed for the next ten years. One was a Frenchman who admitted that his ship sunk the *Patriot* and took Theodosia prisoner. He also confessed he took part in the three month long rape that eventually killed the poor woman. Her body was buried near the pirate's base on Galveston Island, or so he claimed. One confession was uncovered in 1959 by a free-lance writer; Foster Haley found documents in the Alabama Archives building in Montgomery that led him to a shocking discovery.

John Howard Payne was a noted play-wright and actor of his time. Born in 1791, he wrote his first play when he was 15. His finest play, *Brutus: or, The Fall of Tarquin* was performed in the English-speaking world for 73 years. Today he is mostly remembered for his song *Home Sweet Home*. He died serving in a consular post in 1852. Seeking absolution for his past misdeeds, Payne admitted to being the last of a blood-thirsty band of corsairs. He joined the rogue mariners as a youth. One particular ship stood out in his memory. In a quick battle the pirates overpowered an unarmed vessel named the *Patriot*. After looting the ship, all the survivors were made to walk the plank. There was a very beautiful woman that Payne remembered among those he helped to kill. Later in life he realized that she was Theodosia Burr Alston. This story appeared in the Charleston *News and Courier* in 1963.

Theodosia's story does not end with the many confessions of her murder. There are those who believe that "land pirates" or wreckers had caused the *Patriot* to crash on the North Carolina coast. Trinkets, lockets and even paintings from the ill-fated ship are offered as evidence. Several of these items have been found in the homes along the coast of North Carolina. Then there are those who speculate that this was just a normally weird happening in the always mysterious Bermuda Triangle.

A LADY IS FOUND

The first of many derelicts, mysteriously abandoned by their crews, yet left in good working order, was the French ship *Rosalie*. On a clear summer day in 1840 a deserted ship was found floating near Nassau. Everything about the vessel indicated that it had been abandoned by its crew only a few hours earlier. There was no structural damage to the ship and no sign of any leaks. Her cargo of valuable goods including wines and silks was in excellent condition. All the captain's papers were neatly in place. A few

AARON BURR

1756   1836

RICHMOND HILL

DRAWN AND ENGRAVED FOR
THE SOCIETY OF ICONOPHILES
NEW YORK 1902

E.S. KING
DEL & SC

cats, fowls and three half-starved canaries were the only living inhabitants found aboard the *Rosalie*.

Subsequent investigations never turned up any crew member of the abandoned ship. Recently a theory has been put forth that there was a mistake in the original report and the *Rosalie* was actually the *Rossini* that had struck a reef two weeks earlier. Everyone from the *Rossini* was rescued and safely put ashore. Proponents of this idea believe that the ship dislodged itself from the reef and floated for two weeks until found again.

If the *Rosalie* was in fact the *Rossini*, then why didn't one of the most influential human motivations... greed, become a major factor in the story? Here was a crewless ship laden with valuable cargo just asking to be taken. With all those sailors and passengers in port talking about their escape from the *Rossini*, didn't anyone listen to them? Was there no former pirate or semi-retired rogue willing to grab such a rich and easy haul? Was there no one in port curious enough to see what he and his cronies could make off with?

Another strange fact is the lack of damage to the hull. If this vessel recently had a serious close encounter with a reef, one would expect to find signs of the coral damage somewhere in the structure of the ship. When the derelict was found it was in perfect condition, without any gashes. The best that can be said about the *Rosalie* is that on an August morning in 1840 she sailed deep into the annals of unsolved mysteries.

THE QUEEN OF ABANDONED SHIPS

One ship that embodies all of the mystery derelicts found in a seaworthy yet crewless condition is the brigantine *Mary Celeste*. It is the standard to which all similar enigmas are compared. The ship was found off the Azores, although its destination was Genoa. Today it is assumed by researchers that the *Mary Celeste* did, at some point, sail through the Bermuda Triangle. This chapter would not be complete without her story.

In 1861, the *Mary Celeste* was first launched as the *Amazon*. From the moment she was launched at Spencer Island shipyard, Nova Scotia, she was said to be a jinxed ship. Her first captain died ten days after she was registered. For seven years the *Amazon* seemed to go crashing about the seas. When the ship wasn't bashing smaller boats (one which she sunk in the

Aaron Burr spent the last years of his life seeking an answer to his daughter's disappearance. It is a good thing he never heard some of the later stories of her demise. The lurid desciptions would have broken stronger men.

straits of Dover) it was busy beaching herself. Finally in 1867 she had run aground in Cow Bay, Cape Breton Island, Canada. By this time the *Amazon* was uninsurable and she was abandoned in the bay for salvage.

Two years and three owners later she was afloat again with a new name... the *Mary Celeste*. Once more she plied the seas like a drunken elephant; this time the ship had only minor scrapes and no major disasters. Still the captains and owners of the *Mary Celeste*, until 1872, all suffered minor ill fortunes. The real tragedy, shrouded in veils of perplexity, was yet to come.

On her famous voyage from New York to Genoa, the *Mary Celeste* carried a crew of eight and two passengers. Benjamin Spooner Briggs, the captain, was also a partner in the ship. His crew consisted of two mates and a cook from America and the rest of the crew came from either Germany or Scandinavia. The two passengers were his wife and two-year old daughter. It was common practice for the captain and sometimes the mates to bring their wives and children on long voyages.

Captain Briggs descended from a long line of sailors. A man in his late thirties, he had an exemplary record on the seas. Later a court of inquiry would claim that Briggs was a tyrant. This accusation stemmed from his deeply religious nature. He refused to allow his crews to drink alcohol on any of the ships he commanded and it was known he read the Bible daily. Actually, Briggs was rather well-liked by the other crew members who served with him.

On December 4th the harsh grey skies of the Atlantic yielded to a heavenly blue and the choppy misty seas gave way to a rolling calm ocean, as the brigantine *Dei Gratia* made its way to Gibraltar. She was about 350 miles east of the Azores at one o'clock in the afternoon when Captain David Reed Morehouse noticed a ship sailing erratically about 5 miles away. The *Dei Gratia* sailed closer to this strange listing ship. Morehouse noted that the mainsail was furled; some of the other sails were torn; the running rigging was missing; there was no one on lookout or at the wheel. When the two ships were alongside one another, it appeared that the deck of this odd vessel was deserted. Captain Morehouse sent three of his men to investigate.

What was discovered on board the *Mary Celeste* has since been hashed into mounds of confusion. For many years numerous published accounts contained inaccuracies. A subsequent board of inquiry was ineptly handled. Some writers have confused the fictional story of the *"Marie" Celeste*, by the then unknown author A. Conan Doyle, for a factual statement of the discoveries on that December afternoon. It has taken almost a century to arrive at a fair summation of the truth.

When the three men arrived on the deck of the *Mary Celeste* they found it deserted. A further search of the ship confirmed that it was indeed devoid of people. The 17-foot life boat appeared to have been launched and the rail used to send it into the sea was lying on the deck. Conspicuously missing were the ship's register, chronometer, sextant and navigation book. The crew left all their clothing, valuables and money. Several of the seamen had abandoned their tobacco pipes, something that most sailors, of that day, would never do without. The *Mary Celeste* had at least six months food stowed below decks.

Some discrepancies have never been resolved. In the galley the food was cooking, the food was served on the table or everything was put away in its proper place. The captain's bed was either unmade, had his daughter's toys on it or there was a small imprint in the bed as if his daughter had recently slept in it. A sword was found hanging on a wall with blood on it, the sword was found with rust on it, the sword was found under the captain's bed or there was no sword at all. Several reports have blood stains found about the ship, while other reports mention wine stains on the woodwork and of course as some tell the story there were no stains found. By the sewing machine there was\was not an open vial of oil. If this is true it would mean that the ocean was calm when everyone deserted the ship. Some claim that the ship's clock was still ticking. If this is true, then the ship abandoned shortly before being found. Much of how one tells this tale depends on which theory one is attempting to prove.

The *Mary Celeste's* main hatch was secured, but the fore hatch and aft hatch were open. A sounding rod was found near an opened hatch leading to the cargo hold. Inside the hold was 1,700 barrels of alcohol. One of the crew tested the cargo hold with the sounding rod and found it contained little more than three feet of water. Considering the size and construction of the ship this was an insignificant amount. Some water was also between decks. And when the compass was inspected it was found to be broken.

At the time the *Mary Celeste* was discovered she was sailing west, away from her destination. According to the logbook, the last entry was on November 25th. At that time the ship was 100 miles west of the Azores. This meant that the *Mary Celeste* had changed course in nine days and had traveled close to 500 miles in the opposite direction.

Here were two ships in the middle of the sea, one had a crew and one was abandoned by its crew. Opportunism with a shade of greed ran through the crew of the *Dei Gratia*, if not the captain. His first mate and Morehouse discussed the possibilities of claiming the *Mary Celeste* for the salvage reward. It can be assumed the first mate held similar discussions with the crew before speaking to the captain. They all knew the cargo of alcohol would bring a rather tidy price. Morehouse agreed to bring the *Mary Celeste* to Gibraltar, but he could only spare two men to crew her for the 600 mile journey. Lots were drawn or perhaps the two men volunteered and both ships sailed for Gibraltar.

Did Morehouse think about his fellow captain on the trip back? They were close to the same age and knew each other as men who are in the same business usually do. Those who were acquainted with both men said it was more than a casual friendship. Just two days before the *Mary Celeste* sailed from New York, Captain Morehouse had dinner with Captain Briggs and his wife. Now some inexplicable tragedy happened and Ben Briggs and his family had vanished.

Gibraltar was not what the captain and crew of the *Dei Gratia* expected. Instead of being welcomed and quickly awarded a generous salvage, Morehouse and his men were savaged in the press and in the courts. Rumors instantly grew; fact and fiction blended into thick dirty paste that stuck to everything, mostly to Captain Morehouse and his crew.

Certain facts were quickly brought to light. There was little damage to the deck and the hull. The ship did not nearly roll over due to a storm. All of the water found in the hull and between decks was not the result of a heavy storm. Two of the barrels of alcohol were cracked. The investigators concluded that at worst the *Mary Celeste* had encountered a medium- to light storm. All of this should have led to a quick hearing but for one man.

Attorney General Solly Flood, who headed

the Court of Inquiry, was the crux of the problem. Once this man made up his mind not even "The Truth From Heaven" could make him think otherwise. His version of the truth consisted of Morehouse and his men killing the crew of the *Mary Celeste* and seizing the ship for salvage. The press of that day found piracy sold more newspapers than a blockbuster unsolved mystery. These two forces worked in tandem to their own self interest. Flood's accusations made headlines and Morehouse's rebuttals were found at the end of the news articles. Much of the factual confusion about the *Mary Celeste* mystery stems from this hearing.

Flood attempted to stem the tide of facts crashing on his theories. He did not succeed, but he did have the last word. The other investigators came to the conclusion that the stains on the deck were placed there by Flood himself. Rather than showing open hostility to the attorney general, they simply announced that the stains were not blood, but some other red liquid, maybe red wine stains. The investigators determined the sword in question belonged to Captain Briggs and the dark spots on the blade were definitely rust spots. This evidence was suppressed for most of the inquest, which took over three months. In the end there was not enough evidence for Morehouse and his men to stand trial for murder and piracy. Nonetheless the sailors found their reputations blackened and instead of a share of the approximately $80,000 salvage, the captain and his crew received a little over $8,000.

What happened to Captain Briggs, his family and the crew? Were they forcibly taken off the ship? If so by whom? Brigg's friend Captain Morehouse could not have done it. No matter what Attorney General Solly Flood believed, the facts contradict that theory. Piracy runs a close second in this line of thinking. If there were any sea rogues this late in the nineteenth century, they were old men telling tales of their youth; there just weren't any sailing the Atlantic Ocean at this time. Both of these theories needed signs of a struggle. A few stains on the deck and a rusty sword don't count. Were they abducted by a UFO? This is an idea that would not have occurred to anyone in 1872. Extraterrestrials could have taken everyone off the *Mary Celeste* without a fight. Perhaps the stains on the deck were a significant clue that was overlooked. Lacking modern chemical analytic methods, they had no way of knowing what those stains really were composed of. Until

there is more proof of these types of events occurring, it remains an unlikely solution.

A typically nineteenth century notion stated that a sea monster, something like a giant octopus, plucked one and all off of the ship and ate them.

Did everyone jump or fall into the sea, either by accident or intentionally? Some of these theories include scenarios of disease or food poisoning. A few researchers believe that the passengers were poisoned by wheat ergot in the bread. Wheat ergot is a fungus rot which contains a potent and unrefined form of LSD. According to this idea, they all went mad and jumped into the sea. The wood on the *Mary Celeste* was contaminated with a rare form of ergot is a variation on this theme. Plague broke out among the crew of the Mary Celeste and before long everyone was dying, is yet another scenario. In this case the last person alive throws the bodies overboard and commits suicide in order not to spread the disease to those ashore. A macabre theory claims the cook went berserk, poisoned the crew and then jumped overboard after disposing of the bodies.

Several of the accident theories revolve about the idea that a platform was built for the crew to watch: either a swimming race around the ship or the captain taking a swim. The end result in either scenario is the platform collapses and all are killed in some manner. In one case all are attacked by sharks and in the other everyone drowns after a strong wind comes up and the ship sails away. However interesting to contemplate, all of these speculations have no hard facts to back them up.

There is some evidence to support the claim that the *Mary Celeste* was caught in a waterspout. Rarely photographed, waterspouts are tornados that occur at sea. According to this theory the meteorological conditions were just right for a string of waterspouts to be formed near the Azores on the morning of November 25. This date coincides with the last entry in the ship's log.

Suddenly smashing into the ship, the high winds of the waterspout would have torn the sails, ripped the rigging away from the *Mary Celeste* and blown out some of the hatches. Possibly one or two of the crew were swept overboard in those brief furious moments. Gallons of water were flung through the opened holds, much of it settling in the cargo hold.

For the next few minutes everyone left on the ship was confused. Occasional mental confusion has been observed resulting from

HOME SWEET HOME.

Moderato

Mid pleasures and palaces, though we may roam,
Be it ever so humble, there's no place like home.
John Howard Payne.

For a poet, actor and playwright John Howard Payne had a bloodthirsty youth. Had his deathbed confession of his early adventures in the Bermuda Triangle been publicized at the time they would have shocked the nation.

a rapid lowering of barometric pressure. It was in this bewildered state that someone took the sounding rod and incorrectly measured the water in the cargo hold. The low pressure would have also caused an incorrect measurement of six or more feet of water below decks. Briggs believing the *Mary Celeste* was sinking launches the life boat and the crew abandons ship. After a few minutes everyone comes to their senses, realizes the ship is not sinking and they row back to the *Mary Celeste*. But a stong wind comes and the ship sails away without them. Sometime later the lifeboat is swamped by heavy seas and all are lost.

To the end of her days the *Mary Celeste* had bad luck follow her wake like a shark. She once again barged around the seas and in 12 years had twelve captains. Her demise, in 1884, was on a reef off the coast of Haiti. It was rumored her last captain smashed the ship for the huge insurance on the cargo. The captain never went on trial for fraud; he died three months later.

The *Mary Celeste,* queen of abandoned ships, remains an unsolved mystery. She was not the last ship found abandoned in the Bermuda Triangle. In 1940 the *Gloria Colita* was found in a crewless state. A similar incident happened in 1944 when the *Rubicon* was found near Key Largo, Florida. Both cases were not well investigated and both cases were shrugged off as some freak maritime story. Some of the more common sense theories, about these two ships include storms and whole crews being swept overboard. They seem to ignore the time in which these two ships were found...World War II. No one, especially in those dark days, wanted unanswerable questions lingering in the naval annals when most of the world was busy at war.

AN UGLY LADY DISAPPEARS

In 1910 the wonders of the industrial technology were incorporated into a whole new class of marine construction and simultaneously into an innovative concept of marine transport. The U.S. Navy had several colliers built with special box like steel girder superstructures. These elaborate superstructures, containing specially designed derricks, enabled the colliers to refuel coal burning warships at sea. It also gave them an ungainly, top-heavy appearance. Many a sailor thought the specially devised ships were just plain ugly. Soon, coal-fueled, steam-driven warships were going to be replaced by diesel-powered warships. But in 1910 the collier *Cyclops*

and her sisters, despite their looks, were the latest and the greatest advancement in marine technology.

Large for her time, the *Cyclops* was over 540 feet long. She displaced 14,500 tons without cargo. When the ship proudly visited Kiel, Germany in 1911, she was highly praised by the German naval engineers who inspected her. "Outstanding!" was the word used to describe her construction.

On March 4, 1918, the *Cyclops* steamed out to sea from her refueling in Barbados, West Indies. Because of mechanical failure, the ship was powered by only one of her two massive steam engines. The result of this halving of power was the reduction of the *Cyclops's* speed to 10 knots. She was carrying a much needed cargo of manganese ore from Brazil to Norfolk, Virginia. This ore was being used to further the Allied war effort against the Central Powers in the latter stages of World War I. No doubt the naval engineers of Germany had given some thought on how to sink this "outstanding" ship.

The ship was due in Norfolk on March 13th. It never arrived. The first public announcement appeared in the newspapers on April 15th. As usual with any bureaucracy, the Navy was hoping to solve the disappearance before they made the news available to the press. After a month of searching some statement had to be made. At best, all the Navy could report was having ruled out several obvious possibilities. There were no raiders or submarines operating along the *Cyclops's* route; no radio messages calling for help were received by anyone; the weather was not stormy along the route; there were no German mines in the path of *Cyclops's* passage; no one reported finding a shred of debris from the ship. In far too many words the Navy concluded a month later that the *Cyclops* had vanished without a trace. All searches for the ship were discontined in late May.

For a short while, until World War I ended, there were a series of theories that made the rounds in naval circles. German spies and traitors were the central figures in most of them.

During the war, accusations of traitorous activities were made on the smallest amount of circumstantial evidence. Rightly, or in many cases wrongly, these charges were readily believed by the government and the public at large.

The first person to be suspected of traitorous activities was the captain of the

Cyclops. Someone in the Navy department unearthed the fact that Lieutenant-Commander George W. Worley was German-born. Under unclear circumstances, Worley had immigrated alone to America as a small child. At that time his name was George Frederick Wickman. For reasons not shown in official records, he was adpoted by a man in California by the name of Worley. While in his teens, Wickman became a United States citizen and he legally changed his name to Worley.

The circumstantial evidence did not stop there. Further investigation discovered that Worley had sold all his property in Virginia, including the family home, shortly before his last voyage. He told his neighbors that the family was moving to California. There was some talk that he needed an operation and he planned to recuperate in his new western home .

This line of investigation seemed to point to the solution to the *Cyclops's* disappearance. Worley was at the very least a traitor, perhaps a well trained spy. He maintained regular communications with the German Admiralty. His crowning achievement was arranging a rendezvous with a German U-Boat, overpowering the crew of 270 men of the *Cyclops,* capturing the *Cyclops* and turning the ship over to the Germans.

When reporters heard this rumor was making the circuits in the Navy department, they interviewed Worley's wife. When she heard this vicious theory from the newspapermen she was incensed. "Do you think my husband would prove a traitor to America, to his wife and little daughter? My husband was and is an American through and through. He hated Germany..." For Mrs. Worley it would take a year before she would believe that her husband had vanished forever.

After the war ended, it took a thorough search through the German Admiralty records to clear Lieutenant-Commander George W. Worley's name. At the same time several other speculations were put to rest. There were no German agents aboard the *Cyclops* and as far as researchers could tell, the German Navy never incited the crew to mutiny. The mutiny theory never had many adherents anyway. No one acting on behalf of the German Navy planted a time bomb on the *Cyclops.* In fact. except for routine intelligence reports, there was no special mention of *Cyclops* in the German Admiralty records. It was not an act of war which caused the ship to disappear.

An explosion due to the shifting and spontaneous combustion of the manganese ore was the next theory to be shot down. The Navy had very strict rules governing the transportation of potentially dangerous materials. Although, manganese ore could explode in a carelessly maintained environment, during World War I the ships that carried the ore had an excellent record of safety. Many experts have pointed out that if there had been an explosion some wreckage from the *Cyclops* would have been found.

Because of its unusual superstructure, many Naval experts believed that the *Cyclops* capsized. This speculation was based upon the top-heavy appearance of the ship. In heavy seas the cargo might shift and the steel girder superstructure would not allow the *Cyclops* to recover from the list in a normal fashion. In this manner the ship would roll once or twice during a severe storm, the cargo would shift toward the roll and the ship then capsizes before anyone knew what hit them. Of course what was needed for this and other disaster at sea theories was a strong storm. The Navy records show relatively mild weather along the projected course of the *Cyclops.*

Lawrence Kushe's investigations uncovered an overlooked fact. According to the records at the National Climatic Center in Asherville, North Carolina, there was indeed a severe storm at sea during the time that the *Cyclops* would have been in the area. This storm weakened greatly when it traveled over land. Therefore, except in New York City where the winds reached 84 miles per hour, the storm went unnoticed by most of the land-based weather stations. The *Cyclops* could have capsized in the heavy seas and disappeared beneath the waves in one piece. It is also possible for the unstable manganese ore to have caused an explosion under these conditions and there would be no wreckage found. Kushe believes that the ship may have sunk in one piece near Norfolk, Virginia.

One problem with the storm theory is the *Cyclops's* sister ship the *Orion.* Here was a ship that was identical in every way with the ill fated *Cyclops.* In 1925 the Orion was dry-docked after encountering severe storm conditions with a full cargo of coal. The ship showed signs of buckling on the hull and flooding of her forepeak tanks. But she did not capsize because of her top heavy superstructure. In fact, the *Orion* enjoyed a long career in the service of the Navy.

The fact that the *Orion* did not sink in heavy seas does not in itself disprove Kushe's theory. The only way that we will know for sure what happened to the *Cyclops* is to find her intact or in pieces somewhere at the bottom of the ocean. Until then the ugly lady in another member of the convoy of vanished ships that plied the Bermuda Triangle.

A FOOTNOTE

Two other of the *Cyclops's* sister ships disappeared in seventeen days of each other during World War II. Both the *Proteus* and the *Nereus* left St. Thomas, Virgin Islands and both sister ships were bound for Portland, Maine and both ships vanished without leaving any clues as to how they vanished.

Again the world was at war. On November 23, 1941 the *Proteus* left port and disappeared and on December 10th the *Nereus* left the same port. The only crucial difference between the two dates was on November 23rd the United States was not at war and on December 10th she was. Some have claimed that the *Proteus* was sunk by the Germans. If this is true that would mean that the Germans were already attacking American shipping before any formal declaration of hostilities. There is no conclusive evidence of a German U-Boat torpedoing these two ships. Yet it is odd that two ships should join their sister ship the *Cyclops*, in the annals of unsolved mysteries, under similar circumstances, twenty three years later.

THE LADY CARROLL

Sometimes circumstances are so bizarre, no one can satisfactorily pierce the shroud of mystery that surrounds an inexplicable event. Such a case in point is the *Carroll A. Deering*.

On January 31, 1921 a five masted schooner, beached on Diamond Shoals, was sighted by the morning watch of the Cape Hatteras Coast Guard station off of North Carolina's Outer Banks. Because of heavy seas the Coast Guard could not get near the ship until the next day. On February 1st the Hatteras Guard, using their power boat, motored close enough to read the name of the ship and perform a visual inspection. Still the seas were too rough to safely allow the men to board the vessel. What they found was the *Carroll Deering* with sails unfurled plowing itself further into the beach. She was a newly-built ship with little evidence of damage. Missing were the two life boats and on her port side there was a ladder dangling in the wind. It also was evident that it was devoid of any crew. Puzzled, the Coast Guard motored through the heavy seas back to their station.

For the next few days no one could board the stranded ship; the seas remained extremely hazardous. Keeping busy, the Coast Guard checked out the ship in the Marine Register and contacted the *Carroll Deering's* owners, the G.C. Deering Company of Portland, Maine. The only other information to be found in the Marine Register was indeed it was a new schooner of 3,500 tons, built in early 1920 at Bath, Maine. Normally it was crewed by twelve officers and men.

Finally on February 4th the weather broke and the Coast Guard led by Captain James Carlson boarded the *Carroll Deering*. What they found was reminiscent of the abandonment of the *Mary Celeste*, the mystery ship of almost fifty years before.

A six-hour search of the ship disclosed the following facts. The *Carroll Deering* had suffered no collision with any other craft. As well as missing both life boats, both anchors were missing. In the galley, the now cold evening meal was still on the stove and the table was set, ready for dinner. The officers' salon lamps were still lit. Almost all of the luggage and clothing belonging to the captain and crew was missing. Except for the main navigational chart all of the other charts, logbooks, papers, chronometer and dining room clock were missing.

There were no signs of bloodshed on the decks; but since the sea had washed over the decks in the last four days, no traces of blood could be expected. Indications of intentional damage were found. The steering wheel and compass was smashed. Near the compass the Coast Guard found a sledge hammer. Some reports stated that the rudder was deliberately disengaged.

The captain of record was Willis B. Wormell. He came out of retirement in late August, to replace Captain William M. Merritt. Merritt had taken ill near Lewes, Delaware and asked to be relieved of his duties. Captain Wormell had a very distinguished record and was a legend in his own time.

Whatever occurred on the *Carroll Deering* must have involved the captain. Someone had slept in the captain's spare room. Three pairs of different sized boots were found in the captain's cabin; showing there were other men using the captain's quarters besides the captain. The main navigational chart revealed Captain Wormell's handwriting marking the course and then on January 23rd another hand appeared; Wormell's markings never appeared on the chart after that abrupt change.

Waterspouts are essentially water torna-
does, rarely seen, let alone photographed.
But this unusual phenomenia may hold
the key to one of the Bermuda Triangle's
most famous mysteries.

Copyright 1896 by J.N.Chamberlain
Cottage City. Mass.

These clues indicated the captain had lost or shared his command with other men.

A few weeks later the schooner was declared unsalvageable and blown up at sea. As mysteries go the *Carroll Deering* would have been forgotten, chalked up on the dark board of the unexplained, had not new and peculiar facts come to light.

In tracing the last known days of the *Carroll Deering*, the Coast Guard discovered they were anything but ordinary. While unloading his cargo, in Rio de Janeiro, Brazil, Captain Wormell had confided in a fellow captain that his crew drank too much and he could trust only one of his eleven man crew, his engineer Herbert Bates. He then wrote a few letters to his friends and family; these letters hinted at ominous forebodings. Woven into the usual messages of "greetings" and "I'll be back soon" were phrases of death and dying. One such line stated "...the thread of life is slender."

The G.C. Deering Company had ordered the *Carroll Deering* to proceed to Barbados, West Indies without cargo. The ship left Rio de Janeiro on December 2nd. In early January of 1921 the schooner docked in Barbados. During this time in port the first mate was arrested for drunkenness and Captain Wormell had to bail him out. Due to scheduling problems the company's agents in the West Indies ordered the *Carroll Deering* out to sea without cargo. Captain Wormell complained of feeling ill and wished to be relieved of his command. But it was determined that he was well enough to make the last leg of the trip to Norfolk, Virginia. The *Carroll Deering* sailed from Barbados on January 9th, with Wormell as Captain.

Two weeks passed and the *Carroll Deering* was sighted by the Frying Pan lightship off the Carolinas. As far as anyone could see the schooner was fine and sailing as planned to its destination.

After a brief gale in the area the *Carroll Deering* was sighted, four days later, by the Lookout Schoals lightship. This was a mere 60 miles from the last sighting! Something was amiss. Did the ship stop somewhere in the last four days?

It was late in the afternoon on January 29th when the *Carroll Deering* was spotted by the Diamond Schoals lightship. The men on the lightship saw that the crew was assembled on the foredeck. This is a dangerous place for the crew to gather while at sea. A red-haired man shouted to the lightship crew would they please contact the G.C. Deering Company of Portland, Maine and tell them that the *Carroll Deering* had lost both her anchors. Noticeable to the men aboard the lightship was the absence of the captain on the *Carroll Deering*. The ship sailed away and the lightship crew pondered what they should do. Unknown to the men on the *Carroll Deering*, the Diamond Schoal's lightship's radio was broken.

Steaming into view came a possible answer. A steamer moving with great speed, and on the same course as the *Carroll Deering*, was passing the lightship. Here was a chance to have someone radio the *Carroll Deering's* report to the mainland. The lighthouse men sent a message using the emergency signal light. No response came from the mysterious ship. Perhaps it was the darkness, or perhaps there was a tarp covering the bow, or perhaps it was a coat of freshly applied paint on the hull of the ship; at this point the Diamond Schoals crew realized that they could not read the name of the steamer. As a last resort, the captain of the lightship used his number 12 sea whistle. This far-reaching signal is universally understood as a demand to stop and respond. Without any acknowledgement and against the law of the sea, the steamer kept on course and disappeared into the night.

About the same time as the Diamond Schoals lightship's story became known, another mysterious development occurred. A bottle containing a note from the *Carroll Deering* washed up on a North Carolina beach. It stated that the schooner was captured by an oil burning subchaser, the crew of the *Carroll Deering* was hiding on the schooner, those found were handcuffed and the men from the oil burning ship were stealing everything in sight. The handwriting of the note was remarkably similar to that of the engineer, Henry Bates. Mrs. Wormell hired a handwriting expert and he stated unequivocally that it was Bates's handwriting.

Everything seemed to break loose when several newspapers printed articles about sixteen other ships missing in the same area, around the same time. Rumors of piracy and worse began to spread like oil on water. Bolshevik pirates, roaming the seas, capturing ships for the Soviet Union and kidnapping sailors were the worst tales. These popular buzzings grew into a fearful frenzy. It was time for the United States Government to officially investigate the mystery of the *Carroll Deering*.

Nothing can be so wonderful as watching the juggernaut of government move with all due dispatch. In early June the State De-

Legend holds that land pirates operating off the shoals of North Carolina would lure many a ship to its doom by using false beacons. Crews would quickly take what valuables they could carry off the ship before it was reduced to a beached wreck.

partment, Treasury Department, Navy Department and the Departments of Justice and Commerce began their investigations. Around the world consulates were ordered to be on the lookout for the missing vessels and crews. Ships and planes searched the Atlantic and Caribbean. Investigators pored over files and questioned anyone remotely involved with the *Carroll Deering.*

At first government investigators concurred with Mrs. Wormell's expert and declared the note found by Grey to have been genuine. But in September it was suddenly branded a hoax by the government experts. Grey confessed that he forged Bates's handwriting. Many sceptics thought this was a coverup of Soviet piracy. Even today, researchers suspect that, for whatever the reason, Grey was coerced into confessing the forgery.

In the end the vast amount of official time and money spent on the *Carroll Deering* mystery did not find a single new fact. Although investigations led to another piece of the mystery. Among the other ships missing at the same time was a steamer named *Hewitt.* From the description given by the crew of the Diamond Schoals lightship, the mystery steamship could well have been the *Hewitt.* By the end of 1921 the investigation of the *Carroll Deering* was discontinued with the announcement that the schooner must have encountered a heavy storm and the crew abandoned ship. Its only other accomplishment was the discrediting of the Bolshevik pirate theory. Why any pirates would want to take the crew of the schooner and not the ship itself was beyond all common sense and rogue practice, even for politically crazed Bolsheviks.

What happened to the *Carroll Deering?* Some believe there was mutiny aboard the *Carroll Deering.* This may explain the change of handwriting on the main navigational chart, the boots in the captain's quarters and perhaps the breaking of the steering wheel and the compass. This theory does not explain the meal left on the stove and the red haired man calling to the Diamond Schoals lightship. If the crew had mutinied why would they want the G.C. Deering Company to know the *Carroll Deering* had lost two anchors? And why would the mutineers decide to rebel right before dinner? In all the investigations no one ever found out the idenity of the red haired man. He was not part of the crew. Where did he come from? The 1921 official governmental explanation of a heavy storm lacks credibility. It is very unlikely that nothing

not even a piece of the lifeboats would not be found. An amended theory states that the crew was loaded onto another ship and this ship sunk in a storm. Yet no debris from any ship was found. What was the mystery ship that rudely passed the Diamond Schoals lightship later that day? Did that ship rendezvous with the schooner? There seem to be no answers to this mystery. The *Carroll Deering* sailed into mystery one day and left a legion of questions in her wake.

A FAMOUS FLIGHT INTO MYSTERY

One of the problems with designating the Bermuda Triangle as a mystery area is the heavy emphasis placed on the disappearance of Flight 19 by many of the early writers. On the surface it seemed to be a perfect enignma; a flight of five planes and a follow up search aircraft that vanished under bizarre circumstances. The problem arises when someone comes close to solving the mystery... it casts suspicion on all the other events used to prove the case of mysterious happenings in the Bermuda Triangle..

At 2:15 p.m., on December 12, 1945, a routine training flight of five TBM-3 Avengers took off from Fort Lauderdale Naval Air Station. The flight path was a triangular one taking the torpedo bombers over Hens and Chicken shoals on the first leg, turning north and flying over Grand Bahamas Island on the second leg and returning home on the last leg. A low level practice bombing run was to take place when they reached Hens and Chicken shoals. When the training mission flew into the skies over Fort Lauderdale, nobody knew this would be the beginning of a famous and complex mystery.

An hour and a half later, about the time when the flight should have been nearing the airbase, an emergency radio message was received from the flight leader. Lieutenant Charles Taylor. What follows is the most widely reported exchange between the Fort Lauderdale Naval Air Station and Flight 19.

Taylor: "Control tower, this is an emergency. We seem to be off course. We cannot see land. Repeat, we cannot see land."

Fort Lauderdale: "What is your position?"

Taylor: "We're not sure of our position. We cannot be sure of where we are. We seem to be lost."

Fort Lauderdale: "Head due west."

Taylor: "We don't know which way is west. Everything is wrong...strange...We cannot be sure of any direction. Even the ocean doesn't look the way it should."

Communications at this point were broken by static. At 4:00 p.m. a new leader of Flight 19 called Fort Lauderdale.

Leader: "We're not sure where we are. We think we must be 225 miles northeast of base...It looks like we're...It looks like we're entering white water... Don't come after me or..."

This is the last message Fort Lauderdale heard from Flight 19. One more message was heard by the Miami tower at 7:04 p.m., two hours after the flight must have run out of fuel!

Unknown: "FT...FT..."

No one else could have used these call letters. These were the designation letters of Flight 19!

It is unfortunate that this exhange has been used to support theories of UFO kidnappings, Atlantean death rays and space/time warps. The proponents of these ideas point out that the flight was in trouble and although they were experienced pilots they encountered something so bizarre that they either panicked or were taken by circumstances that we have yet to comprehend.

What is usually left out of most reports of this incident is an earlier conversation which occurred at 3:40 p.m., five minutes before Lieutenant Taylor spoke with Fort Lauderdale. The participants in this exchange are Lt. Taylor, Lieutenant Robert F. Cox and occassionally Marine Captain Edward Joseph Powers Junior. Lt. Cox was flying with a group of student pilots near Fort Lauderdale. Captain Cox was a student in Flight 19.

At first Cox overheard part of a conversation in progress.

Unknown: "Powers what is your compass reading?"

Powers: "I don't know where we are. We must have got lost after that last turn."

Cox: "This is FT-74, plane or boat calling 'Powers' please identify yourself."

Taylor: "This is MT-28."

This substition of "M" for the correct "F" T-28 was due to Taylor's recent transfer from Miami. Naval flights out of Miami had "M" designations and flights out of Fort Lauderdale had "F" designations.

Cox: "MT-28, what is your trouble?"

Taylor: "Both my compasses are out and I'm trying to find Fort Lauderdale. I'm over land but it's broken...I'm sure I'm over the Keys, but I don't know how far down."

Cox: "MT-28, this is FT-74, put the sun on your port wing if you're in the Keys and fly up until you get to Miami; then Fort Lauderdale is 20 miles further, your first port after Miami..." What is your present altitude?

I'll fly south and meet you."

Taylor: "I know where I am now. I'm at 2300 feet. Don't come after me."

This conversation puts a different light on the former conversation between Taylor and Fort Lauderdale. Instead of a sudden unknown occurence descending on Flight 19, we see the beginning of a series of mistakes. "Don't come after me or..." takes on a whole other aspect when put in it's proper perspective.

Radio transmissions were heard by Port Everglades until sometime near 6:30 p.m. at which point Taylor gave an ominous order.

Taylor: "All planes close up tight...Will have to ditch unless we reach landfall. When the first plane drops to 10 gallons we all go down together."

According to some very fine research done by Lawrence Kusche, Flight 19 ditched into the Atlantic, several hundred miles northeast of Cape Canaveral, after a series of tragic errors. The Martin Mariner that took off in search of Flight 19 was probably seen to have blown up in the winter skies by at least one ship and an airplane. The follow-up search plane may have had the predisposition to explode because of minute damage suffered during an accident that happened the previous day. Because they carried 2000 gallons of fuel, the Martin Mariners were know as "flying gas tanks." When they exploded there wasn't much to find.

This is not to say that the ill fated Martin Mariner was the only search carried out by the Navy. For six days ships and planes searched for rafts or signs of wreckage. Even though this was one of the most extensive searches carried out in the post war era, only sixty percent of the possible "ditching" area was explored. Kusche points out that when an Avenger ditches in the seas it is entirely possible for the plane to sink in 15 to 30 seconds. Barely enough time for a pilot to escape but not enough time to take a raft out of the airplane.

Much of current speculation believes that somehow Lieutenant Taylor became disoriented. He had been transferred to Fort Lauderdale only two weeks before. Many researchers into the Flight 19 mystery have found indications that Taylor requested to be excused from the flight. His reasons may have been trivial or intensely personal. Much has been made of a letter he took with him on his last flight. Whatever clouded his judgement he confused the Cays of the Bahama Islands for the Keys of Florida and flew north further out to sea rather than

The sea works quickly in reducing a proud ship into a heap of toothpicks and abandoned timbers. How many ships were destroyed by the seas of the Bermuda Triangle? No one will ever know!

west toward land.

Some troubling questions remain. Did the compasses fail or did Taylor mistrust his compass after he became lost? Did the students in the Hens and Chickens exercise make cumulative errors that threw the training flight off course? Did all the compasses fail at once? There still is a tiny mystery left after all.

Many sensationalists looking for the fantastic found Flight 19 their cup of tea. What Lawrence Kusche did is sound fact finding. By exploding some of the more ridiculous speculations surrounding the tragedy of Flight 19 he cast grave doubt on all of the Bermuda Triangle mysteries. Yet many strange things have and still do happen in the BermudaTriangle.

RIGHT BEFORE YOUR EYES

Here is an interesting unverified tale of the Triangle. In early January, 1960 Victor Hayward, a radar operator, was watching five Super-Sabre Jets going through manuevers during lunch hour. It was a warm day at Kidney Field Satellite Tracking Station and many people were enjoying the airshow. As the military jets soared into a cloud the lunch crowd idly watched. Imagine the shock when only four Super-Sabres came out of the cloud. No one heard an explosion nor did any one see a plane crash or debris fall out of the cloud. A search of the shallow waters near the disappearance produced no clues. It was a case of five went in and four came out; the famous vanishing jet magic show.

Hayward told this tale to friends and neighbors and somehow Charles Berlitz found this story for his book. No one has ever denied the story, but no one has come forward to confirm it either. Who the pilots were and what was the excuse given to the missing pilot's family has never been ascertained.

WHERE HAS MY TUG GONE?

Southern Cities was an 85 ton, 67 foot ocean going tugboat. On October 29, 1966 she departed Freeport, Texas bound for Tuxpan, Mexico with a barge carrying chemicals in tow behind her. She kept regular radio contact with her owners. The last report from the *Southern Cities* was on November 1st, when she gave her position as 43 miles offshore and 95 miles south of Port Isabel, Texas. November 2nd came and went and there was no further daily radio contact with the tugboat. Needless to say the *Southern Cities* did not arrive at Tuxpan on November 3rd as she was expected to. In fact she and her crew of six men were never seen or heard from again. The mystery only begins here.

The barge was found on November 5th, 105 miles north of Tuxpan. Attached to it was the 600 foot nylon tow line, intact. The barge and its barrels of caustic chemicals were undamaged. Within two days a cork life preserver, a ring lifebuoy and two pieces of the tugboat's name board were found.

The *Southern Cities* mystery is most perplexing. How could the tugboat breakup and the barge not show any signs of damage? A Coast Guard board of inquiry found no evidence of negligence or foul play. It was also noted at the inquiry that the ship had a large lifefloat, twelve life preservers and plenty of ring lifebuoys. The Coast Guard had no theories as to the fate of the tugboat. Nothing else was ever found of the *Southern Cities* and the Coast Guard closed another case of a disappearance in the Bermuda Triangle.

NEAR BAD NEWS FOR GOOD NEWS

Whatever occurred to the *Southern Cities* may have been similar to a near abduction of the tugboat *Good News*.

Captain Don Henry is a veteran seaman if ever there was one. A ship's captain during World War II, his career also includes deep sea diving as one of his many skills. Up to a fateful day in 1966 he thought he had seen everything the seas had to offer.

On a clear day the 160 foot long, 2,000 horsepower, sea going tug *Good News* was transporting a barge from Puerto Rico to Fort Lauderdale. Everything was going well and Captain Henry decided that this was an excellent time for a nap. He went to his cabin, closed his eyes and began to doze. Shouts and sounds of turmoil broke into his sleep. Instinctively, he bolted from his bunk and ran to the bridge. When he arrived he found the compasses were spinning frantically. Where moments before there was a calm sea and bright sky, now there was an enveloping milky fog and churning waters; the captain could not see any indication of a horizon.

Quickly he walked to the stern to check. All that was visible was a nylon rope extending straight out into a heavy white gauze blanket. With a strong yank on the tow line, Henry confirmed that the barge was still there.

Back to the bridge ran Captain Henry. He pulled the throttle to full ahead only to discover he had lost all power. All the electrical machinery and appliances were malfunctioning; they had no power. The engineer told the captain that the generator was run-

ning but it was not producing any electricity. Suddenly the engines kicked in and Henry could feel the tug strain against some incredibly strong force. Every bit of torque in the 2000 horsepower engine could not move the *Good News* one inch. Henry had a "spine-chilling feeling that somebody or something wanted the ship and crew to be in another place from where it was."

Finally the tug began to move with an irritating slowness. Henry started to see the outline of the barge emerge from the white fog. Abruptly the *Good News* broke free of the malevolent mist and shot forward into the sunshine. As unexpectedly as it began it ended. For miles around there were clear skies and calm waters. The elapsed time of the bizarre incident was twelve minutes.

After Captain Henry and the crew had a chance to catch their breaths, they inspected the tugboat and barge for damage. No structural damage was found, but the hull of the barge was very warm. It was much warmer than any natural forces could account for. Before the *Good News* docked in Fort Lauderdale, Henry attempted to change his dead batteries in his flashlight. It was then he discovered all the batteries aboard the tugboat were dead; a whole case of batteries had to be thrown away.

Did the *Southern Cities* suffer the same fate as the *Good News*? The tow line attached to the recoverd barge had a piece of the *Southern Cities* tugboat at the end of it. If what happened to Don Henry also happened to the crew of the *Southern Cities*, why did they succumb to this unknown force and not the crew of the *Good News*? Of course there may be a perfectly logical explanation for these two incidents.

Other ships have reported sudden electrical power loss. In March, 1971, the *USS Richard E. Byrd* had all its communication and navigation systems fail one by one. In a matter of minutes both systems were dead. The ship was 5 days out on a routine mission from Norfolk, Virginia, to Bermuda. It should have been an easy matter to continue navigating using a celestial fix at night, except for the fact that for 10 days the ship was surrounded by a heavy haze. Finally the *USS Richard E. Byrd* was able to contact a Navy plane that flew by and received the proper coordinates for Bermuda.

The *Vogelgesing*, in March, 1972, suddenly changed course, lost all power from its electrical systems and then came to a stop halfway between Florida and Puerto Rico. It wasn't until morning that they could get

The deadly Grumman "Avenger," work-horse torpedo bomber of the Pacfic fleet. Five of these planes took off one morning, disappearing into the legend the Bermuda Triangle.

Several of Grumman "Avenger" wrecks have been found in the Bermuda Triangle. None of them belong to the famous Flight

underway again.

On it's way back to Coconut Grove from a fishing trip, the diesel powered boat *Nightmare* began to wander off course. It was a clear night in September of 1973 and the captain could see the lights of Featherbed Banks as his compass began to drift 90 degrees away from the magnetic north. At the same time all the boat lights faded to black. Try as he might, the captain could not get the *Nightmare's* head in any other direction but north. Hanging on the north horizon was a black cloud like shape and the boat kept heading toward it. An unidentified light appeared to enter the dark presence, shortly after that the shape disappeared and everything returned to normal.

The strangest story of power loss in the Bermuda Triangle happened in August, 1975. Dr. Wayne Meshejian, a physicist, issued a statement that several weather satellites had temporarily malfunctioned when the satellites were over the Bermuda Triangle. This blackout occurred sporadically over a period of two years and it would only affect the visual pictures, not the infrared scans. Experts from the National Environmental Satellite Service claimed that this was a typical transmission scheduling problem and not some mysterious event linked to the area between New York and Cuba. Dr. Meshejian countered that this area was an important weather region, it would make no sense to blackout pictures from this location. Further, the physicist pointed out, the satellites worked fine for the first six months of service. Why should they all suddenly develop the same problem? The satellite service did not bother to respond to those questions.

JUST SCRATCHING THE SURFACE

There are hundreds of mysterious incidents that have taken place in the Bermuda Triagle. Some of the bizarre events, not mentioned here, include: strange lights of all sizes, ghost ships and planes, columns of water that appear from nowhere and airplanes that glow with an eerie green glow. Theories as to what causes any particular incident or set of incidents are also numerous. Some of the latest thinking on the subject states that electromagnetic forces may affect the mental abilities of a large number of people at a specific place and time. It is this confusion which might have caused much of the odd behavior reported in many of the disappearances in this region. Closely associated with eruption of electromagnetic forces are blackouts of radio communications, calm seas and fog. Sound familiar?

It may be there is not one cause for all of these strange phenomena. Perhaps there are several related events of piracy, another

The Carrol A. Deering, *the last great ghost ship of the Bermuda Triangle, drifted off Diamond Shoals and on to Ocracoke Island. Subsequent storms buried the wreck under several tons of sand. In 1945 a powerful hurricane exposed the hull one more time. A grim reminder of the mysteries of the Bermuda Triangle.*

set of incidents which were caused by sudden weather changes and several cases of human errors which resulted in tragedy, that when totaled together give the Bermuda Triangle an ominous tone. Not every disappearance that happens in this region is the result of UFOs or a Fourth Dimensional door. To make a statement like that is to bring out the super rational in all of us. Yet when all the stories are sifted for the readily explainable there remains a few events for which there are no rational answers. It is those events which may be truly great mysteries of the Bermuda Triangle.

Shoe Size 13+... The Search For Bigfoot

Something is lurking in the woods. When you're by the campfire or in your country home it is watching you. It has the shape of a man, it is covered with hair, it is tall with long strong arms at its sides, it can move through the woods at great speed and if you look real quick you will see him before he vanishes... some witnesses have claimed that the beast's eyes glow in the darkest night.

No, this is not a blurb from a horror movie. It is what is known about an often sighted creature known as Sasquatch or Bigfoot. This humanoid has been sighted in British Columbia, Canada, and the states of Florida, Texas, Illinois, Arkansas, Missouri, Iowa, Indiana, New Jersey, New York, along the Appalachian Trail and in the Rocky Mountains. Countless articles and quite a few books have been devoted to this intelligent creature that seems to share our continent with us and yet remains hidden from view. Once for a short while, a Sasquatch may have been captured by people who did not know how important their find was.

A BRIEF CAREER

On July 4th, 1884, the Victoria, British Columbia, Daily British Colonist, ran a banner headline: "A strange creature captured above Yale!"

It was a Monday morning and a train crew was on their normal run from Lytton. As the train was nearing the end of a tunnel, the engineer noticed what looked like a man lying near the tracks. Quickly he blew the train whistle and almost instantaneously applied the brakes. Within a few seconds several tons of locomotive and rolling stock came to a screeching halt. All this racket awoke the "man" and brought him to his feet, uttering a "bark" of surprise the man began climbing up a steep rocky bank. The train crew gave chase; they believed that this was a "demented indian" who should be captured for his own safety. Finally they cornered the hairy man, who began to bite and scratch at the train crew. They thought of an excellent way of capturing this hysterical hirsute man without getting themselves injured in the process; the train crew hit him on the head with a rock, thus rendering him unconscious.

Only on closer examination did the men learn that this was not an "indian", but something that looked "half man and half beast." 'Jocko' as the creature has been called by his captors, is something of a gorilla type standing about four feet seven inches in height and weighing 127 pounds. He has long, black, strong hair and resembles a human being. His forepaw is much longer than a man's fore arm, and he possesses extraordinary strength, as he will take hold of a stick and break it by wrenching it or twisting it, which no man can break in the same way." Later, some of the townspeople discovered a few of Jocko's eating habits. "His favorite food so far is berries, and he drinks fresh milk with evident relish. On the advice of Dr. Hannington raw meats have been withheld from Jocko, as the doctor thinks it would have a tendency to make him a savage."

When news of the capture reached the town of Yale, by the newly installed town telephone, a large crown gathered to see Jocko. Only a quick glimpse of the beast was caught by the townspeople at the train crew hurried him into the railroad's machine shop. The newspaper article was unclear how Mr. Tilbury became Jocko's keeper. It was written that the humanoid became quite fond of Tilbury. After an undisclosed length of time, Jocko left with his keeper and went east. Eventually both man and beast were to end up in London, England, where Tilbury planned a permanent sideshow for Jocko. Their departure was the last time that either the creature or Tilbury was heard from. The rumor that lingered after their disappearance was that Jocko died in his cage aboard the train and Tilbury quietly buried him somewhere between British Columbia and New York. Afterwards Tilbury lost himself in America looking for another act to promote.

Was this a young Bigfoot? Many investigators believe it was. The Colonist published two other accounts about Sasquatch, once in 1901 and again in 1904. Although the circumstances varied greatly, in essence the articles ended with the same questions that the discovery Jocko prompted...."Does he belong to a species hitherto unknown to this continent, or is he really what the train men first thought he was, a crazy Indian?"

IN OLDEN DAYS

Anthropologically speaking Indians have very little facial and body hair. The towns-people knew most of the tribes lived in the vicinity of Yale and none of these Indians remotely fit that kind of description. It is highly unlikely that this hairy humanoid was an Indian.

Many of the Indians of North America have had some chance encounters with the Sasquatch, as reflected by their legends and stories. Certain tribes inhabiting the region from British Columbia to Northern California incorporated Bigfoot's likeness in their totems and ritual masks. These Indians noted that the female Sasquatches were observed all to have had large breasts. They did not question whether what they have seen was a hairy white man. They also knew it was to be left alone.

An early Spanish explorer noted some description of Bigfoot as told to him by the Northern California Indians. Almost all the tribes had a great fear of the Sasquatch. As well as being tall, covered with dark hair and ugly, the explorer was told that Bigfoot was equipped with "sharper and stronger fangs than those of a bear,...toes and fingers armed with long curved claws, any unfortunate body he slaps is broken into a thousand pieces." This sounds quite ominous. Is it possible that the Sasquatch is a creature that resorts to violence?

TEDDY TELLS A TALE

In his youth, Theodore Roosevelt roughed it for several years in the Dakota badlands. Perhaps it was here that he heard the violent tale of Bigfoot from an old frontiersman known as Bauman. Roosevelt was so impressed by the man's sincerity that he included the story in his book The Wilderness Hunter, published in 1893.

The only life that Bauman ever knew was in the wilderness, at the edge of North America civilization. A small frontier town was too hectic for the hunter/ trapper; he preferred the company of few people and the open skies of the woodlands, prairies, and mountains.

When Bauman was a young man, sometime in the mid 1800's, he was trapping with a friend near the Snake River. They were in a wild and little known mountain pass that had a small stream running through it. Other trappers told them that this particular pass was known to be home to a large number of beaver. Bauman was also told about a hunter who was savagely killed by a bloodthirsty creature the year before in this same mountain pass. His partially devoured remains were found by some prospectors. Since the attack on the hunter hardly anyone ventured into the gorge. Ignoring the implications of the grisly tale Bauman and his friend made camp in a small meadow. Next they explored their new trapping grounds. After setting a few traps along the stream they returned to camp. They were surprised by what they found.

"....During their short absence something, apparently a bear, had visited their camp, and had rummaged among their things, scattering the contents of their packs and with sheer wantonness destroying their lean-to. The footprints of the beast were quite plain, but at first they paid no particular heed to them..."

Once the lean-to was rebuilt, Bauman's partner became intrigued by the pattern of the footprints. These animal tracings appeared to be bear tracks with one major exception ....they indicated an animal which walked exclusively on two legs. Bears generally walk and run on four. This seemed to be a joke to Bauman but to humor his friend they examined the tracks. His friend was right, the tracks belonged to a large animal that walked upright. By now the sun had set and there was not enough light to follow the footprints. The two men settled inside the lean-to and fell asleep. It was not a restful sleep.

"At midnight Bauman was awakened by some noise and sat up in his blankets. As he did so his nostrils were struck by a strong wild-beast odor and he caught the loom of a great body in the darkness at the mouth of the lean-to. Grasping his rifle, he fired at the vague, threatening shadow, but must have missed, for immediately afterwards he heard a smashing of the underwood as the thing rushed off into the impenetrable blackness of the forest and night."

The two men spent the rest of the evening wearily watching the opening of their shelter in case their unknown visitor returned. It did not bother them again that night. In the morning, while they worked their traps, the men kept together and kept a watchful eye out for the animal. Bauman and his friend almost forgot about the creature until they returned to their camp in the small meadow. Again the beast had struck and again everything was torn up and again there were footprints in the soft mud around the stream. This time Bauman closely scrutinized the tracks and decided whatever this creature was that walked on two legs it was not something to fool around with.

That evening the two men slept in shifts with a roaring campfire burning through the night. As if the creature had a demonic clock in its head, he returned around midnight. For an hour it roamed the forest on the opposite hillside. Bauman could hear the crackling of twigs and branches as the beast moved. The worst moments came when the animal made a low moaning sound, it was the kind of sound that could chill the bone no matter how hot the campfire was or how close one sat. As abruptly as the creature had come it vanished further into the woods. Both men prided themselves on being able to take a hint and decided to leave the mountain pass as soon as it was light.

Daylight is a marvelous booster of morale and courage. The trappers felt childish leaving the gorge so quickly. As they picked up their empty traps they heard rustling in the small pines and an occasional twig snap in the distance. They told themselves these noises were just the normal woodland creatures going about their business. By noon Bauman and his friend were brave frontiersmen once more, who had faced all kinds of danger and had come through without any serious problems. Bauman decided to retrieve the last three traps from a small pond while his friend returned to the camp and finished packing their belongings. To Bauman's surprise there were beaver in the traps and he spent a few hours preparing the skins. The sun was beginning its final journey toward sunset and Bauman realized he should be getting back to his friend.

"He came to the edge of the little glade where the camp lay, and shouted as he approached it, but there was no answer. The camp fire had gone out, though the thin blue smoke was still curling upwards. Near it lay the packs, wrapped and arranged. At first Bauman could see nobody...Stepping forward again he shouted, and as he did so his eyes fell on the body of his friend, stretched beside the trunk of a great fallen spruce. Rushing toward it, the horrified trapper found that the body was still warm, but that the neck was broken, while there were four great fang marks in the throat."

Bauman quickly deciphered the newest set of beast tracks and realized that his friend was attacked from behind while sitting on the spruce log waiting for his return. This was not the worst part of the tale told by the footprints. "It had not eaten the body, but apparently had romped and gambolled around it in uncouth, ferocious glee, occasionally rolling over and over it; and had then fled back into the soundless depths of the woods." Leaving everything but a small pack and his rifle Bauman ran from that terrifying mountain pass believing that this forest devil would come for him next.

This story as told to Theodore Rossevelt is unusual in the annals of Bigfoot. There is very little of this kind of violence in most accounts of the Sasquatch. In fact, sometimes these creatures can be very friendly in an odd sort of way.

SUMMER CAPERS

Toba Inlet, British Columbia was as primeval a wilderness as one could find in 1924. It is a sizeable fiord about 100 miles north of Vancouver. This was to be a well deserved vacation for construction worker and lumberjack Albert Osterman. It had been a long hard year without a break. During that time he set as a goal not only enjoying a few weeks of hunting and fishing, but also finding a lost gold mine he heard existed somewhere near Toba Inlet.

Osterman hired an Indian guide to take him to the head of the inlet. On the way the Indian told Osterman about a white man who regularly came out of this region laden with gold. Visions of glittering golden nuggest dazzled in his mind's eye. When Osterman asked what became of this white man the guide told him that the white man disappeared; he was probably killed by a Sasquatch. The Indian went to great lenghts to describe the Sasquatch for Osterman, who clearly didn't believe a word of it.

When they reached the site of the base camp Osterman paid the Indian and told him to return in three weeks. For the first week he hunted for food a little, searched for the lost mine a little and enjoyed being out in nature very much. Then one day, upon returning to camp, he noticed his equipment was disturbed, not stolen, just slightly askew. At first he thought this was a porcupine looking for food. For two nights he lay in his sleeping bag attempting to catch the animal. Each night he fell asleep and each day he discovered some food missing. Osterman was able to exclude porcupines from his list of night visitors by the types of food not taken. Porcupines love salt and his salt was untouched. Determined to confront the nocturnal pest Osterman loaded his rifle and put it along with a few other possessions in his sleeping bag. He would stay awake, fully dressed, for the entire evening and end this petty larceny once and for all. Little did Osterman realize that this night was going

Years of Indian legends and fireside tales have yielded drawings like these. In the absence of firm photographic evidence this is the best image availible. Most of the personal observations have a remarkable similarity to stories of the Himalayan Yeti.

to end up, not as a wilderness misdemeanor but as a felony...kidnapping.

With all his intentions of staying awake, Osterman fell asleep anyway. In a half dreamy state he felt himself being picked up still wrapped in his sleeping bag. Suddenly he realized this was really happening; he had been lifted off the ground and was being carried on the back of some large animal. As much as he tried to reach his hunting knife or rifle, the position of his body in the sleeping bag would not allow him any such movement. After an hour Osterman understood that he was being carried by an eight foot giant and was not on the back of a horse. This giant also had taken his pack sack too; every so often the pans would rattle in the pitch black woodland night.

After a journey of many hours and an estimated thirty miles inland, Osterman was dumped on the ground. He slowly crawled out of the sleeping bag into the darkness. His whole body ached from the uncomfortable trip and he began to massage the soreness in his legs and arms. The sun rose soon afterwards and Osterman could see his captors. They were hairy giants, four of them to be exact. These creatures must be the Sasquatch that the Indian guide mentioned. Somewhat at a loss for words Osterman said, "What do you guys want with me?"

This was beginning to sound like a comedy, "How I spent my summer vacation." Here was Osterman an unwilling guest of a family of Bigfoots thinking how he could escape their hospitality. It was not as easy as it might seem. There were two older Sasquatches, one male and the other female and two younger ones, also male and female. The oldest Bigfoot was about eight feet tall and weighed 750 pounds. He had longer eye teeth than the others and his arms looked very powerful, but well proportioned to the rest of his body. Slightly shorter was the elder female, she was about seven feet tall and 550 pounds. Osterman noted that of the two females the older one had large hanging breasts. At slightly less than 300 pounds, the youger female had very small or no breasts at all and was about seven feet tall. The young male was the same height as the young female and he weighed about 350 pounds. Each of them had coarse black hair covering their bodies, except for their eyelids and the soles of their feet.

When he first arrived at the Sasquatch forest household "the old lady," as Osterman called the elder female, objected to his presence. With a lot of "chattering" back and

forth, the old man won the day and was allowed to keep his prize. After that the old lady tended to stay away from Osterman. She spent her days hunting for roots, grass, berries, twigs and nuts. The young man was very inquisitive and the old man a little less so. They both found the contents of Osterman's pack sack fascinating. He had food, his rifle, a few pots and pans and his knife. Often the young man would look at these items, he never touched them, just looked. The old man was keenly interested in the snuff box and its contents. This eventually proved to be Osterman's method of escape.

Two days into his captivity Osterman tried to run away. The Sasquatch home was in a small 10 acre basin cut along between two cliff walls. A narrow break in the rock was the only entrance. When Osterman tried to escape through this opening the old man caught up to him and threw him back into the small valley. He had considered shooting his way out. He also considered the size and strength of the old Sasquatch; if the first few shots couldn't kill the creature then he would surely be killed by it.

After six days Osterman had an idea. The elder Bigfoot was very interested in the snuff. Every day he gave the Sasquatch some to chew. The old man really liked to chew the tobacco. Osterman planned to give him enough to kill the Bigfoot. He really didn't want to, but he really didn't want to remain the guest of the Sasquatch family.

For the first time since Osterman arrived, he made a fire. It was the morning of the seventh day and he wanted some good hot coffee. Naturally the older and younger Sasquatch joined him to see this hot new development. Osterman finished his breakfast and was drinking a tin of coffee, when he decided to try out his idea. He offered the old man some of his snuff. Some versions of this story say that this was an unplanned action and others say that this was indeed Osterman's plan. He held on tightly to the snuff box so the elder Sasquatch could not take much of the tobacco. Miffed the elder Sasquatch grabbed the whole snuff box and proceeded to devour all the tobacco. He liked the taste so much that the old man licked the inside of the container. After a few minutes the old Bigfoot became violently ill and ran to the stream. At the same time Osterman grabbed his rifle and few things and shot toward the narrow entrance. His escape attempt was noticed by the old woman who set off after him. Osterman managed to get through the opening before the elder female

Mysteries
in Color

Mermaids could be the descendents of the elusive manatee.

Plesiosaur Elasmosaurus may well have been one of the ancestors of lake monsters in Lake Champlain and Loch Ness.

Many UFO's have been sighted in the neighborhood of Mount Rainier, Washington.

Some believe that bigfoot is a lineal descendent of Neanderthal man.

These reconstructions of Neaderthal man bear a striking resemblance to some of the photos and sightings of bigfoot.

Crater Lake. Numerous sightings of bigfoot have been reported in the surrounding forests of this beautiful high-mountain lake.

Crater Lake.

*Legend has it that Captain Kidd's treasure is buried at Rye Beach,
New Hampshire.*

could catch him. Quickly he turned and fired his rifle over the head of the pursuing female. She stopped dead in her tracks and let out a squeal, but she did not follow him.

Using his compass and familiar landmarks, Osterman made his way back to civilization. His first meeting with his fellow humans would give rise to a dilemma. Should he tell anyone about his encounter with the Sasquatch? Shortly before he met a group of lumberjacks he had made up his mind. Three days after his escape Osterman walked into a logging camp and told a story of finding himself lost while he was prospecting. In essence this was almost the case. For thirty years he said nothing about the Sasquatch. Fear of ridicule was his reason for keeping silent. This is very understandable. To admit having taken part in a bizarre adventure is to invite classification as, at best, a crank. It was only when other people began talking about their experiences with Bigfoot that Osterman recounted how he spent his summer vacation in 1924.

These three incidents are classics in the search for an answer to the Bigfoot mystery. Jocko is especially noteworthy since it appears to be the only time that a creature like or similar to the Bigfoot has ever been captured. Although the sightings of the Sasquatch in North America continued after Osterman's holiday, not much was made of them until the Yeti or Abominable Snowman of the Himalayas made the headlines in 1951.

THE MEDIA HAS A PICNIC

Eric Shipton and Michael Ward were doing reconnaissance for an attempt to finally scale the top of Mt. Everest. In the course of their work they found and photographed a series of footprints on the Menlung Glacier near the Tibet-Nepal border. These were not human footprints but of a creature that no one but the Sherpa porters could identify. They called it the "Yeti." Using an ice-axe as a point of reference Shipton photographed the 13 inch long and inch wide footprint. This was not just an isolated print in the snow but one of a series of two trails that led across the glacier. Shipton closely examined the tracks in the crystalline snow and concluded that both of them were made at the same time...only a few hours before the expedition arrived! The trails led to the edge of a crevasse where upon both creatures appeared to have leaped across and used their toes to gain purchase on the other side.

Eric Shipton's photographs of the Yeti footprints were given a greater credibility because of his standing as an explorer and his work that helped in the successful conquest of Mt. Everest by Sir Edmund Hillary and Sherpa Tenzing in 1953. It took this evidence to set an explosion around the world in Abominable Snowman stories. Russia had a creature quite like the Yeti and so did China, but the biggest surprise was North America had one too. Reporters and researchers in the United States and Canada began looking into legends, old newspaper files and eyewitness accounts of the Sasquatch. There was a large body of sightings that were never taken into consideration by anyone. It was as if the Daily British Colonist had never published its story about Jocko until the 1950's. In this more accepting environment Albert Osterman came forward with his encounter with the Sasquatch. The name Bigfoot wasn't coined until 1958, when a set of North American "Yeti" footprints were discovered.

BIGFOOT IS BORN

In August, 1958, a construction crew was working on a series of logging trails north of Klamath, California, when one of the workers noticed some strange tracks on the freshly laid dirt roadbed. Noting that these were unusual footprints he promptly smoothed them over with an earth moving machine. For the next week the Sasquatch returned to the site and left a new set of tracks. By now everyone had noticed them.

The footprints came down from the surrounding hilly woodland, across the road, and to the small stream opposite the road. On the trip back to the woods the Sasquatch always avoided the heavy machinery. These were not small Yeti type footprints, these measured 16 inches long and 8 inches wide. Everyone might have forgotten this episode had it not been for a bulldozer operator named Jerry Crew. He made a plaster casting of the footprint and took it to a local newspaper in Eureka. Crew told the reporters not only had he seen these kind of tracks at his present construction site, but over the years at other locations in Northern California. Within a few days the Associated Press ran Crew's story with a photograph of the plaster casting. Here's where some anonymous caption writer made a little history. When the picture of the 16 inch casting was distributed, it appeared with the caption of "Bigfoot." Thus a name was born for the North American cousin of the Abominable Snowman.

Crew's casting was made in the Bluff Creek Valley region of California. This area

This is the famous and controversial Patterson photograph of Bigfoot. Some skeptics have called this picture nothing more than a man in an ape suit. Other Bigfoot investigators who have carefully examined this photo have noted many characteristics which could not be duplicated by a human.

was to become famous in Bigfoot annals in 1967.

Roger Patterson, a former rodeo cowboy, had been on the trail of Sasquatch for many years. In 1966 his book about the possibility of an Abominable Snowman in America was published. It was not what one could call a scholarly tome, but it did establish his credentials as a bigfoot buff.

One year after his book was published, Patterson and his friend Bob Gimlin were searching the Bluff Creek region for signs of the Sasquatch. Patterson had been near Mount St. Helens, another famous Bigfoot area, when he received word from his wife that new tracks were found at Bluff Creek, and so he and Bob Gimlin rushed to the area. In order to cover more ground they chose to explore in the crisp autumn air on horseback. It was almost three weeks that they were out in the back country. The only tracks they found were usual deer, bear and cougar. Patterson had brought with him a 16mm movie camera and was learning how to use it. He took movies of the changing fall colors and the both of them roamed the wild.

It was a Saturday. Patterson and Gimlin were riding around a bend in the Bluff Creek, abruptly both horses began to rear. Both men were startled. Both men knew horses and Gimlin quickly got his under control and Patterson using all his rodeo talents slid off his, at the same time he pulled the movie camera out of the saddlebag. In front of them was a Sasquatch crossing the creek and making tracks for the woods. Unable to focus the camera immediately, Patterson began shooting and adjusting as he ran toward the creature. The film records a good deal of confusion at the beginning of this famous footage. One of the functions that was never corrected was the film speed; this accounts for the jerkiness of the image. But in spite of the technical drawbacks, the film became clear enough to see a human like creature, covered with black hair, striding towards the woods. Still filming Patterson stopped running at a distance of 80 feet. The Sasquatch, without breaking stride, turned and faced him for a split second. It was in these few frames that one can see that it was female with large drooping breasts. Her face was flat and hairy with a thick brow ridge. According to the film she had almost no neck with her head sitting practically on top of her shoulders. The female Bigfoot continued her getaway through the creek bottom and into the woods. She walked with a smooth powerful motion while gracefully swinging her arms. Then she was gone.

Excited, Gimlin and Patterson followed the Bigfoot's tracks for a short time. But the further they went the more they became cautious and finally they became fearful. What if the Sasquatch decided to turn on them? She may not like to be followed by two strange hairless human beings. They turned back to photograph and make castings of the Bigfoot's footprints. From the depth of the tracks in the creek sandbar they estimated her weight at 350-400 pounds. From their own height and the height of some of the surrounding trees they figured that she was close to seven feet. Still lingering in the air was the Sasquatch's unpleasant odor.

The air has yet to be cleared of the controversy enveloping the authenticity of the Patterson-Gimlin film. Patterson's passion as a Bigfoot buff has become a reason for some critics to call the film a fake without ever viewing it. If Patterson was not so passionate on the subject of the Sasquatch then he would not have been there to film the momentary appearance of the creature.

Some of the valid criticisms of the film involves the walk and physique of the creature as well as the overall appearance of the hairy skin. To some who have seen the film, the Bigfoot seems to have a masculine build and the movements of a female ape or humanoid. In a point and counterpoint, some scientists take motion and the fluid stride of the Sasquatch into account and come to completely opposite conclusions. Point: the gait is smooth but it seems to support an enormous weight and therefore the physique is strong and appears less femine to humans but perhaps it would not seem so to the Sasquatch. Counterpoint: the walk is of a modern man who walks in an exaggerated manner which gives the appearance of the top half of the body floating while the bottom half is strenuously moving, therefore it is a man in a costume. Some overweight humans will approximate the same walk to compensate for the added heaviness on the top part of their skeletal frame. These contradictory viewpoints mainly come from scientists who used biomechanics to analyze the footage.

The hairy skin which looks like a bad ape costume is also a minus and at the same time a plus. If it is a costume, then it is worn by a powerfully built man who never had the seat of the garment tailored. To all who have seen the film the rear of the Sasquatch does look rather baggy but this could also be Bigfoot fat collecting in a most unflattering manner. The Smithsonian Institution called this film a joke in 1971. They

The world first became aware of Bigfoot-like creatures when Sir Edmund Hillary, conqueror of Mt. Everest, held a news conference to announce the formation of expedition into the Himilayas to capture this elusive creature. Needless to say he did not succeed.

said it was all too obvious that this was a man in a bad ape costume walking in an unnatural manner. Yet the findings of two Soviet anthhropologists found the interactions of the creatures movements in the Patterson-Gimlin film to be ".... Absolutely non-typical of man."

How much can be discovered by this film remains in doubt. Bob Gimlin can shed no more light on the circumstances surrounding the filming. In fact, even though he readily affirms the authenticity of the film, he also gives the impression, to those who have interviewed him, he wishes all the notoriety would just go away. Roger Patterson has only the film to speak for him. He died in 1974.

WHO WILL GUARD THE GUARDS?

By now you are probably thinking that all the Sasquatch occurrences only happen in the Pacific Northwest and people who don't live in that region never have to worry about encountering one. That may have been how three Michigan National Guardsmen felt in the summer of 1976.

Northwestern Michigan is noted for its endless ridges and valleys of pine, oak and aspen. Located in this sparsely populated portion of the state is a military reserve used by the region's National Guard for summer bivouac. Into these idyllic forests march thousands of young men practicing the art of war. They carry, ride and tow weapons of fierce destruction through scenes of pristine beauty. And sometimes they will stop in their maneuvers to watch a deer or a hawk or the sun setting behind a hill. Even if they rarely fire these weapons they are secure in the knowledge that there is nothing here that can harm them.

The sun had dropped below the hills hours ago. For the three men stationed inside the armored personnel carrier it was a time for guard duty, light conversation and a cat nap. They did not hear the heavy footsteps approach their vehicle. What each of the three men did hear was a horrible growl and a vicious pounding on the carrier's door. One of the men peeked out of the side view-slit. In front of him was a large human like creature. First panic broke out as each man tried to get a look at the Sasquatch and managed to catch a glimpse of their assailant. Then the panic was sustained when the pounding became a rocking motion of the whole vehicle. The radioman made his way to his device, crashing from side to side like a sailor caught in a terrible sea. To his horror, he discovered the radio couldn't function...the

Bigfoot had snapped the antenna! Orders stated they were to remain on watch until morning. But orders never considered a Sasquatch trying to pry the hatch off with its hands. While they were deciding on a course of action the rear view mirror was torn off the carrier. Orders may be orders but survival is best. The driver waited until the creature stopped rocking the carrier; then he started the engine and drove down the trail, leaving the Bigfoot in the dust.

Stopping at the first house they could find, they began honking the horn. John Howe heard this racked and peered out his window. There was an armored personnel carrier in front of his house, lights on and horn blaring. Howe shouted a, them to be quiet and went back to bed. Now the guardsmen were trying his patience, the honking wouldn't stop. He didn't mind if the young men wanted to get drunk; he did mind if they were going to make a racket in his front yard. Howe was not prepared for the Guardsmen ringing his doorbell, something must be wrong he thought. When he opened the door there stood three frightened men blurting out the most incredible story that Howe had heard.

The subsequent investigation by the Sheriff's Department of Kyle Lake found no tracks or evidence, except for a snapped antenna and a smashed rearview mirror. All who interviewed the Guardsmen did conclude that they were sincere and seemed to be telling the truth.

THE RABBIT THIEF

The Northeastern corridor that includes Boston, New York City and Washington D.C. is one of the most densely populated urban and suburban areas in North America. This is not what one might call Bigfoot country. There may be a few strange people in New York City, but the Sasquatch is not among them. Yet 50 miles from the Big Apple is a very small town of Wantage, New Jersey. It is situated on a rural and hilly countryside with three heavily forested state parks nearby. This area of the state has been rumored to have at least one Bigfoot in residence.

On may 22, 1977, the Sites family discovered something had broken into their barn. Whatever it was, its approach was direct. The barn door was ripped off and the boards of the rabbit hatch were smashed. Inside Mrs. Sites found several rabbits squeezed to death and a few were missing.

That evening the family heard an uproar coming from the front yard. Taking no

chances, Mr. Sites turned the yard lights on from inside the house. Through the windows the family could see a hairy creature pacing about the yard. Mrs. Sites thought the Sasquatch was showing off in the bright lights. It was brown, humanoid in appearance, with enough hair in it's face to approximate a heave full face beard. What looked odd about the creature was the apparent lack of a neck and the demonic red glowing eyes.

Bob Jones made this plaster impression of a Bigfoot print in a northeastern New Jersey swamp. Is civilization pushing Bigfoot into extinction? Will the New York Jets and Giants football teams draft the creature for next year's front line?

The family dog either attracted by the noise or lights came slowly into the yard, keeping its body low to the ground and ready to spring. When the dog let out a snarl, the Sasquatch turned and faced his attacker. Gleaming sharp teeth were bared, muscles coiled, in one huge powerful effort the dog propelled itself at the spot where there should have been a neck on the creature. With a casual flick of its arm the Bigfoot stopped the dog in midair and deflected the canine's trajectory 20 feet to the side. Stunned, but not badly hurt the dog ran into the shed. Like something that dwells in a nightmare, the creature stared at the house with those glowing red eyes and then it turned and lopped off into the darkness beyond the glare of the front yard lights.

On the following night the Sites family was prepared for the night visitor. Mr. Sites had a few of his friends come by to see the Sasquatch. Waiting inside the house, with the front yard lights blazing, Mr. Sites and his friends were armed with shotguns. The Sasquatch appeared later in the evening. Staring from the front door the guests had a chance to marvel at this incredible sight before the whole group blasted the Bigfoot. It howled as if it was badly wounded and ran away.

Several inquiries were made into this incident. One of the groups involved was the Society for the Investigation of the Unexplained. No blood was found in the Site's yard. The investigators did view the barn door, the rabbit hutch and the dead rabbits. While the SITU team was there, they heard howling from the nearby swamp. The creature was observed a few times since then.

THE BEST GUESS

To think about the existence of Sasquatch is either to believe that all the stories, all the footprints, all the eyewitnesses are either liars, fakes and have had hallucinations or there is a creature living on the North American continent that doesn't want to make itself known except in brief encounters. As with most other unexplained phenomena, the search for Bigfoot lends itself to the quick brushoff by sceptics. They readily point to this hoax or that prank, perpetrated by teenagers and publicity seeking individuals. Sometimes, as in the case of Sir Edmund Hillary, honest people are fooled by circumstances of which they did not initiate. In 1954, Hillary discovered the existence of several "Yeti" scalps while on an expedition to photograph one of these creatures in Tibet. He was told by the Sherpas some monasteries had these items and the monks revered them as the holiest of relics. Hillary's reputation in Tibet was such that he was allowed to borrow one of the scalps for further research. It took a few years, but the final word on these Yeti relics was they were unintentional fakes. It seems these relics were made from pieces of the same animal and molded into the cone-like shape. All of this happened over 300 years ago. Why it was done has been forgotten and it was assumed, by those in possession of the scalps, these items once were the top part of the Yeti's head.

Two classes of theories are currently being considered by experts who believe in the existence of Bigfoot. There is either a relic human or a descendant from a prehistoric ape.

Neanderthal man vanished from the face of the earth over thirty thousand years ago. The disappearance of this predecessor of modern man has never been solved. Our direct ancestor Cro-Magnon man may have the key to the mystery, but there are none around for us to ask. Some experts theorize that Cro-Magnon man took advantage of the hairlessness, appearing almost childlike in comparison to the Hirsute Neanderthal, to ingratiate themselves with this older species and then slaughter the unsuspecting competitor. In any case it is quite possible Neanderthal man did not die out completely. Bigfoot and his other cousins may be the direct descendant of the Neanderthal as we are of the Cro-Magnon.

The prehistoric ape theory describes a descendant from Gigantopithecus. His remains were discovered in 1930 by Dr. Ralph von Koenigswald. It is surmised that the ancestor of the giant ape migrated away from early man, a creature that Gigantopithecus could not successfully compete with proto humans for survival. Its long journey through time included mutations to the Yeti, Sasquatch and other elusive species. Yet the one instinct from its ancestors remains...wariness of humans.

If there is to be a solution to this mystery, then it must be in the form of a living Sasquatch or the body of a dead one. Until that moment, tracks will be found, pictures taken, eyewitnesses will tell their stories and sceptics will scoff. It is a cycle which is familar to all who attempt to solve the unexplained.

Dressed like the frontiersmen he much admired, Teddy Roosevelt spent part of his youth in the Dakota badlands. It was here that the future president heard an early tale of Bigfoot.

Some Open Files on Murder

Whodunit? Whenever this question is asked in books, in the movies and on television, we expect that in the end we will find out who really dunit. In real life sometimes its true and sometimes it's not. A murder that has been solved has a certain satisfaction to it. Bringing the criminals to justice reaffirms our faith in society's ability to protect us all from those people who would do us ill. Yet it is the unsolved murder that captures our imagination. Here is a horrible crime, the taking of a human life, for which there is no neat ending. It is like an accident on the highway. Deep inside one has the suspicion it could happen to them too. It is the grownups version of the bogeyman.

There will always be questions about some murders. Law enforcement agencies and the press may feel reasonably sure, in some crimes, of who but never be able to prove it. Other cases have no suspects and plenty of clues. And other cases have only the victim and a multitude of questions littering the scene of the crime. Many of these cases become famous the longer they remain unsolved. This chapter is dedicated to all those who attempted to solve these heinous crimes.

Let us begin our study of unsolved murders in a place where no one ever hoped to solve any of the thousands of killings that were committed there. Our perception of the rising crime wave in North America is easily dwarfed by this one building, where murder was the rule and not the exception. All this took place in a city that prides itself today for being tough. New Yorkers have forgotten about a time when being tough simply was not enough.

The Five Points area of New York was the worst slum, or as they were called in the 1840's, rookeries, in the city, perhaps in all of North America. Five streets, snaking their way across Manhattan Island, met in a wide space that created a lopsided star. This star was the center of the district. Today there is a quiet park and court house adjacent to the infamous site. Once it was a center of "amusement" with beer halls and theaters. It was this reputation as an entertainment area that earned the Five Points the nickname of Paradise Square. As the nightlife moved uptown, in the 1820's, to the Bowery, gangs of criminals moved in. Ironically, the transition was hurried by the arrival of the green groceries. Seemingly a welcome addition to any neighborhood, these establishments were not a place to do your vegetable shopping, rather it was a place to do your drinking. Most of these stores abused the term grocery to display rotting greens on the outside and sell cheap alcohol in the back room. In short order the green groceries became hangouts for gangs of rough hoodlums. By 1840 the area was a terrifying place to walk in the day and during the night it was absolutely out of the question, unless you really belonged. Being a native of the Five Points meant being a member of a gang.

A typical gang had names like The Roach Guards, Shirt Tails and Dead Rabbits. These were serious names and no one laughed at them, even if they lived uptown. An early history of crime in New York City described one particular gang in a matter of fact manner. "The Plug Uglies were for the most part gigantic Irishmen, and included in their membership some of the toughest characters in the Five Points. Even the most ferocious eye-gougers and mayhem artists cringed when a giant Plug Ugly walked abroad looking for trouble, with a huge bludgeon in one hand, a brickbat in the other, a pistol peeping from his pocket and his tall hat jammed over his ears and all but obscuring his fierce eyes. He was adept at rough and tumble fighting, and wore heavy boots studded with great hobnails with which he stamped his prostrate victim." These guys are nice in comparison to the nameless fiends who lived about 200 feet away from the center of the Five Points.

It is an odd twist of fate that the present New York County court house occupies about two thirds of the land that was known as the Old Brewery. Originally known as Coulter's Brewery, it produced rather good beer from the first day it opened, in 1792. But business fell off after thirty years and the yellow five story brick building fell into disrepair. In 1837 it was renovated and became a hundred room tenement house. Different ethnic and racial groups had their own territory inside this hell. The Irish lived on the upper floors, the Germans and Italians lived on the middle floors and the

By 1859 the worst visible signs of decay in the Five Points area of New York City was not readily apparent by day. But at night it was a very dangerious place to be.

BACKGROUNDS OF CIVILIZATION.—MRS. CROWN'S FIVE POINTS BAR-ROOM, ON CROWN'S CORNER, WORTH AND CROSS STREETS.—See page 222.

blacks, usually runaway slaves, lived in the
basement. Unlike todays worst slums, most
of those who lived in this desperate building
had no windows in their rooms and no
ventilation. Some children who were born
in the Old Brewery did not see the outside
world until they were teenagers; they never
saw sunlight, never heard rain and never
knew of the blue sky. In the middle of the
building there was a long hallway. It was
the same on every floor and each level had
the same name for it...Murderer's Row.

When it came to fun and games inside the
Old Brewery murder was the most popular.
Those who dwelled in this abyss of the human soul could sink no further on earth.
Day and night the sounds of insane laugh-
ter, whines, wails, screams and shrieks
were all punctuated with the thud of
slamming doors and crack of smashing
bricks. A chilling drunken symphony always emanated from the building and could
be heard for blocks around.

Inside no crime was too ugly to commit.
In one of the fifteen by ten foot rooms a little
girl lived with her starving mother and
twenty six other unrelated people. One day
she had come into possession of a single
penny. This might mean a bit to eat for both

mother and daughter that day. An
unidentified "roommate" saw this pitiful
sum and broke the girl's neck for it. The assailant casually tossed the body in the corner
of the room, then left to spend the penny.
For several days the body lay in the corner
until the mother had enough strength to
drag her daughter's body to the basement.
With only a spoon she dug a shallow grave
and buried her child.

Leaving the Old Brewery unaccompanied
could mean one's death. Even some of the
gangs of the Five Points found the building's
inhabitants undesirable; they killed them
whenever it was possible. Entering this hell
was to attempt suicide or admit defeat in
one's life. Although everyone in the Old
Brewery had at least one criminal skill;
some entered willingly, seeking sexual
thrills. It was a place where quite a few of
society's failed offspring went for a last fling
of debauchery. There was no time inside the
joyless building, no day, no night; orgies of
any combination, with willing and unwilling participants took place at all hours. In-
cest, homosexuality and rape were common
forms of accepted behavior. It was claimed
that many a missing woman could be found,
if anyone was brave enough to search,

within the confines of the Brewery's brick walls.

The New York Police entered the building infrequently and when they did it was with the reassurance of great numbers. Casualities after these raids were always greater for the police than for the criminals. In the last years of the Old Brewery, it was said that one person a day was murdered inside this citadel of depravity, each and every day, for seven years. In its life span as a tenement, the building was witness to over eight thousand killings.

If all good things must end, so must all evil things and the Old Brewery was no exception. Too long had this moral blight been allowed to exist. The Ladies' Home Missionary Society was a political and social power in 1852. In its constant fight with Tammany Hall and other stalwarts of corruption, they won a small but important battle. Together with financier Daniel Drew they bought the Old Brewery. Their plan was simple, tear down the building and erect a mission in its place.

On December 2, 1852, hundreds of policemen surrounded the Old Brewery; one hundred more boldly marched inside to evict the fiendish tenants. Criminals who were wanted for more than fifteen years were snagged in the waiting police chain outside. Women and children who had been forced to live in the foul building were freed from their immoral prison. Later when the work

of demolishing the Old Brewery was begun, the workmen made a discovery no one was prepared for. Under every floor and between every wall they found human bones. Before the building was finally destroyed, over two hundred sacks of human remains had been removed. No one will ever solve the mystery of who these people were let alone who murdered them.

A COUPLE OF INEXPLICABLE MYSTERIES

If Sherlock Holmes really existed the next two mysteries would have been solved. They were exactly his cup of tea.

A HOLE IN THE SHIRT

On a hot summer evening in July of 1872, the body of Captain George M. Colvocoresses was found on a busy Bridgeport, Connecticut street. He was shot to death. Next to the corpse lay a revolver and a satchel. Not too mysterious thought the Bridgeport police, a clear case of murder...that is until they examined the body. Colvocoresses was wearing a three piece suit but there was no bullet hole in his jacket or vest; the bullet tore through the man's shirt. Another examination of the body revealed powder burns on the inside of the vest and on the outside of the shirt. This bit of evidence pointed to the fact that Colvocoresses was killed by someone putting the gun inside the jacket, wedging it between the vest and the shirt, and shooting the victim in the heart.

Imagine if you will a gang fight like the one reported in this July 6, 1857 edition of the New York Times. We just cannot conceive of such a large gang fight taking place in any of today's urban areas.

Why, wondered the police, would anyone kill someone in this bizarre manner?

For a few days the police and the press speculated on the idea of suicide. This notion was fueled by the discovery of a $193,000 life insurance policy, taken out by Colvocoresses a few months earlier. The police began finding technical problems with this theory. What did Colvocoresses want to achieve by killing himself in this manner? Did he want to be buried in his favorite suit, therefore he wanted to keep it spotless? How could he be sure he would not die before he got his hand, let alone the pistol, out in time? In attempting to duplicate the obvious method of suicide the police could free both gun and hand in only forty percent of the trial runs. The biggest unanswered question was why would Colvocoresses want to make his death appear to be a murder? The press independently conducted an investigation of Captain Colvocoresses's character. No one ever said anything bad about him. He had no enemies. His will bequeathed small amounts of his sizable estate to friends and relatives; the rest went to charity.

If someone murdered Colvocoresses, what was the motive? If someone had a motive, why choose such an exotic style of murder? And why would the murderer shoot Colvocoresses on a busy street in the early evening? And why didn't anyone hear the shot that killed the captain? If only Sherlock were there he would have solved the mystery...wouldn't he?

THE ORIGINAL LOCKED ROOM MYSTERY

Legions of mystery writers have at one time or another included a locked room murder in their fiction. Many never heard of Isodore Fink, the original locked room murder victim.

It was 10:30 p.m. on March 9, 1929 and Mrs. Locklan Smith heard screams and shots coming from the Fifth Avenue Laundry next door. The store was located on East 132 Street just off of Fifth Avenue. Within minutes the police arrived and easily gained entrance to the laundry, but could not get into the back room; the door and all the windows were locked. After a quick canvas of the street, the officers enlisted the aid of a small boy, which they hoisted up and through the transom window. The boy unlocked the door. Once inside the police found Isodore Fink shot dead, lying on the floor.

Investigators discovered that Fink had been shot three times at close range. Powder burns were found on the victim's shirt. Two bullets had lodged in his chest

and one had passed through Fink's left hand. Death was caused by one bullet that smashed into the heart. Substantial amounts of money were found in the cash register and in Fink's wallet. A thorough search of the small room yielded no further clues.

At first some of the police thought the shots came through the transom. It seemed like a reasonable idea. No gun was found at the scene of the killing. Yet the powder burns indicated that Fink's assailant was standing close to him. Another theory

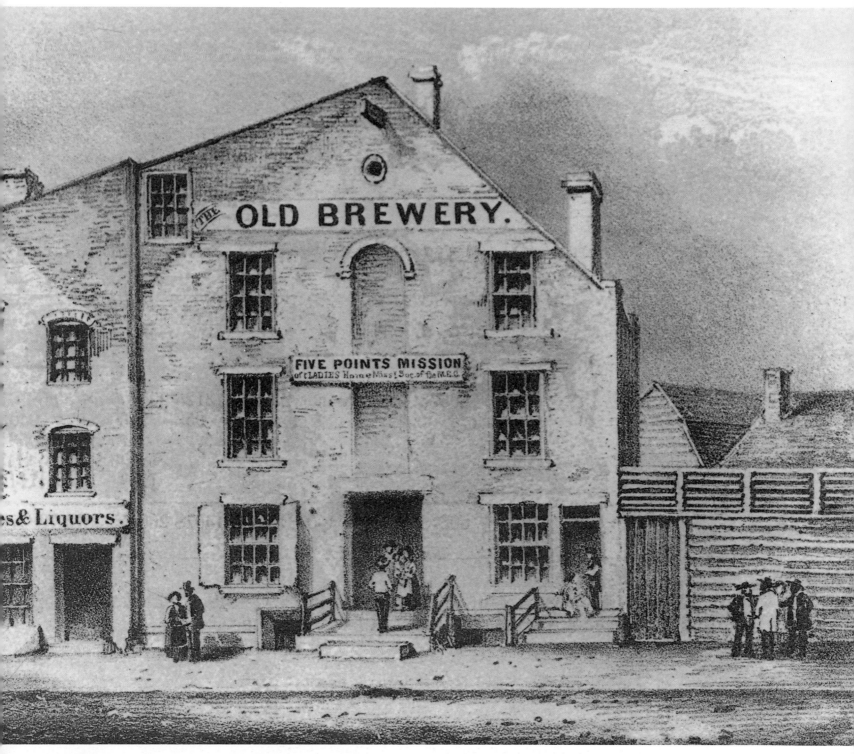

stated the murderer exited by the same transom the boy entered through. The killer might have known that Fink locked himself in the room when he worked late at night and the only way to kill the store owner was to climb through the transom. But the angle of the gun shots hinted at a person of average height. Only a very small man or boy could have navigated the tiny window. Of course there was the nagging question of motive. The only motive the police could rule out was robbery.

Two years after the crime Police Commissioner Edward P. Mulrooney said the Fink murder case would never be solved. He was probably right.

Showing none of the its former infamy, this picture was drawn shortly before demolition uncovered the full extent of the horror that went on day after day in this building.

SCENE AT THE FIVE POINTS RIOT.   WOMEN AND MEN TI
THE POLICE.

A FAMOUS CHOPPER

Lizzie Borden took an axe,
Gave her mother forty whacks;
When she saw what she had done,
She gave her father forty-one.

The question still lingers to this day, "Did she or didn't she?"

The victims were Andrew Jackson Borden, sixty-nine, and his wife Abby (Grey) Borden, sixty-five.

About Abby Borden there is little to say. She was Andrew Borden's second wife; his first wife died when Lizzie was quite young. Abby Borden had a friendly relationship with her two stepchildren, Lizzie and Emma. Wealthy Andrew Borden is another matter, everyone had something to say about him.

For the time, 1892, and the place, Fall River, Massachusetts, Andrew Borden was considered a proper member of society. His contemporaries saw him as hard working and temperately thrifty. By the standards of nearly a century later he would be seen as a workaholic and somewhat of a miser. He was the president of several banks, owned most of the high income producing real estate in Fall River and spent very little of his money. His house lacked gaslight, a bathtub and a library; material goods of that day found in less wealthy homes. The victorian house the family lived in was not in the affluent part of town.

Borden did provide for his daughters by purchasing land and setting up bank accounts with substantial amounts of cash in them. In his will he left almost everything to his daughters, very little was to be left to his wife. Unlike Willie Loman in Death of a Salesmen, Borden was not well liked and he didn't care if anyone liked him at all. What he had was respect, respect built, in no small way, on fear and loathing.

It is easy to say that bank presidents can, in the course of business, make enemies, but Borden collected them like postage stamps. One week before he was murdered Borden was visited by an unidentified man with whom he argued with for close to an hour. Finally the shouting became too much for Borden and he kicked the man out of his house. Burglaries were occurring with a frightening frequency at the Borden's home. The last burglary was in daylight, almost unheard of in the best of homes.

When you have next to nothing in this life you defend what little you have with a furious energy. Inhabitants of the Old Brewery fight off another police raid on their pitiful corner of the world.

The Borden sisters lived a very sheltered life. Their father was a very strict parent. Lizzie was thirty-two and Emma was forty-one; they were both well into spinsterhood. No one has ever mentioned either of them ever having been courted or having boyfriends. Perhaps their father preferred it that way.

On his last day alive Andrew Jackson Borden sat down to breakfast with his wife and his daughter Lizzie, the other daughter, Emma, was away visisting friends. It was a hot August morning, but Borden insisted that all the windows in the room be closed. They were served by their maid, Bridget Sullivan, an Irish immigrant, who was never treated as a member of the household. In the case of this breakfast she was lucky. The meal consisted of week old mutton, mutton soup, week old pungent bananas, bread and coffee; waste not, want not, as Borden would say. He left the house at 9:00 a.m. sharp to collect rents.

The women went about their routines for the next hour and a half. Abby Borden was upstairs making up the guest room for an unknown amount of time. Bridget was outside cleaning the windows, several neighbors had seen her, but not during the whole hour and a half. Lizzie inside the house doing little personal chores.

When Andrew Borden came home the front door was locked and he had to be let in by Bridget who used the side door to gain entrance to the house. At that time Andrew was informed by his daughter that Abby had gone out. "She received a note from a sick friend," said Lizzie. Bridget noticed that Lizzie was on the bottom steps of the main staircase leading upstairs.

From the time that Andrew Borden came home until 11:10, the family was in and out of the house. Bridget cleaned and then went to her room in the stifling attic for a nap. Lizzie did some ironing and then went outside for either some fishing sinkers or to eat some pears. Borden settled into the sofa in the sitting room to rest. Abby had at some point returned to the homestead. Lizzie was about to discover that she was an orphan. Some will say later on that she already knew.

Bridget was awakened by Lizzie's frantic calls for help. "Come down, quick! Father's dead! Somebody came in and killed him!" When the maid got downstairs, Lizzie was in a confused state. She was standing in the middle of the door to the sitting room. Lizzie pleaded with Bridget not to go inside but go to Doctor Bowen's house and get him. The

next few minutes were as confused as poor Lizzie asked the maid to get this neighbor, the doctor and yet another neighbor, when it was learned that the doctor was out on a house call.

By the time the police, Dr. Bowen and several neighbors came to the Borden house, Lizzie had mentioned to various people she was outside eating pears when it happened, she was outside and heard a groan and came inside, she was in the barn looking for fishing sinkers.

Nothing can prepare someone for the sight of a brutal murder. Dr. Bowen and the police walked into the sitting room, and were greeted by the sight of Andrew Borden lying on the sofa with his face all but chopped away and his skull bashed in. Splattered on and behind the sofa there was an enormous quantity of Borden's blood. There was no sign of a struggle. It was noted by Dr. Bowen that Andrew Borden's hands were not clenched, indicating that the victim did not even have time to protect himself. Accustomed to gory sights, this one made Dr. Bowen ill.

Lizzie was sitting in the kitchen, mumbling in her anguish. She was being comforted by several of her neighbors. At one point Lizzie was asked where was her mother. Her reply must have brought a chill to the good women attending Lizzie in her confused grief. Lizzie told them that her mother went out to visit a sick friend and she must have returned and had been killed also. She also added that her father had enemies and because of that fact the milk was poisoned. In all fairness to Lizzie, the family was made ill from the dinner the preceding evening. Unfortunately this and certain facts brought out in the trial would come back to haunt the distraught woman.

Upstairs in the guest room, facing the wall with her rear in the air, prostate as if in Islamic prayer, was Abby Borden with her skull crushed and brains laid bare. As one would expect the wall in front of the dead woman was heavily speckled with her blood. The medical examiner counted head wounds on Mr. and Mrs. Borden. Abby Borden was the winner in this macabre lottery. She had twenty one head wounds; her husband had only eleven. What the police did not bother to do was to check for fingerprins. At the turn of the century fingerprinting was considered un-American and therefore was just not done. Law enforcement in the town of Fall River was somewhat lax. The original list of blood stains was lost before the trial and was

Daniel Drew provided the funds to purchase the Old Brewery, and with The Ladies Home Missionary Society, brought an end to the daily madness that took hundreds of lives.

Not only did Lizzie Borden inspire nursery rhymes, there were also plays, novels and movies. No one to this day has been able to answer the all important question, "Did she or didn't she?"

rewritten from the officer's memory who first answered the call.

At first no one in this small protected New England town knew what to make of the worst crime of the century. While the citizens of Fall River went about bolting their doors, buying rifles, and watching each other very carefully; the police and the town officials busied themselves questioning Lizzie Borden as to her whereabouts at the time of the murder. The answers that friends and relatives received, let alone the police, were the same jumble as on the day of the murders.

An inquest was held and before the District Attorney could decide on a course of action, Bridget Sullivan volunteered herself as a witness for the prosecution. Suspicion slowly surrounded Lizzie as innocuous circumstances took on ominous meanings in light of the murders. A few days before the killings Lizzie attempted to purchase hydrocyanic acid to clean a fur coat; the pharmacist refused to sell it to her. Several experts testified that hydrocyanic acid was easily absorbed through the skin, deadly in small doses and would leave hardly a trace in those who were poisoned by it. Because of its toxicity hydrocyanic acid was not used as a cleaning agent. This line of questioning led to the family's illness the night before the murders and Lizzie's ramblings about the milk being poisoned. Further, in the course of the investigation, it was discovered a day before the murders that Lizzie bought a small axe. Since there were no other suspects and circumstantial evidence pointed to the Borden woman, it seemed only right that Lizzie stand trial for murder.

The trial of Lizzie Borden attracted national attention by reason of her position in society. She was a thirty-two year old spinster heiress, who devoted much of her time to the Woman's Christian Temperance Union and other such organizations. A pillar of old respectable New England stock was on trial for brutually murdering her parents with an axe; it was unbelievable that such a lady could do such a horrible crime, the trial was guaranteed to sell newspapers across the country.

Ten months after the killings of Andrew and Abby Borden their daughter was fighting for her life in a Fall River courtroom. Initially some of the inquest findings were thrown out by the judge. This was an axe murder trial and all the suppositions about poisoning and attempting to purchase hydrocyanic acid were ruled irrelevant because it was not the cause of death.

The prosecution began with a motive .... money. Both sisters were going to be disinherited by Mr. Borden in favor of his wife. They knew this and it was Lizzie who did something about it before her father's will could be changed. There was actually no factual basis for this motive, but the motive was not the crux of the district attorney's case, Lizzie's erratic behavior was.

Where was the ubiquitous Lizzie Borden at the time of the murders? Harping on her answers concerning her whereabouts before and during the trial, the prosecution was beginning to think the case could be won. Where was the note from your mother's sick friend? Why doesn't your mother's sick friend come forward? Why can't you remember if you were eating pears or in the barn at the time of the murders? A neighbor testified that a few days after the murders Lizzie burned a dress similar to the one she was wearing on the day of the killings. An axe was produced that was found under a pile of ashes in the Borden's cellar; the shape and size of the blade fit the wounds exactly. And Bridget, the maid, was the prosecution's star witness, always ready to substantiate the district attorney's assumptions.

For the defense Lizzie had several lawyers, one of whom was a popular ex-governor of Massachusetts, George D. Robinson. Quickly the axe from the cellar was discredited. It had rust, not blood stains on it. Any number of Borden axes and hatches could have caused the same wound. Lizzie and her sister both had substantial amounts of money without the inheritance. It was impossible to murder someone with an axe and not get splattered with blood. This point was shown by Robinson in a graphic courtroom demonstration. There was no time for Lizzie to change her clothes and wash. Police reports verified that the wash room and basin were dry whey they arrived. Neighbors corroborated the defense statement that Lizzie was wearing the same spotless clean dress after the murders as earlier that morning. Robinson made Bridget verify, under oath, that the dress that Lizzie burned had paint on it, not blood. At the end of his summation Robinson said, "... To find Lizzie Borden guilty you must believe she is a fiend. Does she look it? She is a lady, and a Christian woman, the equal of your wife and mine."

After a trial of fifteen days and a jury deliberation of ninety minutes Lizzie Borden was found not guilty. The courtroom, filled with spectators from Lizzie's church and social clubs, broke into applause.

After the trial life was different for the sisters. With their inheritance they moved to the best section of town. Lizzie was able to grow and enjoy her new found freedom. Although she never married, she threw herself into a life of social clubs. Emma could not adjust to her sister's new life style and left twelve years later. Many in town were surprised at her investment acumen. Some of the old bank president was in Lizzie, at her death the family fortune had grown close to a million dollars. In her will she left the sum of $30,000 to the Animal Rescue League.

Did she do it? No one will ever know for sure one way or another. A motive not discussed at the time was Andrew Borden's less enlightened ideas of child rearing. For his time he was seen as a little strict with his daughters. Today he is seen as a possessive monster. One can imagine attempting to date either of the Borden girls with Andrew Borden looking on. He could have made life extremely difficult for any

possible suitors. Lizzie may have decided she had enough and in a unpremediated frenzy cut herself free from her father's intolerable bonds. In a similar murder case in the 1920's, it was shown that a murderer doesn't have to get him or herself splattered with blood when killing someone with an axe.

One person whom the prosecution implied could have killed the Bordens was Emma. A popular theory surfaced in the twenties that the elder daughter came back to the house from Fairhaven, fifteen miles away, killed her parents and returned to her friends before anyone knew that she was gone. Her motive also may have been her father's possessiveness.

In some mystery fiction the butler really does do it, in the Borden case it very well could have been the maid. Bridget Sullivan was unhappy in the Borden household. She had complained to her friends that she was never part of the Borden family. In fact both

Andrew and Abby constantly went out of their way to point this out to the maid. She was never allowed in the bedrooms on the second floor. She was never allowed to eat with the family. She was shrewdly paid just enough money to live on but never enough to allow her to leave the Borden's employment. She was more of a slave than a servant. It is not difficult to imagine all her pent up animosity bursting forth in an axe wielding rage. Let us not forget that Bridget was very enthusiastic about being the prosecution's star witness.

But this is all conjecture, until someone uncovers a lost letter or a misplaced statement, we will never be sure whether or not Lizzie Borden deserves to be the central character of a morbid children's nursery rhyme.

MURDER UNDER THE APPLE TREE

The year was 1922 and Prohibition was in full swing. After a long struggle, the Temperance Movement had won its battle over the evils of alcohol; Lizzie Borden, an old Temperance member, probably approved.

What the good tea totalers wanted to accomplish was the banishment of drink from those, whom it was believed, abused it the most, the ignorant lower classes. In an odd way they were successful. The lower classes did curtail a good deal of their drinking, they began to make money from the sale of booze to the middle and upper classes instead. As the Jazz Age began its rhythmic dance through the roaring twenties, a search for pleasure brought new forms of behavior to many who felt the time was right to explore new freedoms. Yet there were those who felt that if some respected member of society were going to "fool around" they would have to to pay the price.

Unlike today's straightforward discussion of relationships and sex, the fun loving people of the twenties invented euphemisms for amorous activities. Spooning was a popular word and if that was too blatant, a walk in the night air to "pick mushrooms" would do just right. It was on a warm, 1922, September evening that a young couple found themselves walking down De Rossey's Lane in New Brunswick, New Jersey. Any couple who walked down this tree lined dirt road were obviously out for a session of picking mushrooms. They were about to find one of the great murder mysteries of the decade.

At first it was a minor nuisance; another couple was under their favorite apple tree. Pearl Bahmer, all of fifteen, wanted to let the unknown couple make love in peace. Raymond Schneider was more experienced at twenty-two; he noticed that the couple was not moving in a loving fashion, perhaps they had fallen asleep. If he could awaken the man and woman, they might be embarrassed into leaving his happy spooning tree.

Raymond coughed, made loud crunching footsteps in the dry spots in the grass and finally spoke to Pearl so that the couple could hear his voice. Nothing would stir them. Slowly Pearl and Raymond walked over to the couple, drawn by an invisible aura that certain horrible events radiate so magnetically. It was close to dawn and there was enough light for Pearl and Raymond to discern much about the still couple. They could see that the couple were well dressed, they could see that the woman was nestled in the man's arm, they could see that the man had a bullet hole in his head and the woman had been shot in the face three times as well as having her throat hacked from ear to ear.

They could also run to the nearest house to call the police, which is what they did.

Reverend Edward Wheeler Hall was the murdered man and the woman was the lead choir singer in his church, Mrs. Eleanor Mills. The bodies were carefully placed under the apple tree which meant they had been killed somewhere else. Their clothing was too tidy which led the police to believe that they were killed while naked and carefully dressed afterwards. Scattered like leaves around the couple were Mrs. Mills' love letters to Reverend Hall. Purposefully propped up against Hall's shoe was one of the Reverend's business cards. There was no doubt that the Reverend and the choir singer were lovers for some time.

In 1909, Hall became rector of the St. John the Evangelist Church, New Brunswick, New Jersey. Two years later he married the wealthy Frances Stevens. At thirty six she was already matronly; at twenty nine Hall was quite handsome. Rumors that the good Reverend married for money were heard over the town telephone lines and back yard fences. Perhaps their marriage lacked excitement, but over the years they were known as a stable and peaceful couple. Time was good to Hall, he aged gracefully. Frances Hall appeared and acted as if she was well into her sixties. In 1922 she was all of forty-four.

Mrs. Hall's family was a trifle peculiar. Willie Stevens, her brother, was a strange man. His hair, which included his mustache and eyebrows, were in a perpetual state of chaos. It was thought Willie had never know the function of a comb or a brush. Not a man who cared about clothes, Willie would dress himself in suits at least a size too large. He never held a job; he had a large trust fund instead. It was thought by his parents that he was incapable of managing his own finances. Each week Willie received a tiny portion of his fortune. He never needed much money since he lived in the family mansion with his sister and her husband, the wandering reverend. To keep himself busy he became a self-taught recognized expert in entomology and botany. For fun Willie Stevens was a volunteer fireman. Occasionally when things were too dull for Willie, he would make a large fire in his back yard and then rush into the house. Quickly he would return dressed in his fireman uniform and hose down the flames.

By comparison his brother Henry was positively normal. He lived sixty miles away in his own home. Henry, a taciturn man, managed the family investments and avidly pursued his passion, hunting and target shooting; he was an excellent shot. A close cousin, Henry de la Bruyere Carpender, a member of the New York Stock Exhchange, was a frequent visitor to the Stevens estate. Every family has a competent member who is always there when trouble brews; Henry Carpender performed that function for the Stevens family.

James Mills was employed as the sexton and handyman at Reverend Hall's church. He knew that his wife had some sort of relationship with Hall, but thought it was their love of music and religion that brought them together, rather than physical attraction. Many was the night the right reverend would have dinner with his choir singer and sexton. Mills was the same man who would later sell his wife's torrid love letters, from Hall, to the press for five hundred dollars.

For their time the letters were hot stuff, they are still pretty good today. When they were published in The New York Daily Mirror, millions read Mrs. Mills declaring: "Oh honey, I am fiery today. Burning flaming love, it seems ages since I saw my babykin's body and kissed every bit of you." A typical answer from Hall went something like this: "I want to see you Friday night alone by our road; where we can let out, unrestrained, that universe of joy and happiness that is ours."

In short order, the news of the murders spread like butter on a hot frying pan. Mrs. Hall first heard about her husband's death from a reporter seeking an interview over the telephone. She hung up on him without comment. As crowds began to collect at the murder site, the police and authorities began a weird battle of denial of jurisdiction. It turned out that the bodies were found just inside of Somerset County line, although the victims both lived in Middlesex County. Each county prosecutor was claiming that the case belonged to the other county. It would take years before the matter was settled.

While this was happening Henry Carpender arrived at the scene with the family lawyer, viewed the bodies and left almost unnoticed. Several 32-caliber shells were recovered by investigators. By this time the crowds had begun taking souvenirs; the apple tree was losing it's bark, the grass was being pulled up in large patches and some of the hardier seekers were digging out the tree's roots. All the police could decide was to take the bodies to the Somerset County morgue before even they disappeared.

Could this love affair have been so invisi-

ble, that Mrs. Hall and Mr. Mills were ignorant it was going on? When the police first investigated the matter they found many indications this may have been the case.

Mrs. Hall had befriended Eleanor Mills, to the extent that the older woman was almost a mother to her. It was not uncommon for the matron to buy clothing for the younger woman as well as inviting her to some of the finest social affairs in New Brunswick. Shortly before Eleanor's death, Mrs. Hall had paid for her appendectomy. On the night of the murders, Mrs. Hall last saw her husband at 7:30 p.m., when the Reverend left the house, "on business." She spent a sleepless night when he did not return and went to the church the next day. Mr. Mills was there and they realized, in the course of conversation that both their spouses had not returned the previous evening.

According to Mills his wife also left the house at 7:30 p.m. When he asked her where she was going she replied, "Why don't you come with me and find out?" He declined, but about 2:30 a.m. he awoke to discover his wife had not come home. He dressed himself and their two small children and went to the church to search for his wife. Of course he didn't find Eleanor and he returned home to a fitful sleep.

Digging a little deeper, investigators unearthed several new facts. On the night in question, neighbors had seen Mrs. Hall leave the mansion at about 2:30 a.m., with her odd brother, Willie, in tow. Her story changed a bit when detectives questioned her again. Yes, she did go out that night; she went to the church looking for her husband and saw the lights were out. The reverend must be with a sick parishioner, she told Willie. Next they went to the Mills house, but the lights were out there too, so they returned home.

The police felt the stories they gathered from Mr. Mills and the Hall clan were not quite right. Yet each had an alibi that could not be broken. With nowhere else to turn investigators took a closer look at Raymond Schneider and Pearl Bahmer. What followed was another bizarre twist in a weird murder case.

Raymond claimed a young man named Clifford Hayes had killed the couple. The motive was jealousy. According to Raymond, Clifford had dated Pearl several times and in a rage he thought it was Pearl with her father under the apple tree. Unable to control himself the young man killed the couple. After the couple was dead, Clifford discoverd he made a mistake.

Mrs. Francis Hall toured Europe after the trial. Here she is at customs after returning from a trip to Italy. As usual, she appears not to be having a nice day.

It did not take long for the incredulous police to find the accusation groundless. Raymond promptly confessed to fabricating the tale, but he refused to give any reason as to why he did. None of the authorities liked Raymond or Pearl very much. At fifteen Pearl was already a very loose woman. A pool hall hustler, Raymond had recently walked out on his pregnant wife. He was the kind of misfit all good people despised. In rapid succession Raymond was tried, indicted, convicted and sent to jail for perjury.

After weeks of dead ends, the next turn in the case occurred. Her real name was Mrs. Jane Gibson, her profession was hog farmer and thus she was known by the nickname "The Pig Woman." Gibson came forward and told the police she witnessed members of the Stevens family kill the lovers near the apple tree. During the grand jury investigation however, Gibson only admitted to having seen the murders on the ill lit night. She would not say under oath it was definitely Mrs. Hall, Willie, Henry Stevens and Henry Carpender who committed the crime. It was too dark and misty for her to see clearly any face that well. The grand jury could not return an indictment and the case gathered dust for awhile; everyone went about their usual business.

The power of the press was responsible for the last break in the Hall-Mills killings. Four years had passed when Philip Payne, managing editor of the New York *Daily Mirror*, received information that made him use his considerable influence to have the murder case reopened.

One of the newspaper's reporters was routinely covering a divorce case when he realized that the defendant was formerly employed as a maid in the Hall mansion at the time of the murders. The maid's husband was suing for divorce on the grounds of adultery. Among the men he claimed his wife slept with was Reverend Hall. It was further charged that Mrs. Hall gave the maid the sum of six thousand dollars to keep quiet about the affair and confirm her alibi that she was home at the time of her husband's murder. He informed Payne of this interesting judicial tidbit. Pressure was put on the New Jersey governor and he in turn pressured the state's district attorney to reopen the investigation.

Like a bolt of lightning in the night, the police made simultaneous arrests, Mrs. Hall and her two brothers. Events moved quickly from that point and the trial began on November 3, 1923.

Although the actual figure was seven hundred thousand dollars for the Stevens family legal expenditures, it was billed as the "Million Dollar Trial". It had a bewildering cast of characters. As expected, the defendants were the Hall family, who made good copy because of their strangeness. The key prosecution witness was the Pig Woman. She was dying of cancer. Unable to move, she had to testify from her deathbed which was wheeled into the court room each day. New to the Hall-Mills trial was Mrs. Hall's mother, who sat behind her daughter and repeatedly droned "liar" at any testimony she disapproved of. An extra added attraction was Charlotte Mills, daughter of the murdered Mrs. Mills. She had become a reporter in the last few years. Because of her relationship with the victim, Charlotte was given the assignment to cover the trial for a big city newspaper. She was anything but unbiased, practically every article had a reference to Mrs. Hall's dowager wardrobe and dumpy appearance.

Many witnesses were called to testify for the state, but the prosecution decided to hinge its case on the Pig Woman's evidence. It was high drama, Gibson's moaned testimony from her deathbed, Mrs. Hall and her brothers silently staring at her and Mrs. Hall's mother loudly punctuating each statement with "liar, liar, liar."

The Pig Woman stated that she was riding on her mule that evening, chasing corn thieves from her property. From a short distance she saw the defendants get out of a car and quietly walk into the apple orchard. It was then that Gibson dismounted and followed the trio. Suddenly there were five people among the trees instead of three, they were yelling at each other. "Explain these letters!" was heard clearly by the Pig Woman hidden in the nearby bushes. There was some cursing and sounds of someone being beaten. A wild scramble ensued and the next thing Gibson knew two men were struggling on the ground. A flashlight was shown on them and the Pig Woman recognized Henry Stevens and Reverend Hall wrestling for some shiny object. A shot was fired. A woman began screaming "Oh God!" Three more shots rang out and the woman was silent. It was then the Pig Woman began to make her way back to her mule. Once she looked back and saw Mrs. Hall bending over what appeared to be a body. She had something long and silvery in her hands. Mrs. Hall began making slashing motions with her hand. Gibson got on her mule and speedily road away from the scene.

Under cross examination the Pig Woman's memory proved faulty. The defense could not break her account of that evening. They did show that Gibson could not remember her three husbands names, nor when she was divorced. Her memory outside the events of the murders was hazy at best. The jury found Mrs. Hall and her brothers innocent.

Gibson lived until 1930. Until the day she died, she maintained that her version of the murders was the truth. Mrs. Hall and her brothers sued The New York Daily Mirror and received an out of court settlement for an undisclosed amount. No one ever solved the murders of Reverend Hall and Mrs. Mills.

IN THOSE SILENT DAYS

Movie studios had their birth in West Orange, New Jersey. The first one belonged to Thomas Edison. But it is Hollywood we associate with all the glamour and major film productions. In 1922, New Jersey may have had the sensational Hall-Mills murders and the resultant "Million Dollar Trial," yet it is Hollywood which that same year stole the limelight. If the Hall-Mills case had everything but the kitchen sink, the William Desmond Taylor murder included the whole kitchen.

He was thought to be one of the greatest silent film director's by Adolph Zukor, head of Paramount Studies. William Desmond Taylor could do no wrong in Hollywood as long as he made films for Famous Players Lasky Studios, a profitable division of Paramount. He did many things that even shocked members of the fabled land of celluloid make believe.

When it came to sexual prowess Taylor was an athlete of Olympic proportions. Starlets and stars beat a path to his bed. Sometimes there were as many as three or four different sexual encounters a night; some of those nights it was three or four participants at the same time. Many well known female leads were linked to Taylor. Notable among them were Mabel Norman, the Max Sennett comedienne and Mary Miles Minter.

He was one of the wealthiest directors of his day. What money he had, he earned by making movies. Unlike many other residents of the nascent tinsel town, he read books, collected real works of art and had a fine eye for expensive antiques. Taylor was tall and very British, complete with a distinctive well bred English accent. During World War I he left Hollywood in 1915 to fight in the Royal Canadian Air Force. He returned in 1917 having attained the rank of captain, an accomplishment which he was

always proud of.

His past, before his film career, was shrouded in attractive mystery. Taylor appeared out of nowhere in 1910 acting in bit parts. By 1914 he was a lead player and he made transition to director with all due speed and ease. No one knew much about the dashing director before Hollywood, yet everyone wanted to hold on to their romantic notions about him. They all had their reasons to leave his past unknown. On the night of February 1, 1922, he was well on his way to becoming a legend when death stepped in and changed the script.

The evening started out as just one of those nights. Mabel Normand stopped by to pick up some books. It was part of the director's education campaign for his lovers of long standing. She was greeted by Taylor's effeminate and reputedly homosexual butler and shown into the lage living room. The director with the large sexual appetite was on the phone, in his study, having an argument with someone. At times the conversation was quite heated, although Mabel couldn't make out the subject. Taylor hung up the phone and kissed Mabel after coming into the living room. Mabel was not staying the night. She was tired and staying over would definitely mean she would be tired the next day. He gave her books by Freud and Nietzsche.

The butler was given the rest of the night off and he left the house at 7:15 p.m. Taylor spent the next half an hour complaining how his former butler, Edward F. Sands, had stolen jewelry, forged his checks, charged lage sums to his accounts and smashed up one of his cars. All of this larceny was done while the director was in Europe. When he returned Sands was gone. There were several more burglaries and more forged checks were cashed since then. He showed her two forged checks. Normand commented that the forgeries were very good indeed, like someone who knew Taylor a long time had done them. He made an odd face at her statement.

At 7:45 Mabel left the Taylor mansion. At 8:15 a loud crack was heard. None of the neighbors thought it was anything more than a car backfiring. It sounds trite today, but automobiles did backfire a lot in the 1920's. About 10:00 a neighbor seeing the lights still on stopped by to say hello. Taylor did not answer the door. This was not unusual when he was otherwise engaged. The neighbor left. A half an hour later his chauffeur returned his car, knocked on the door, received no answer and left imagining the bawdy action in the mansion.

Little did William Desmond Taylor realize, when this picture was taken, that his romantic entanglements would cut short his brilliant career.

Arriving at his usual time, 7:30 a.m., the butler started in with his duties. He began breakfast as usual and while the coffee was being made he went to tidy up the living room. What he saw in the room was to abruptly change his life forever. On the floor next to the desk was Taylor's body, stiffly lying on the rug with his arms at his side, like a fallen wooden soldier. From his mouth ran a rivulet of dark crimson dried blood. On top of the body was an overturned chair. The butler, in his high pitched voice, ran screaming from the house. Outside he started to yell that Taylor was dead. He was to continue running though the streets yelling his precious head off for a half an hour, but the shock would eventually drive the poor man insane. He would be committed to an insane asylum and die there in 1931. Although, it was also reported that he died impoverished, in 1937, hiding from those who would kill him if he told the terrible secret he knew.

Those neighbors who first heard the news called Mabel Normand who in turn called the studio, who in turn notified Adolph Zukor of the news, who in turn sent some of his executives to the house. He was to follow them shortly. As word spread, many studio chiefs converged on the Taylor mansion.

A doctor was found in the area and brought to the house. He took one quick look at the body and pronounced that Taylor died of a gastric hemorrhage. Having given his diagnosis from the hip, he promptly left.

The Taylor mansion looked like a meeting of the studio executives. They were mulling about the body trying to figure out what they should do next, when Adolph Zukor breezed in. One glance at the body was all it took for Zukor to tell his employees to search out and destroy anything that could hurt the studio's reputation. Instantly the executives raced through the house gathering up letters, papers and booze. Even Hollywood had to give the appearance of abiding with the new prohibition laws. All the papers that were found suspicious were thrown into the fireplace and a fire was started. Mabel Normand arrived; she was scarcely noticed as she raced upstairs to the bedroom in search of her love letters. Meanwhile the butler was still running around the neighborhood screaming that Taylor was dead. Finally someone called the police to get the man to stop making all that racket.

Finally the forces of law and order arrived on the scene. For about a minute they were barely noticed. One by one all the studio executives were restrained from further self-serving vandalism. People had to pay attention to Taylor's body, the assistant coroner was examining the victim. In all fairness to the studio executives it was one of them who suggested that the body be turned over. There, to everyone's shock, were two bullet holes. Taylor didn't die of natural causes, he was murdered!

Murder was a hotter topic than the peaceful death of a lecherous director. That news made the rounds even faster than the news of Taylor's death.

Mary Miles Minter heard the news from her mother. At the time Minter was as famous as Mary Pickford. On screen she appeared as a teenager, to the press she was about twenty years old, yet her birth certificate said she was thirty. Not too many people knew of her affair with Taylor. Her mother knew and did not approve of the director. His rakish reputation gave the woman anxiety attacks when she thought of her daughter spending time with the man.

Mary had recently broken away from her mother's control and was living at her grandmother's house. When Mary saw her mother approach the house she locked herself in her room. Her mother shouted word of the director's death through the bolted door. She also demanded to know where her daughter was last night. Shocked, Mary unbolted the door and raced past her mother who was attempting to stop the actress from going to the Taylor mansion, which is exactly what Mary did.

The police were not allowing anyone into the mansion. The studio people had done enough damage to the murder investigation. Mary pleaded and began to weep, it was a better performance than she did on the screen. Her uniformed audience was not affected by her show of emotion; too many people had wandered through the house already. Minter left the mansion and went to Mabel Normand's house. She stayed there until dark. No one knows what they said to each other for those many hours, but they had a common bond in the man they loved and the letters they could not find.

What the actresses did not recover the police found. Some of Normand's letter were found in Taylor's boots. Some of Mary Miles Minter's letters were so well hidden they were found days later. Some of the letters found their way to newspapers. Those who read them in the tabloids agreed that the Minter/Normand love notes were hot stuff. What Zukor hoped to avoid happened anyway. Ever widening ripples of scandal washed over the movie colony. Mary Pick-

ford was included for a short time as one of Taylor's fun loving night callers. There was no truth in that rumor, yet it did make the rounds for awhile.

Investigators uncovered what few clues remained after the tinsel town scavenger hunt. Cigarette butts were discovered outside the kitchen door, indicating someone may have waited there until the director was alone. Taylor was killed at close range with a .38 caliber pistol. The alignment of the bullet holes with the jacket and wounds proved that the director was shot in the back while sitting at his desk. One of the neighbors reported to the police they saw someone dressed as a man, but with a distinctly feminine walk, leave the Taylor house just after the "backfire." Beyond those paltry findings the police had little to go on.

Lacking clues, the investigators theorized that perhaps someone or something in William Desmond Taylor's past may have led to his murder. They began the arduous task of tracking down Taylor's pre-Hollywood life. In this endeavor they were successful.

The man behind William Desmond Taylor was an Irishman named William Cunningham Deane Tanner from County Cork, born in 1877, the eldest son of a wealthy family. Instead of following the family tradition of military service, Deane Tanner joined a theatrical company after he graduated from Oxford in 1895. Although Taylor thought the theater was in his blood the company did not want him in theirs. He left and traveled to the New World.

For a while he and his younger brother Dennis worked on a ranch in Harper, Kansas. Soon afterwards he and his brother came to New York and started a successful antique shop. The money for the enterprise was borrowed from members of the New York upper crust, who readily took a liking to the "English" gentleman. He married actress Ethel May Harrison in 1901 and moved to Larchmont. Rumors, that were still circulating in the best of New York circles, stated that Taylor lived above his means and in turn his brother had to do with drawing less than an equal share of the business. There was no doubt the elder brother always lived in a high style. Another explanation for Taylor's flamboyant life style was that he borrowed heavily from his wife's uncle, the real estate magnate Daniel J. Braker and never bothered to pay back what he owed.

No one knows exactly what happened in October, 1908, but whatever occurred, Taylor changed his whole life's course. He left his

Almost ageless in her appearence, Mary Miles Minter often played parts of women fifteen years younger. Her biggest role may have been off-screen as William Desmond Taylor's lover.

The wife and daughter Taylor deserted to find fame and fortune in Hollywood. When this picture was taken Mrs. Taylor had become Mrs. Edw. L. C. Robbins and his daughter had become Ethel Daisy Dean Tanner.

wife, his young daughter, Daisy, his business and his brother. It was all rather sudden. Right after he was seen quite drunk at the Vanderbilt Cup Race, he took five hundred dollars from the shop till and disappeared.

Taylor aimlessly wandered about the United States and Canada for five years. It is known that he worked alternately as a hotel manager, prospector and a mine timekeeper during his travels. After he disappeared his wife obtained a divorce from Taylor. His younger brother, unable to run the antique shop on his own, deserted the business and his wife too.

Both of the Taylor brother's wives found out that their spouses were alive by accidentally seeing them again. In each case they were seen acting on the silver screen. Needless to say both wives were rather shocked. Only Dennis Tanner's wife made the trip to Hollywood to track down her husband. When she met with Taylor, his directorial star was rising. He could not or would not tell her the whereabouts of her errant husband, but he did send the woman some money each month for Dennis's daughter's education.

From this historical research the police concluded that the thieving butler, Edward Sands, was none other than Taylor's younger brother, Dennis. This was never fully proven but for awhile he became a prime suspect in the murder. Edward Sands was never found and there are those who believed that he murdered Taylor for running out on the lucrative antique business in New York, thus ruining Dennis's life.

Drugs, the illicit American pastime of the latter part of the twentieth century may have played a part of Taylor and Mabel Normand's lives too. There are several different versions to the story. One states that the two lovers would regularly partake in opium parties. They would buy the drug in Chinatown and later smoke the sticky substance with friends in Taylor's house. Another version has Taylor and Normand taking the drug alone. Some believed that opium was only Mabel Normand's vice. Taylor thought it was a filthy habit and did his best to make her quit. No matter which story was told the outcome was the same; a drug dealer killed Taylor to protect himself.

Recently a new development in the case may have come the closest to solving the mystery. Author and filmmaker Sidney Kirkpatrick, in the course of writing a biography of the noted film director King Vidor, came across an astonishing discovery. Locked away in Vidor's private papers was a solution to the mystery that evaded trained detectives for sixty years. Vidor was fascinated with the Taylor murders; he wanted to do a movie about it. In 1967 he began his own investigation of the crime and may have uncovered the killer in the process.

The possible solution pins the murders on Mary Miles Minter's mother Charlotte Shelby. She was a strong woman who would let nothing come between her and her control of Mary. The young actress was more than a daughter to Shelby, she was her livelihood. Mary's mother was also her manager. Her fee was an above standard thirty percent of earnings. Taylor was a very strong personality and as such became Shelby's rival for her daughter's affections and/or control of those emotions. On the night of the murder it was Shelby who was seen dressed as a man walking with a feminine gait away from the Taylor house. Shelby got away with the murder by paying off one of the chief investigators. Mary Minter's life was destroyed by her mothers overprotectiveness, if not her self interest. Her last words to King Vidor was, "My mother killed everything I loved."

The only problem with the solution, so excitingly written in Kirkpatrick's book A Cast of Killers, is the circumstantial and hearsay nature of the evidence. It is a fifty/fifty propositin whether or not Charlotte Shelby would have been convicted in a jury trial on such evidence.

Many of the lives touched by the William Desmond Taylor murder were ruined by subsequent publicity.

Although it was never proved that Mabel Normand was a drug addict, her career began to tumble. In 1923 she was involved in another violent incident. This time her chauffeur shot an oil tycoon who was dating her at the time. It was said they were both in love with Mabel and the chauffeur knew he could not compete with the millionaire so he decided to rid himself of his rival. Fans quickly turned against Normand; Max Sennett was forced to drop her as his leading comedienne. In 1930 she died, a broken woman, of tuberculosis.

In 1984, Mary Miles Minter died in obscurity. Her career was all but ended by the murder. Her life after Hollywood and stardom was one of litigation, successfully fighting her mother's bid, as her former manager, for part of her estate and also suing those who would include her as a suspect in the Taylor murder for libel.

Bitterness was her constant companion for the rest of her life.

Charlotte Shelby was reported to have died at least twice. The first time was in 1957 and later under an assumed name. Never did she say anything about the murder than "Why would anyone wish to shoot such a man?"

SHREDDED PETALS

Los Angeles has always been a Mecca for aspiring young actresses, few have succeeded in finding fame and fortune in the movies. With her "stage name," Elizabeth Short found notoriety in death which had been so elusive to her while she was alive.

On the morning of January 15, 1947, a mother was walking with her young son past a vacant lot. Garbage dumping had recently been a problem in the lot. At first she thought the carelessly discarded item encroaching on the sidewalk was just someone's sloppy littering. The mother was prepared to ignore whatever it was and walk by. As she strolled closer, her mind began making sense out of the fragmentary nature of the object. It was half of a woman's torso! A second passed as if it was an hour. In slow motion her mouth began to open, her heart started to quicken and forcefully pound, the muscles in her throat constricted and the air from her lungs slid through the fear tightened vocal cords. Her scream could be heard for blocks.

Wailing sirens answered the incoherent mother's frantic call to the police. First to arrive were several radio patrol cars; they were followed by the coroner and lastly by Detective Harry Hansen, an officer who would attempt to solve this crime for the rest of his law enforcement career.

Hansen and his partner were veterans of many murders, but this was the most savage and sadistic they had ever seen. The body was surgically dismembered and disected. On the victim's skin were razorlike cuts and cigarette burns. Carved into the thigh were the letters "B.D." What was left of a beautiful face showed signs of prolonged beating. Her mouth was cut from ear to ear, forming a macabre smile. It was determined that the woman had been hogtied and continuously tortured for some time; she died about eight hours before being found. Two other ghoulish facts were noted about the body; it was completely drained of blood and then the skin was scrubbed spotlessly clean with a brush.

From the woman's fingerprints, her identity was learned; from a reporter's

dogged hard work a sensational unsolved murder case was born.

Tall, thin with creamy white skin, blue grey eyes and thick black hair, twenty-two year Elizabeth Short was born in Hyde Park, Massachusetts on July 28, 1924. Her last known address was in Long Beach, California, where she was best remembered for her black attire. Every article of her clothing, underclothing and accessories was black, even her ring was black jade. A little more digging, at the neighborhood bar, found the name most men knew her by...the Black Dahlia.

The dahlia is a flower native to Mexico and Central America. In North America, the exotic plant, is cultivated for show and decoration. Most garden dahlia varieties need rich soil for optimal flowering in the summer and must be stored in a cool dry place in the winter. Elizabeth's childhood was impoverished, emotionally as well as economically and her remains were being kept in a cold refrigerator at the city morgue waiting for a next of kin to claim them.

For the next week a thumb nail sketch of Short's life emerged from Hansen and the Los Angeles Police Department investigators. Elizabeth ran away from home at the age of seventeen. Originally, she planned to go to Hollywood and become a movie star. Short missed her mark and found herself, in 1944, working in an army post canteen in Santa Barbara instead. It was there the popular Elizabeth became engaged to a handsome major. As tragically typical in World War II, he was killed in the Pacific a few months later. A routine police sweep of the army canteens netted the underaged Elizabeth. She was arrested and sent home to her mother in Massachusetts. By simply getting off the bus when no one was looking, Elizabeth failed to reach her destination again and this time she ended up in Hollywood.

It was in Hollywood that Elizabeth Short became a high priced call girl; she became well known by many film producers and one of them named her Black Dahlia for her beauty and the unusual monochromatic color of her clothing. All the trappings of the good life were hers, but she could not land a film role from her sexual efforts. That one unattainable goal made Short very bitter and she left California in early 1946.

In the last year of her life, Elizabeth Short returned to Massachusetts, visited her mother, drifted back to Los Angeles, briefly had a lesbian affair and posed for nude photographs. Elizabeth began living for the

It takes a film director to solve the murder of a film director. Author and filmmaker Sidney Kirkpatrick belives that the legendary director King Vidor may have solved the Taylor murder and kept quiet about his findings.

moment as she played on the sympathies of elderly women by posing as a poor war widow, thereby gaining free room and board. By the end of 1946, Short had told her friends she finally found a boyfriend who loved her for more than just her body.

When the police tried to trace Elizabeth's whereabouts on the last week of her life, they got nowhere. The investigators struck out with the several sets of tire tracks found near and in the vacant lot. Tracing the cars seen at the lot on the night of January 14th proved equally futile. No leads could be developed from the fact that the murderer possessed considerable medical and surgical skill. The whole case began to crawl to a halt. Whomever and wherever the killer was, he must have sensed this, his next move took everyone by surprise.

Three weeks after Elizabeth's body was discovered, the city editor of the Los Angeles Herald Examiner received a phone call from a man who spoke in mellifluous tones about the moment by moment horror that was inflicted upon the poor victim. The eerie contrast of voice and subject matter sickened the editor. At the end of the sadistic chronology the caller claimed he was the killer and would turn himself in after he watched the police squirm a little longer. His last words to the newspapermen told him to watch the mails for "...some souvenirs of Beth Short."

A few days later an oversized envelope arrived at the Examiner's office. The address and the message on the front of the correspondence were words and letters cut from assorted Los Angeles newspapers. Clear for all to read was the following pasted message, "Los Angeles and other Los Angeles papers. Here is Dahlia's belongings, letter to follow." Contained inside the envelope were Elizabeth's birth certificate and address book. Needless to say, her address book was black. At the same time detective Hansen and his partner found Short's suitcases in a bus terminal locker. Besides the expected articles of clothing, Hansen found a packet of love letters from her boy friends. Most of the letters were dated within the last eighteen months.

Where just days ago the police had run out of leads, now they had over ninety names and addresses of possible suspects to investigate. The task force assigned to the case grew to fifty detectives and they quickly spread out to hunt for the men in Elizabeth Short's life. As the investigation began to pick up momentum, the killer mailed his poison-pen communication to the Examiner. He was not going to give himself up; "You would not give me a square deal. Dahlia killing justified."

New facts became known to the police. Elizabeth took a bus from Santa Barbara to Los Angeles early in the morning on January 14th. That afternoon she was seen in San Diego driving with a red headed man wearing what seemed to be a Marine uniform. Some of the detectives had their doubts about these witnesses' statements, but the red headed man had become a reoccurring theme in the last days of Elizabeth's life. Several of her friends had reported that she had been in the company of the red headed man in the past few weeks. Hansen found, hidden in one of Short's suitcases, a wire, dated January 7th signed by someone called "Red,, asking her to meet him the next day. This telegram led Hansen to the only prime suspect the police ever had in the case, Robert "Red" Manley.

Manley was a married twenty four year old salesman, who lived in Huntington Park, California. At first he denied knowing Elizabeth, but he quickly changed his story when he was shown his signature on the telegram receipt. Manley told the police he lied to them because he was having fights with his wife. She was suspicious of his having an affair with another woman, which in this case was the now famous Black Dahlia.

According to Manley, the last time he saw Elizabeth was for the twenty-four hour period between January 8th and 9th. He met her early in the morning at the San Diego bus station. At that time she had scratches and light bruises on her arms. Short claimed it was her jealous, black haired Italian boy friend, who also lived in San Diego, that roughed her up a bit.

Hansen had discovered that Elizabeth had become a sexual tease in the last year and this had, at times, made some of her admirers furious. He suspected this was what might have been the cause of what happened to Short before she met "Red."

After breakfast, Manley helped Elizabeth pick up her suitcases from a friend's house. In the late afternoon he took her to a motel where they had a terrible time together. They did not have sexual relations that afternoon or evening. Short spent most of the time alternating between getting drunk and being sick. Than morning Elizabeth and Manley drove to Los Angeles. The last time "Red" saw The Black Dahlia she was checking into the Biltmore Hotel.

The police checked Manley's story with a fine-tooth comb. Everything he said was verified by clerks, friends and a parking

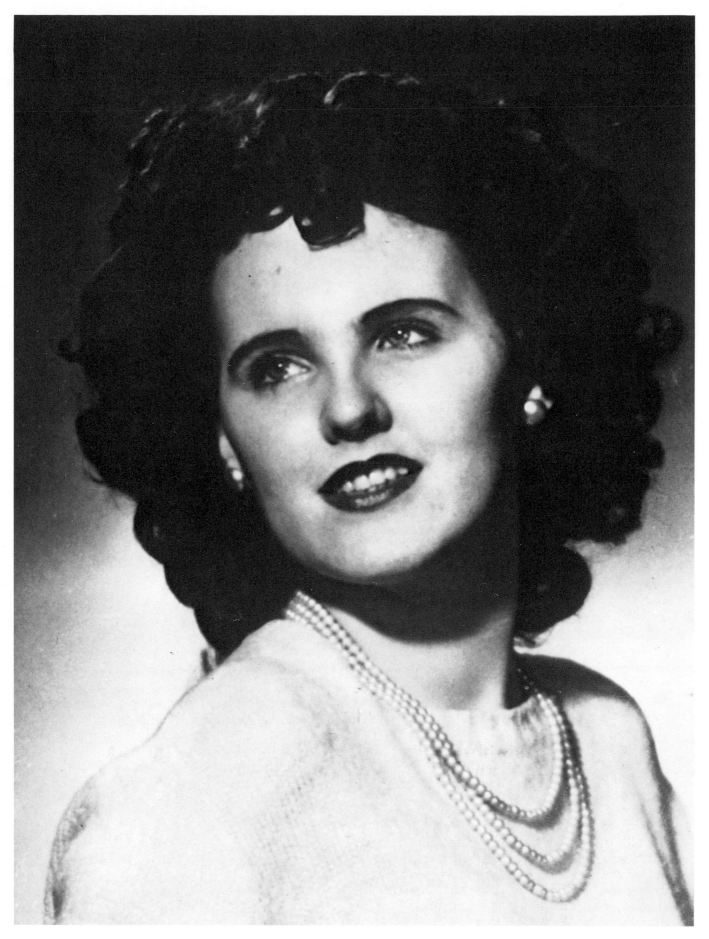

The beautiful and confused Elizabeth Short, a.k.a. Black Dahlia, became famous for the way she died, not the way she lived.

The gruesome murder of the Black Dahlia would eventually destroy her last boyfriend, Robert "Red" Manley, shown here with his wife Harriet.

ticket. When the Los Angeles police released Manley they were letting their best lead go. Years later he would be committed to an insane asylum.

Other than the full moon, the best way to bring the cranks and weirdos seeping out of the woodwork is a sensationally gory murder. The Black Dahlia case was no exception. There was the man who roughed up women when he was drunk. He believed he killed Elizabeth in one of his blackouts. A former WAC confessed to killing The Black Dahlia because she stole her man. Another confessor was a man who was arrested for carving his initials in a woman's hip. Each year for ten years someone admitted to the murder. They all lacked credibility and a missing piece of evidence. To this day the exact condition of Elizabeth Short's body as it was in the vacant lot on January 15th has never been reported. None of the headline seekers could fill in the grisly blank. The only people who know the full details are the Los Angeles police and the killer.

When Harry Hansen retired in 1971 he went over the case for reporters. In his estimation, every possible measure was taken to prevent the murderer from escaping justice, yet that is exactly what the fiend did. Some of the Los Angeles police believe the killer might still be alive today.

BAD ALBERT AND THE COMPANY HE KEPT

The Bible states "He that lives by the sword shall die by the sword." In the case of Albert Anastasia, the former head of Murder Inc., the statement was certainly true.

Born in Sicily in 1903, Albert Anastasia immigrated to the United States in 1917. He soon found work on the New York docks. Albert did more with his hands than just work as a longshoreman, he used them to savagely beat anyone who was unfortunate enough to get in his way. Anastasia's style attracted notice of the local Mafia bosses. In 1920 he was put in charge of liquor smuggling on the waterfront. His boss was no other than the young Lucky Luciano.

His first killing was at the behest of Luciano and Albert managed to bungle it. The murder was committed alright, the victim died, but Anastasia committed it in front of four witnesses. These men helped to convict him and send him to Sing Sing prison to await execution. Luciano wanted his friend out of jail, so he hired the best lawyers and made the appropriate payoffs. The result was another trial for Albert. This time the witnesses did not testify in court, they

seemed to disappear off the face of the earth, they were never seen by anyone again. Albert was found not guilty due to a lack of evidence. Anastasia was now free to control the docks and personally commit 62 more murders in his lifetime.

Albert reached a stage in life where he wanted to make lots of money. Step one in his personal wealth campaign consisted of taking over six union locals and having all the members kick back to him part of their salaries for the right to work. Some longshoremen didn't take this laying down. But eventually after the protestors were laid to rest, having been found murdered in one location or another, the union membership reluctantly went along with Albert's hiring practices.

The next step was easy for Anastasia. He became a professional killer. Albert was used as an enforcer by the mob bosses and this helped him rapidly rise in the Mafia hierarchy. He liked his work, his favorite tool was the ice pick, although he was also known to occasionally use a scarf to dispatch his assignments. When Albert became the chief Mafia enforcer, he moved his operations to the Brownsville section of Brooklyn. This promotion put him under the command of gangster Lepke Buchalter. Together they made a great team. Lepke was the powerful and smart leader who was on the board of the newly formed crime syndicate. Albert was the expert killer who took care of the day to day operations of their new business, Murder Inc.

We have Anastasia to thank for adding colorful new meanings to the words hit (a killing) and contract (the order to kill someone). Murder Inc. became a nationwide syndicate killing service, it made money and it generated the myth that no matter where you hid, the syndicate would get you.

Things went well until the early 40's when Buchalter's racketeering empire fell apart because of police and FBI harassment. Already convicted of narcotics peddling by the local police, Lepke was tried for murder by the federal government. Their case was based on the testimony of one of Murder Inc.'s staff murderers, Abe "Kid Twist" Reles. Lepke was convicted and sentenced to die in the electric chair. For his trouble Reles was thrown out of a hotel window by persons unknown. After Buchalter was executed in 1944, Anastasia became a syndicate boss and headed Murder Inc. by himself.

Throughout the early fifties, many in the syndicate believed that Albert was getting out of control. An apt example was the murder of a non-mob innocent honest citizen, Arnold Schuster. Willie Sutton was a legendary bank robber of the day and Arnold was the young man who spotted him on the subway. Schuster went straight away to the police who arrested Sutton within hours of Arnold's tip. It was Arnold's bad luck to have his television interview seen by Anastasia. While Albert was watching the thin bespectacled young man, he went into a rage and said to his underlings, "I can't stand squealers. Hit that guy!" The next evening Arnold walked up the driveway of his family's house in the Boro Park section of Brooklyn. He never knew what hit him. Three Murder Inc. gunmen stepped out of the shadows and shot him to death.

Before Albert met his end, he had managed to make many enemies in and out of the syndicate. One of them was Mafia boss Frank Costello, who Albert had unsuccessfully tried to remove from the gambling rackets. Another was Meyer Lansky the financial wizard of the mob. Anastasia wanted to move in on the syndicate's Cuban gambling operation. It was rumored that Albert would raise an army of a thousand men to take over the Cuban action by force, if he couldn't have his way by persuasion. Although he wasn't a target of Albert's expansionist plans, Vito Genovese made clandestine maneuvers against Anastasia. It was a matter of greed, Vito wanted Albert's rackets.

To kill Anastasia one had to be very careful. If you did not put him in a grave with the first attempt, there would never be a second chance. As the story goes, on October 24, 1957, Albert had dinner with Mafia under-boss Sam Trafficante at the Park Sheraton Hotel, New York. At the end of the meal Sam leaned over and gave Anastasia the ritual kiss of death. This was supposed to be a warning that he was soon to be hit.

According to statements of middle level Mafia members who knew Albert at the time, he had other warnings. A method which Anastasia had developed to test the target's possible reflexes was the seemingly innocent setting off of firecrackers near the victim. If the target jumped or reacted with alertness then the use of guns was ruled out as a mode of execution. If the victim did not react to the loud popping sounds, you knew that he would stand still long enough to make an easy hit with a gun. One of Albert's associates was throwing firecrackers near him for a whole week and telling Anastasia to be careful. Twice his friends left wires sticking out of his car door

pretending there was a bomb inside. Albert was taking everything in stride. He had reached the pinnacle of hubris, he believed no one could touch him in any way. Albert, of course was wrong.

The morning after his dinner with Sam Trafficante, Anastasia walked into the Park Sheraton basement barber shop and asked for a quick haircut and shave. Only one barber was on duty at the time. Albert casually sat down and the barber put a hot steaming towel around his face in preparation for a shave. The unusual aspect about this tonsorial visit was the absence of Albert's bodyguard. When questioned by police, the bodyguard said that Anastasia let him take a coffee break at the hotel's coffee shop. All things considered this in not a likely explanation for his absence.

No sooner had Albert relaxed in his chair than two men with scarfs covering their faces entered. One of the men motioned to the frightened barber to keep quiet. Both men pulled revolvers out from under their top coats and began firing at Anastasia. Albert, mortally wounded, jumped out of the chair and tried to grab one of his killers. His injuries made him lose control of his body. Instead of lunging forward, Anastasia spun into the wall length mirror behind him, smashing it. Albert fell to the floor and his killers used one of his own murderous innovations on him, two shots to the back of the head. Not only does this action usually insure the death of the victim, but if for some unknown reason the person should survive, he would virtually be a vegetable for the rest of his life. In Albert's case there was no cause for alarm. He was very dead.

Did Vito Genovese or Meyer Lansky or Frank Costello have Anastasia killed? Everyone in the syndicate seems to know and at the same time no one really knows. Depending on who's talking to the authorities each former gangster has a different version of the mob rub out. This is strange, since many stories of the murdered underworld luminaries have come to light over the years with very little factual disputes, except for minor details. In Anastasia's case this is not so.

When mobster Joseph Valachi became a government informer, he claimed that Carlo Gambino was one of the gunmen who shot Anastasia. Careful Gambino would not have taken that kind of risk. He was a Mafia don of the old school. Keeping a low profile, not taking unnecessary risks and being smarter than the competition were Carlo's guiding principles. It is unlikely that the man who would take over the Anastasia op-

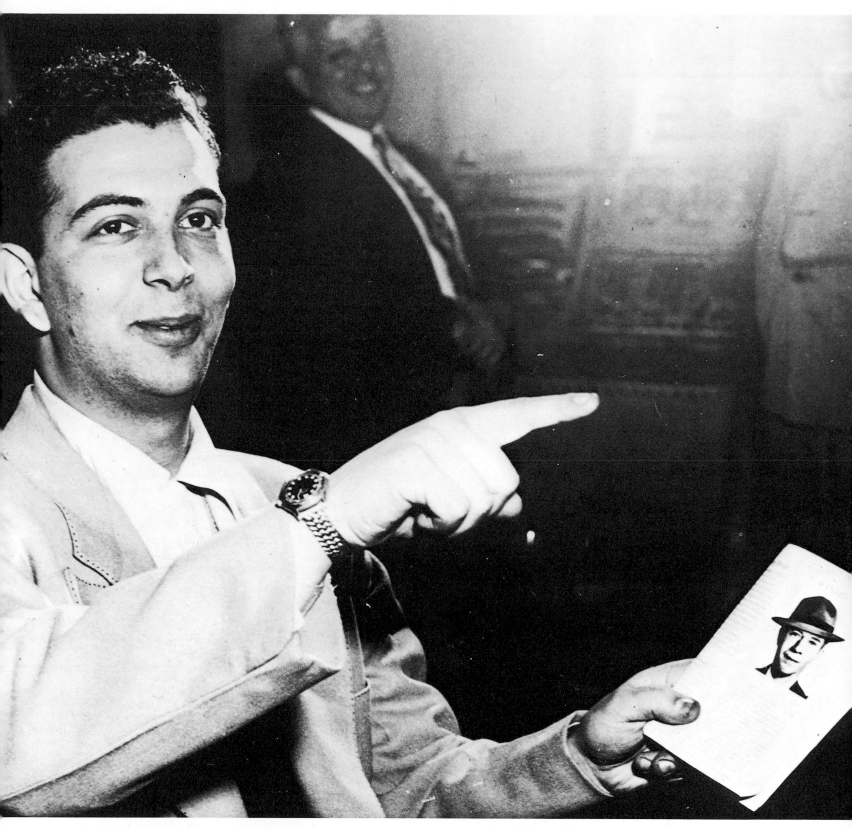

erations would risk everything just to have the honor of killing Albert.

The reputation of Murder Inc. and Albert Anastasia was and still is such, that many of the older syndicate members claimed to have had a hand in his murder. If you added up all those who claimed they were near the Park Sheraton barber shop that cold January morning, it literally would

Arnold Schuster displaying the innocent bravado that incurred the wrath of Albert Anastasia. For his identfication of Willie Sutton, shown in the small photo in Arnold's hand, Anastasia had him murdered.

In an unusual moment in Frank Costello's life, he is shown here arriving at a police station late at night to look at a suspect in an unsuccessful attempt on his life.

have been a mob scene outside the hotel. Who ordered him killed and who actually did the murder may someday be truthfully revealed. But don't hold your breath waiting.

WRITTEN IN THE STARS

In the latter part of the twentieth century serial killings have become more of a common occurence in America than most people would like to admit. Maybe it started with Charles Starkweather and Carol Ann Fugate's murderous rampage through the plains states in January of 1958. Perhaps it was the obsessive killings of Harvey Glatman in 1957. But whatever started the waves of serial killings they increased in violence and victims over the years. One particularly nasty killer, who is still at large, terrorized the west coast states for six years before he vanished.

On December 20, 1968, David Faraday and Bettilou Jansen were seventeen and sixteen years old respectively. They were high school sweethearts out on a pre-Christmas date. David parked his car on lonely Lake Herman Road, outside of Vallejo, California, just north of San Francisco. The couple were kissing each other when someone stealthily crept up on the driver's side of the car. Suddenly the assailant popped up and fired several shots with a 22 at point blank range into David's head. Bettilou bolted from the car and ran down the road. The killer never changed his position; he just stood by the car and fired five shots at the fleeing teenager. Each shot found its mark and Bettilou fell dead in her flight like a doe in deer hunting season. When the police investigated the crime they had no leads, no clues and not even a theory as to who committed the murders.

July 4, 1969, another holdiay season and another shooting. This time it was a young teenage couple making love in Blue Springs Park near Vallejo. The killer crept up and shone a flashlight at the startled kids. As they looked up, shots were fired and quite a few nine millimeter slugs tore into their bodies. The girl died but the boy lived with four bullet holes perforating his body. He could not give a description of the killer. The intense flashlight beam had blinded him and he passed out after he was shot. Because of their age their names were not released to the press.

For three and a half weeks the Vallejo investigators had only one lead in this case. A few hours after the shooting, a phone call was received by the police; a flat monotone voice announced that he shot the Blue Springs Park teenagers. He correctly identified the caliber of the gun used in the shootings, a fact not released to the press and promptly hung up to avoid a telephone trace.

The faceless killer surfaced on August 1, 1969, by sending letters to the Vallejo and San Francisco newspapers. Now he had a name of sorts; each letter began with "This is Zodiac..." Enclosed in each of the letters was a cleverly conceived cryptogram. Zodiac wrote that if the newspapers did not publish the cryptogram, he would run amok in San Francisco, killing as many innocent people as he was able, until they changed their minds. Nobody wanted to challenge the madman on this point. The next day every paper that received the Zodiac letters published the cryptogram.

It turns out that publishing the cryptogram was actually a good move. The police experts spent days trying to crack the code and they failed to decipher it. Two amateur cryptologists succeeded in overcoming the problem that stumped the experts. The basic difficulty with the code was the, perhaps intentionally so, misspellings found littering the cryptogram. When deciphered the cryptogram yielded a glimpse into a very sick mind. Zodiac wrote: "I like killing people because it is more fun than killing wild game in the forest because man is the most dangerous animal of all. To kill something gives me the most thrilling experience. The best part of it is that when I die I will be reborn in paradise and all I have killed will become my slaves. I will not give you my name because you will try to slow me down or stop my collecting slaves for my afterlife." This is kind of a twisted version of the ancient Egyptian belief of the afterlife.

A San Francisco reporter noticed Zodiac's handwriting matched a note left at the scene of a 1966 unsolved coed murder. Fear spread throughout the Bay area like the famous San Francisco fog coldly padding its way in from the sea. Invisible among the population was the fiend's intent on random murder and the police had no clues as to his identity.

The building anxiety, caused by waiting for Zodiac to strike again, was quickly relieved in September. It appeared that Zodiac was dropping deeper into his personal fantasies. This time the monster was seen wearing a makeshift fifteenth century executioner's hood as he ritually tied up and stabbed a young picnicking couple near Lake Berryyessa. The man was knifed six times and the woman was stabbed twenty-four times. The wounds made the sign of a cross upon her body. Again the man survived and the woman did not.

The surviving victim could only give a sketchy description of the killer who called himself Zodiac. He was said to be about five foot eight inches tall and overweight. To the police this information was better than nothing. Tragically a better description would follow another murder on a crowded afternoon street. A cab driver was killed by his would be passenger in the Presido Heights section of San Francisco. When Zodiac ran away from his victim, about ten people got a good look at him. In addition to being five foot eight and overweight, Zodiac was also seen to be a man in his late twenties, with reddish brown hair, who wore thick glasses.

Although the citizens of the Bay Area remained frightened, for a long while Zodiac's activities seemed limited to an occasional killing and mostly writing macabre letters to the newspapers. One of his letters threatened to shoot out the tires of a school bus and use the children for target practice. He never carried out his threat, but he did start playing a numbers game with the police. Zodiac began to credit himself with more killings than law enforcement agencies knew about. At first he claimed seven murders when the police count was only five. When the official count was six, Zodiac had boasted of thirteen killings. The San Francisco police were soon dismayed when the madman claimed thirty six murders and they had, at most, eleven possible unsolved killings that might be attributed to Zodiac.

Zodiac's letters stopped in 1974. In 1975, Don Striepeke, the sheriff of Sonoma County, began a study of unsolved killings in five western and Pacific states. It began as a test of his new computer's capabilities. He fed in data of Zodiac's style of ritualistic killings and correlated the profile with hundreds of open murder cases. The unexpected answer that came out of the computer threw Striepeke for a loop. Over 40 unsolved killings had over a ninety percent chance of being the work of one man and there was an equally high probability that man was...Zodiac.

Where is the demented murderer who called himself Zodiac? Some believe he may be dead, having collected enough slaves for his morbid fantasy of an afterlife. Others think he may have snapped into another self which has forgotten about his career as a murderer. And there are those who say he is still at large, killing at random, with all of North America as his hunting ground. We may never know which of these theories is true.

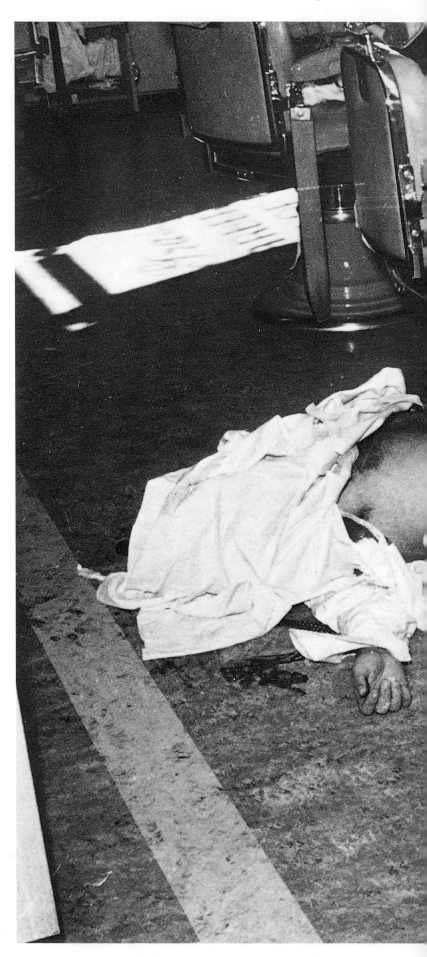

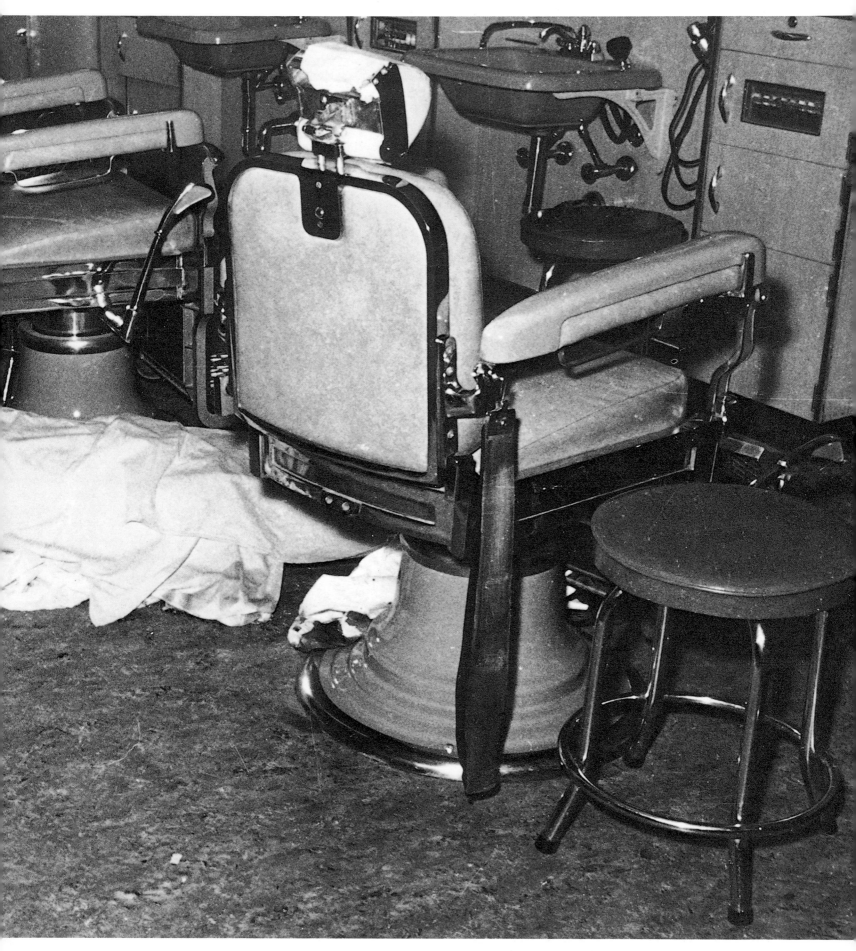

Some people call their escapes from danger "close shaves." Albert Anastasia went for shave and never survived.

UFO's
in Color

Motion picture film taken by Fred Svihus from airline flight near Lomax, California, 11 April 1977.

Photo taken by Squadron Leader Robert J. Childerhose, Royal Canadian Air Force while setting a cross-Canada speed record. Photo made above storm clouds at 47,000 feet on 23 August 1956.

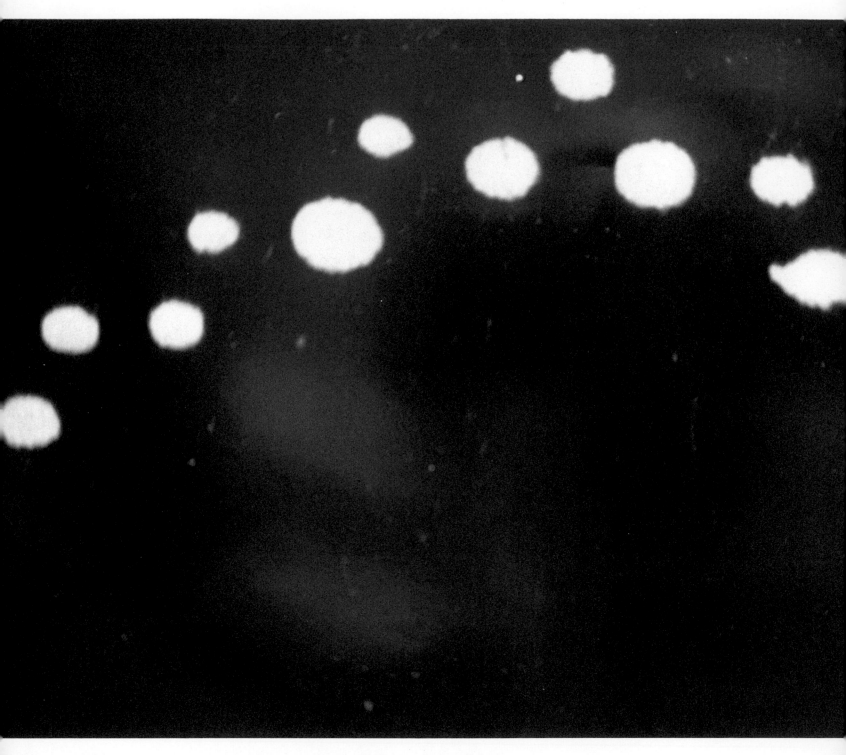

Popularly referred to as "Lubbock Lights," this photo was taken by
Carl Hart, Jr. in August 1951 in Lubbock, Texas.

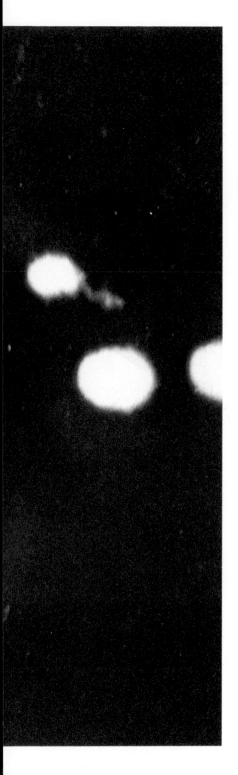

Near Calgary, Alberta, Canada.   This photo was taken by Warren Smith on 3 July 1967.   There were two other witnesses.

The Oregon photograph, nr. Diamond Peak, on 22 November 1966. Three views of object in one exposure, taken by Los Altos, California scientist.

Martin B-57 photo taken for promotional purposes by the Martin Company ca. 1954. Disc in the upper right-hand corner went unnoticed until photo was developed.

NICAP·9

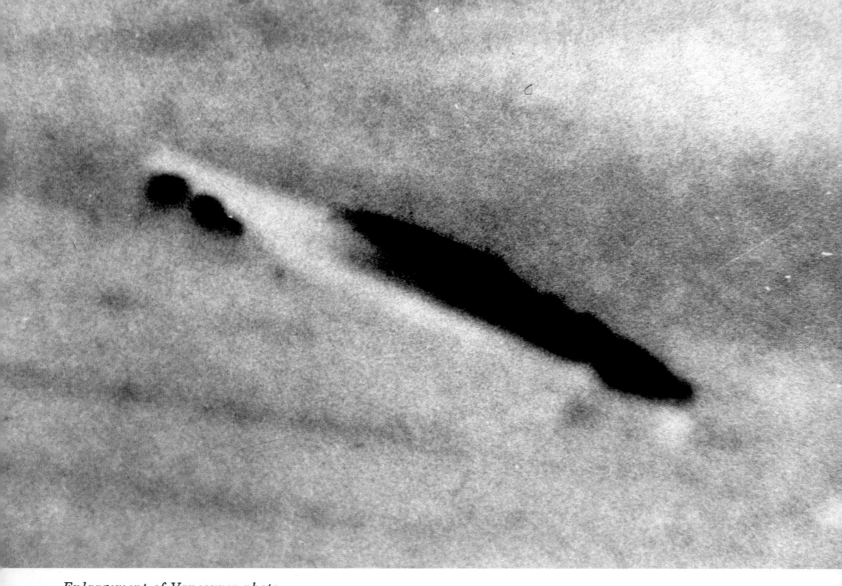

Enlargement of Vancouver photo.

Photo taken 8 October 1981 on Vancouver Island, British Columbia,
Canada.

Enlargement of disc in B-57 photo.

Two photos taken by Paul Trent at McMinnville, Oregon on 11 May 1950.

Blow-up of Doss photo.

Preceding spread:
Paul Doss photos taken at the University of Illinois Vermillion
River Observatory near Danville, Illinois on 9 May 1971.

Photo taken by Rex Heflin of the Orange County, California Highway Department near the Santa Ana Marine Corps Air Station on 3 August 1965.

Second shot by Rex Heflin taken through his pick-up truck wind-sheild

Going, Going, Gone

People always lose things. Keys, watches and other such items have a habit of disappearing. One of the minor perplexing problems of the twentieth century is the unexplained vanishing of one sock when a pair of socks are washed in an automatic washing machine. Many writers have ventured a guess as to what happens, in the washing machine, to the missing sock and more than one scientist has attempted to observe what has been termed "sock cannibalism" to no avail. But with all kidding aside, the matter of vanishing acts becomes quite serious when people disappear. In the latter part of the twentieth century people vanishing without a trace has been more common place than we would like to admit and is usually a prelude to tragedy. However, there have been classic, if not bizarre, disappearances in North America which have defied definite solutions.

OH WHERE, OH WHERE, HAS MY COLONY GONE?

It was to be a new venture in the new world, but instead it became one of North America's first disappearances. Discovered in 1584, Roanoke Island, off the Virginia Coast, was considered to be a prime location for a farming colony, according to the best logic of two sea captains financed by Sir Walter Raleigh. It was an ideal location to grow sassafras, an herb prized for its medicinal qualities in England at that time. In the early spring of 1587 the colony of Roanoke was founded by Governor John White. He led the hundred men and women in the establishment of a small village on this beautiful island. But winter was coming and supplies were running low. White decided to sail back to England and return with enough provisions to last the colonists at least two winters. Before the governor left the colony his daughter gave birth to the first white child born in North America, Virginia Dare.

White was delayed three years by circumstances beyond his control, namely by a British war with Spain. Even when his ship finally approached the island colony in 1509, White knew something was wrong. No one answered the ship's trumpet call. As the ship sailed closer not a living soul could be seen in the village or on the shore greeting the ship. When the sailors landed and investigated, they found the whole colony mysteriously deserted. There were no signs of battle, no bodies and no destruction of property. Everything was intact, yet there were no colonists.

Before White sailed back to England, he devised a signal that was to be used in case the colonists found they had to leave in great haste. A cross was to be carved on a tree near the fort gate and if time allowed an arrow was to point the direction in which the colonists were forced to flee. No such mark was found. Instead the word "CROATAN" was found carved in a tree bark near the fort's entrance. On another tree, stripped of bark, the letters "CRO" were inscribed in the bare wood. That's all that was ever found of the Roanoke colonists.

For a while it was believed the colonists migrated to nearby Croatan Island, built a small ship and attempted to sail back to England. According to this theory the ship they built was either sunk at sea or was attacked by the Spanish, who wanted to wipe out English claims in North America. Another notion involving the Spanish, had the Spaniards taking the Roanoke colonists captive and holding them on Croatan Island until another ship could take them away to work as slaves in some South American mine.

For some unknown reason it did not occur to White to find the Croatan Indians and ask them about the missing Roanoke colony. A few years later some English official did have this idea, but all efforts by the British to locate the tribe failed. They vanished into the wilderness seeking a life free of the white man's hustle and bustle. No one believed that the Croatan Indians had attacked the colony. Governor White remembered them as quite friendly and even helpful in setting up the colony.

About 100 miles inland from Roanoke Island and adjacent to the South Carolina border was an area called Robinson County, North Carolina. In 1719, colonial hunters and trappers wandered into this hilly land and found a tribe of Indians who had light skin, grey/blue eyes and light brown hair. Even more surprising was the fact that they spoke nearly perfect English. This discovery gave rise to the theory that the colonists at Roanoke, who were nearly starving, took refuge with the Croatan Indians during the first winter when White did not return with the much needed supplies. Later they intermarried and the tribe became an assimilated group which was neither purely Indian or English colonist. In 1934 a local historian visited the tribe and found indeed they were still fair skinned and had grey/blue eyes, but much to his amazement, he also discovered that ".....they used phrases of speech that have scarcely been heard since the days of Shakespeare. Unfortunately this tribe of Indians have assimilated into the American Culture since then and there is no way to test this theory today.

Did the colonists leave the village and live with the Croatan Indians? One can imagine after several years of waiting for White to return the men and women at Roanoke came to the conclusion that they were abandoned. It is also possible the colonists actually saw, from their vantage point on Croatan Island, the ship returning from England and just watched the crew search the village without calling attention to themselves. The existence of fair skinned Indians in Robinson County, North Carolina, lends credence to the theory that the Roanoke colonists melded with the Croatan Indians. If they did not do this, then what did become to these brave men and women?

IN THE WINK OF AN EYE

Legend has it that Houdini made an elephant disappear on stage, right before the audience's eyes. In reality he pulled the curtain around the pachyderm and then proceeded to make the one ton mammal vanish. It was a great feat of magic, only duplicated in this century by Doug Hemmings when he made a Lear Jet and the Statue of Liberty vanish on network television. What all these fabulous magic tricks have in common is a showmanship, curtains and elaborate preparation. But in 1880, on a farm in Gallatin Tennessee, David Lang was the central character of a seemingly impossible vanishing act, he disappeared, involuntarily, before the eyes of startled witnesses.

It had been a dry spring and even drier summer. The grass in the pasture was a tan/brown, On that late September morning, Mr. and Mrs. Lang went to Nashville to buy their children a toy wagon and now George, 8, and Sarah, 11, were playing with it in the backyard. David Lang had just finished telling his children to be careful playing on the new toy, when he decided to take a walk through his pasture. His wife was putting up some clothes to dry in the sun and down the lane, leading to the house, came a buggy driven by Lang's good friend Judge August Peck and Mrs. Lang's

brother. It was one of those rare instances where everyone's gaze was fixed on the same object, in this case the object was Lang walking through his field. Without any warning David Lang vanished into the air! There was no flash or loud noise; he just silently dematerialized in a wink of an eye. The startled on-lookers rushed to the site where Lang vanished. What they were hoping to find was a crevasse or a hole in the ground. That area of Tennessee is known for its limestone caves and it was immediately assumed Lang had fallen into a small depression or a cave. But when the Judge, Mrs. Lang's brother and Mrs. Lang arrived at the spot where David vanished, all they found was unbroken earth covered with grass.

Mrs. Lang became hysterical, she started to wail and had to be carried into the house. Someone rang the Lang's fire bell, in short order neighbors came running to the house. Soon there was a pack of at least 50 people jostling each other to stare at the spot where Lang disappeared. Judge Peck organized the group to search the pasture for any sign of Lang's whereabouts, but nothing was found to indicate what happened to the poor man.

A week later a county surveyor and a geologist from Nashville examined the disappearance site and surrounding field. They concluded there was no crevasse or cave under the spot where Lang vanished. In fact they found that the whole pasture had a large limestone bedrock floor just three feet under the soil. About this time larger search parties rummaged about the countryside seeking a clue for a reasonable explanation for Lang's disappearance. While all this activity was going on, the Lang servants, who had also witnessed David's vanishing into thin air, quit. After several months of fruitless endeavors, the search parties gave up all hope of finding any trace of David Lang.

If this was all that occurred on the Lang farm, it would still be a bizarre disappearance, but almost a year later something truly incredible happened. In August 1881, Mrs. Lang and her two children were standing at the spot where David vanished. It already gained a reputation for being different from the rest of the pasture. One very noticeable fact was that in a 20 ft. diameter circle around the spot where Lang disappeared, the grass grew taller, thicker and faster than the adjacent grassland. Although this might should have been attractive to the grazing cows, they avoided the

Engraved for
Middleton's Complete
System of Geography.

SIR WALTER RALEIGH ordering the STANDARD
of Queen Elizabeth to be erected on the Coast
of VIRGINIA.

Taylor delin. et sculp.t

Sir Walter Raleigh could not have known at the time that the colony he financed in Virginia would become famous in the annals of unsolved mysteries.

area, as did the birds and even the tiniest of insects. The circle was devoid of animal life. It was in this strange area the tearful children started calling out "Father! Where are you?" They repeated the question in union and then the family began to sadly walk away. Suddenly they all heard David Lang's voice answer their question by crying for help. He was no where to be seen, but his voice could be clearly heard. Judge Peck was one of the witnesses to this chilling phenomena. This situation continued for about one month, but with each passing day David Lang's voice grew fainter. And one day there was no answer to the children's cries. He was gone forever.

Where did Lang disappear to? Did Lang somehow fall into a parallel dimension? Was he kidnapped by an invisible UFO? These are some of the possible solutions that various investigators have used to explain this strange mystery over the subsequent years. Unless someone else disappears in full view of reliable witnesses it is unlikely that any more clues to this incident will be found.

DO YOU REAP WHAT YOU WRITE?

A similar incident as the Lang mystery occurred several decades earlier in 1856. In this case the man's name was Orion Williamson and the disappearance took place on a farm outside of Selma, Alabama. Williamson's vanishing act, like Lang's was witnessed by his wife, children and three neighbors. What made this story different was the very young notable reporter who covered it, Ambrose Bierce. A few years later, the writer included his description in his short story "The Difficulty of Crossing a Field". It is ironic that one of his first newspaper stories was about peculiar disappearances and his last great project in his long and eventful life, should end with his own.

A man of many talents, Ambrose Bierce was born on June 24, 1842, in Meigs county Ohio. He was an excellent student and skipped a few grades in his primary education. But he grew bored with the pace of his learning when he reached high school. After a year of secondary education he quit school and found his first job in journalism as a printer's devil. For a man who was to become known for his wit, satire, journalism and short stories, his formal education was very short. During the Civil War he served in the Union Army and fought in the famous battles of Shiloh, Stone's River and Chickamauga. Bierce was wounded in 1864 at Kenesaw Mountain. When he left the Army in 1865, he had risen from a private to a first lieutenant. In 1867, he was given the rank of Major in appreciation for his meritorious service.

Over the next thirty years, Bierce was a journalist, satirist, engineering attache, mining entrepreneur and a newspaper editor. His various careers took him to the Dakota Territory, England, and San Francisco. Two months before he left for England, he married Mary Ellen Day in a pre-Christmas ceremony in 1871. It was while writing for the London satirical magazines Fun and Figaro, that he became known as "Bitter Bierce". He settled down in San Francisco in 1887 and joined the staff of Hearst's San Francisco Examiner, an association that lasted for 20 years.

When Bierce was 71, he had written two famous collections of short stories. "The Devil's Dictionary" and innumerable articles reviling religion, big business and the human race in general. It was time for Bierce to find something new to write about and the Mexican Revolution appeared to be the perfect subject. It had the potential to provide a new vista in journalism, one he had not tried before. He would witness history in the making, with all its excitement and danger. Not every man in his comfortable later years would undertake such adventure. But for Bierce covering the Mexican Revolution was better than the alternative. In one of his last correspondences with his literary secretary, dated December 16, 1913, he wrote, "I am going to Mexico with a pretty definite purpose which is not at present disclosable...... If you hear of my being stood up against a Mexican stone wall and shot to rags, please know that I think that's a pretty good way to depart this life. It beats old age, disease or falling down cellar stairs. To be a Gringo in Mexico-ah, that's euthanasia!"

Many people have commented on this note. It would appear that Bierce did not want to return from his last adventure. His fear of dying in a slow and debilitating manner may have overpowered his common sense, or perhaps for someone with Bierce's point of view, it was the perfect way to end his career.

Did the Indians native to the Roanoake area hold the key to the disappearance of the colonists? Some modern experts believe this to be the case.

Raleigh's Expedition zu Roanoke.

In 1924, several of Bierce's friends went to Mexico and talked with Pancho Villa. The bandit revolutionary told them Bierce did visit his camp in the spring of 1914. But the "Gringo" journalist was asked to leave when he made favorable remarks about Villa's enemy, Carranza. Villa said he did not know what happened after the man left his camp. It looked like his friends had reached a dead end in their search for the solution of Bierce's disappearance. Sometime later they spoke with Villa's brother, Hippolito, who suggested it was very possible Pancho had sent some gunmen to kill the journalist for his inappropriate remarks. Not everyone believes this was the case. Hippolito may have tried to ease the anguish of Bierce's associates by giving them a successful, if not truthful, conclusion to their quest. This story was never corroborated by any other witness or by any hard evidence. Ambrose Bierce simply went to Mexico during a turbulent time and disappeared.

THERE GOES THE JUDGE

Born Joseph Force Crater, he became famous by his occupation as magistrate; the news media and public knew him as Judge Crater. He was born in 1889 in the small town of Easton, Pennsylvania. After graduating from Lafayette College he came to New York and graduated from Columbia University Law School. In 1913 he settled in New York and began to practice law. In 1916, he represented a woman named Stella Wheeler in a divorce action and a year later he married her. His ambition and hard work made equally as successful in the legal and political professions. When he became president of a Democratic Party club in Manhattan his law practice began to flourish. Crater's leadership position within the Democratic Party gave him access to many of the party's leaders in the corrupt Tammany Hall organization. This association with Tammany Hall led to Crater being appointed as a New York Supreme Court judge in April 1930.

As with any such appointment made with the influence and blessing of Tammany Hall, there was a fee to be paid to the graft ridden entrenched powers. In Crater's case it was a simple $20,000 which was arrived at by a formula of 90% of his first years salary. He paid the money with withdrawal from his savings account. In those dark early days of the depression, $20,000 was a considerable sum. Some may ask why would any-

one pay such a large premium for a judgeship? The answer can be found in one of Crater's first actions as state Supreme Court judge. Within weeks of his appointment Crater became the receiver of a bankrupt hotel. He sold it to a bond-and-mortgage company for $75,000. A few months later the city agreed to buy it back for a condemnation price of $3 million. It just so happened that the building's plot had miraculously become a vital part of a street widening project. For his time and effort Crater received a percentage of the profit. It was a small percentage, anywhere from 2 to 5 percent, or from $60,000. to $150,000. Not a bad return on a career investment.

That June the judge and his wife went to their summer cottage in Belgrade, Maine. In the decades before air conditioning much of the city agencies would crawl to a halt in the sticky summer heat and those who could afford to leave the urban steam bath, did. In late July, Crater received a phone call from New York. According to some reports he told his wife he had to return to the city to take care of some urgent business; other sources quote him as telling his wife he had to go to New York ".....to straighten those fellows out." The only known fact about his whereabouts and/or business during those few days, was a trip he took with a showgirl to Atlantic City on July 30th. He returned to Maine on August 1st. On August 3rd, he received another phone call and returned to New York yet again, without explanation to his wife.

Nothing out of the ordinary was noted in his behavior for the next few days. But on August 6th Crater had his assistant, Joseph Mara, cash two checks for him amounting to $5,150. He spent the morning going over files in his courthouse chambers. At noon, Mara delivered the cash, packed into two locked briefcases, to Crater's home. The judge then told Mara to take the rest of the sweltering day off.

Shortly before 6 o'clock, Crater purchased one ticket for a comedy at the Belasco Theater. He took a short walk to a steakhouse on West 45th Street; there he had a chance meeting with two friends of his. One of them was a lawyer named William Klein and the other was a fashionably beautiful showgirl named Sally Lou Ritz. He joined them for dinner, there were no outward signs suggesting that anything could be amiss. But there was one peculiarity, he showed his companions the theater ticket on which was printed a curtain time of eight o'clock. Crater left them at 9:10 P.M., indi-

Jimmy Hoffa, former Teamster Union leader, left his house one morning and disappeared. Throughout his career there had been rumors of his links to organized crime. Many investigators see these links as part of the chain that pulled Hoffa into an unmarked grave yet to be discovered.

If one picture can truly speak a thousand words then this photo of Judge Crater and his wife would contain several paragraphs about a confident man and his adoring spouse vacationing in Maine. Three days after this was taken, the self-possesed judge vanished without a trace.

cating he did not want to miss the show. He stepped into a taxicab and was never seen again.

One would think from all the publicity Crater's disappearance had received over the years that the day after his vanishing into thin air, the story instantly made headlines. Actually it took almost a month before there was any public reaction. At first his wife began to worry when she did not hear from her husband for 10 days, but after she phoned a few of his friends, she was reassured that all was well and the judge would eventually reappear. On August 25th, the first day of the fall court calender arrived and there was no Judge Crater on the bench. Everyone suspected something was amiss. His fellow judges conducted their own investigation, but after a week of fruitless searching they decided to notify police. The day after the police began their in-vestigation into Judge Crater's disappearance, the story finally made its way into the newspapers and was featured on page one, preceded by large headlines.

Many theories have been proposed as to the fate of the missing judge. Mrs. Crater and her friends favored those possible solutions that made the judge a victim of circumstances beyond his control. Some of those theories involved Judge Crater being killed by someone hired by his Tammany Hall associates for not paying money he owed for: either his judgeship or his portion of the hotel deal. The judge's wife maintained her husband was murdered "....because of a sinister something that was connected to politics." Another explanation, popular at the time, said the judge was killed to prevent him from testifying at a grand jury investigation into graft ridden Tammany Hall politics. Of course there was

a wide spread belief that Judge Crater simply disappeared to live a richer life elsewhere. Some of the evidence, which includes his withdrawal of funds and strange theater going habits, could be seen as backing up those theories. There is another fact which is not often mentioned in articles about his mystery; three weeks after Crater vanished, Sally Lou Ritz, the showgirl he had so accidentally met for dinner, also disappeared. Some of the newspaper accounts of the time had speculated that the Judge and the showgirl had made Rio their permanent trysting place.

In 1937, Mrs. Crater sued several insurance companies for double indemnity on her husband's life insurance policies. Insurance companies, then as now, were reluctant to pay anything let alone double the face amount of the policy for a murder, where there was not one shred of a body as proof of death. The Crater family lawyer claimed that Sally Lou Ritz or perhaps another showgirl was blackmailing Judge Crater. According to Mrs. Crater's lawyer, the judge withdrew the $5,150. on the last day of his life to pay the showgirl's gangster beau the blackmail. But the payoff went sour and Crater was accidentally killed. The Ritz showgirl was murdered later because she knew too much. The court did not buy this rather thin idea and Mrs. Crater was denied the double indemnity. Two years later, the courts did declare Judge Crater legally dead, allowing his wife to collect the normal value of the insurance policies. The New York Police Department, however, never officially closed the case in their files.

Profitable Mysteries

Delving into an unsolved mystery can bring a certain self-satisfaction to the sleuth. He may even find some reward if he takes the time to write about his possible solution to the investigated mystery, that is if he has managed to unravel the many twists and turns associated with most great unsolved mysteries. And of course if he happens to be lucky and have a UFO land in his back yard and visit there for awhile, or capture a Bigfoot, or even make a pet out of a friendly lake monster, he will become rich and famous. There is one class of mystery which does reward successful detection with wealth and sometimes with fame, that is the discovery and recovery of treasure.

THE TREASURE HUNTER

Stereotypically the treasure hunter is portrayed as either an old prospector, out in the wilderness with a tattered map in his pack, seeking his last desperate chance to make a killing; or the treasure hunter is an adventurer who stumbles upon a map, or clue and against all odds, attempts to recover the loot before the unsavory competition. Let us not forget about the bored playboy for whom the search is another means of keeping busy. The true hunter is an altogether different breed.

It takes hard work and perseverance to be a treasure hunter. Usually it begins with some new clue to the whereabouts of a particular hoard of gold, silver and/or gems. These clues often come from historical research, legends, a phrase in an unpublished diary, a notation on the edge of an old manuscript or the proverbial treasure map. Next the treasure hunter must decide if his information is accurate. Often this is a matter of intelligence and experience and reinforced gut instinct.

The professional seeker doesn't rush out looking for the treasure right away. He plans what measures he should take to recover the hoard. Is it under water? Could the original position have shifted over the years? Could the landmarks have changed? Once he is satisfied the undertaking is within his capabilities, he may try to get the financing from investors or finance the expedition himself.

Time and money are important ingredients in searching for treasure. Even a vacation trip to Superstition Mountain will incur expenses for transportation, lodging, food and elementary tools; it is also underwritten by the amateur treasure hunter's full-time job. How much time does one spend on a lead depends upon the encouragement one finds in the search. If the treasure is underwater and the seeker finds an anchor in the suspected area of the booty, it might be a reasonable assumption that the hoard may be nearby and worth the extra time to search further in the area. Conversely, if the same anchor is found in a location that has swift currents, the treasure hunter may not be near the depository of riches at all. The professional treasure hunter knows when to quit a search when, like a detective, he runs out of encouraging leads and the additional expenditure of time will not be justified.

CREATING TREASURE

Before it is hidden, treasure is someone's wealth. The earliest recorded reason for turning riches into treasure has to do with burial rituals and customs. Many are the tombs of the ancient Egyptians, Chinese, Greeks, Etruscans, Persians, etc., in which noblemen and lesser ranks were buried with their prized possessions, in many cases these afterlife baubles did not outlive their usefulness in the here and now. When some tombs are opened for the storehouse of knowledge within, it is called archaeology; when some tombs are opened for the wealth alone, it is known as grave robbing. The larcenous, clandestine visits to newly sealed tombs seem to have started concurrently with the initiation of burying riches with the owner. Treasure doesn't have to be old, just cached.

Keeping riches safe from invading hoards, curious occupying troops and unpredictable raiders, is good reason for stashing valuables away for safe keeping. It is only when the owners, owing to regrettable circumstance, are not around to retrieve their goods that they become treasure. Somewhere in Braddock Heights, Maryland, a British Army payroll lies buried in a large chest. General Edward Braddock had every intention of coming back for it once he and his troops either won the battle or escaped from their pursuers during the French and Indian Wars. The chest is still there somewhere because Braddock and his troops never lived through the battle to retrieve it.

Illegally gotten gains can often become treasure. Pirates were notorious converters of loot into treasure and they made North America their hiding ground. Captain Kidd, Jean Laffite and Blackbeard were the piracy superstars of their day, at least in legend if not in fact. Many pirates buried their loot in order not to share with their crews and sponsors. Others saw fit to keep a nest egg for retirement from a dangerous occupation. They chose places, like General Braddock, that they could find at some later date, sometimes the pirate's schedule was upset by foreign navies, other pirates and the hangman's rope. They never claimed their carefully hidden pension, and the loot became the treasure that is sought today.

Criminal proceeds, other than those from piracy, are another way treasure is created. Occasionally a thief or burglar must hide

During the French and Indian Wars British General Edward Braddock had his men bury the large army payroll rather than let it fall into enemy hands. He's shown here after being mortally wouded during the battle that followed. The French and their Indian allies were victorious and not one British soldier survived. The treasure remains unfound.

the objects of his attention in order to escape detection as the perpetrator or just plain escaping by not being weighed down while quickly fleeing the scene of the crime. A famous case in point is former Public Enemy Number One, John Dillinger. A few months before his death in the attempted capture by the FBI, Dillinger and some of his cohorts found themselves surrounded by the Feds. They were hold up in a little roadhouse near

Mercer, Wisconsin. In the confusion of the ensuing gun battle, Dillinger and his gang escaped. Not wanting to be slowed down by the large suitcase, containing close to a quarter of a million dollars in small bills, he buried it. As the story goes, it is still in the ground near the roadhouse. Unfortunately, the paper money was only protected by a leather suitcase, which would not provide any long term preservation from water damage. It has turned back to worthless pulp by now.

A LOUISIANA LEGEND

Quite a few people, in Arkansas, Mississippi and Missouri believe there is gold in "them thar hills." This is due to a legend that keeps circulating among those who, even on a part-time basis, seek to make themselves wealthy by finding treasure. As tales go it is not a concise story, it has many versions and many possible sites for the gold to be found. It may be there is no treasure. On the other hand, because of the persistence of the legend, it may be everyone has searched in the wrong locations and the Spanish gold is waiting for some lucky hunter to pluck it from the earth.

Once upon a time the Spanish Conquistadors ran rampant over present day Mexico. They were adventurers who came as grave robbers to a tomb, they sought wealth not enlightenment and the indigenous populations were crushed in the process. But England did not let this exploitation go unchallenged. She commissioned privateers to raid the Spanish galleons and seize this wealth on the high seas for the greater good of the English Crown.

Nine Spanish treasure laden galleons were sailing for home when several sleek and fast English privateer ships swooped down upon them. A short inconclusive battle took place and the galleons ran away not wanting to risk their precious cargo. The English followed at a distance for the galleons were still formidable fighting ships. Toward dusk, when the visibility was shortened, the Spanish sailed toward land and up the Mississippi River. They anchored around a bend in the river which has since disappeared. The next morning the privateers realized they had lost the galleons. Not wanting to lose a good opportunity, they decided to hang around in the area in case the Spanish treasure laden ships should reappear.

After the Spanish made camp and surveyed the land, they began to hear rumors from the docile river tribes of a gold mine to the north. According to some versions the Spanish heard this tale from Indians who actually worked in the mines. Since wealth was their reason for coming to the New World, it was only logical they find this mine and take all the riches found therein.

Large rafts were built, loaded with the Mexican booty, and the galleons were sunk. The gold seekers traveled up the Mississippi stopping at various places to trade with the natives and gain further information on the whereabouts of the mine. It was found, by the Spaniards, nestled in the quartz cliffs of present day Arkansas, slightly north of the confluence of the Arkansas and Big Mulberry Rivers.

The Spanish seized the mine and enslaved the Indians. Mining continued as usual except all the proceeds went to the Spaniards. They were harsh masters and word of their cruelty spread to the neighboring tribes. Soon the adventurers found themselves fighting a guerilla war with the natives. Attacks upon the Spanish increased in ferocity, at the same time their supplies and ammunition ran low. The only option left to the Spaniards was to abandon the mine, hide the treasure they brought with them and make their way back to Mexico. The adventurers did this in their usual style. After they buried the Mexican treasure in the mine, they buried the Indians alive in the same mine and after the entrance was well hidden, they set off down stream.

Luck was not in their favor. The French put a kink in the Spaniards' plans. While the adventurers were busy collecting gold at the mine, France sold the Louisiana Territory to the former English colonists, the Americans. Now, in order to escape undetected, the Spanish had to sneak by the newly built and numerous U.S. Army outposts to make their way back to Mexico. As the legend ends, all the unfortunate Spaniards die from a combination of Indian attacks and swamp fever.

The problem with the legend as told, is the time-frame in which it allegedly occurs. It seems to begin in the middle to late 1500's and jumps at the end to the 1800's. Clearly this is an amalgam of two different versions. There is an interpretation which states the Spanish discovered the mine in the late 1500's under the already described circumstances and secretly kept mining operations going for over two hundred years. The French were lax in patrolling and protecting their New World lands. It was relatively easy for the Spaniards to keep the mine going for all those years, taking small amounts of gold back to Spain on each voyage. But the Americans were a different matter, they lived on the continent and were intent on developing the new addition to their country. In a few years the Spanish presence would be discovered and ownership of the mine would be taken away. This version ends the same way with the natives being killed and the mine sealed.

Spanish explorations of the Mississippi River has been historically verified. In fact it is the descendants of the Spanish horses that became the wild mustangs of the plains that the Indians tamed and rode so well. It is possible for a band of Spaniards to have found an Indian mine and even made the natives work it for them. The question is....did they?

THE VERY, VERY BAD LANDS

Discovered in 1540 by Vasquez de Coronado, while searching for the Seven Cities of Gold, Superstition Mountain, Arizona is not one mountain but a range of volcanic peaks, mesas and cliffs. During the day, temperatures can rocket above 100 degrees Fahrenheit and plummet to below freezing after sundown. It is a tough rugged country and difficult to explore. Coronado originally named the region, "The Range of Foam" after the ubiquitous grey speckled pumice, which adds an eternal feeling of rubbing against sandpaper; even a casual walk through the area can rub exposed skin raw. Everything is sharp and abrasive here, the cliffs are steep, the rocks are jagged and the plant life seems to have grown thorns just for the sake of blending into the hard edged landscape.

While exploring The Range of Foam, several of Coronado's scouts were killed by persons unknown. It was probably the Apaches who ambushed them. Their bodies were found headless and the heads were never found. It turns out the Indians of the area believed their gods lived in the inhospitable land, they would do anything to insure the good graces of the deities. Coronado thought it best for all concerned to leave and not return. Taking a last look at the other worldly scenery. he christened it Superstition Mountain. It was a name that stuck through the centuries.

Miguel Peralta, set out in 1845 to find a new source of income for his family. In the seventeenth century his forebearers were given a huge land grant by the Spanish Crown, which included a few profitable silver mines and Superstition Mountain. After two centuries of exploitation, the mines began yielding less and less silver each year. Peralta read the down turning line on the production chart and decided it was time to see what other wealth there was in the rest of the family holdings.

Some people are plain lucky, everything they touch becomes gold. This was true for Peralta. Within six months of exploring the Superstition Mountain, he discovered a rich vein of gold. It was located somewhere in sight of a prominent feature now known as Weaver's Needle. He made a map using the landmark as a guide to the gold and left Superstition Mountain to raise the necessary capital for men and equipment. Peralta returned to the area with over three hundred men, tons of mining equipment and a hundred mules. He set up a large base camp on a level plateau a few miles from the mine. The camp became the center for refining the gold ore.

For three years he mined and shipped gold back to Mexico. During this time, it is fair to say, the natives were getting restless. More to the point they were getting furious, the Spaniards were seen as violators of holy ground, as men raped the scared earth for mere gold. It didn't help the Spanish any that some young Apache girls chose to visit the camp at night trading pleasure for material goods.

Foremost among the angry and vengeful Apaches was a charismatic tribal chief called Cochise. He, along with the other Indian leaders, planned for weeks to destroy the sacrilegious foreigners. Rumors of the impending attack were spread to the Spanish by the Apache girls in their nightly visits. Thus warned, Peralta shut down the mine, buried what gold was not packed near the mine and sealed the entrance of the mine. He and his men retreated to the base camp and fortified it against attack. But the Spaniards soon realized they could not stay holed up forever so they planned to escape.

Now it was Peralta's turn to be betrayed by the nightly visitors. Either an Apache girl volunteered the information or she gave it up under torture. In any case Cochise found out the exact route Peralta was using to make his escape. The Spaniards loaded most of the mules with gold, some had to carry provisions for the expected long journey, and set off for Mexico down a wide valley at dawn.

Peralta's progress was watched by the Apaches. Knowing the area better than the Spaniards, the large band of Indians could follow them without indicating their presence. The Apaches, under Cochise's leadership struck while Peralta and his men were passing a cliff. With Indians on three sides of the Spaniards and a steep mesa at their backs, they were wiped out to a man, but the burros bolted and were spared the same fate as their owners. Two years later the Spaniard's bones were discovered by the U.S. Army on a routine search for some errant Apaches. It was called, by the army officer in charge, the Massacre Grounds, a name it is still known by today.

Peralta's death marks the beginning of a period in the history of Superstition Mountain which could be called the "Gold, Gold, Everywhere There is Gold" epoch. Remnants of that haphazard golden era are still happening today.

The next big find of Superstition Mountain treasure was not Peralta's much sought after mine, but his almost forgotten gold laden burros. Although the animals were spared the wrath of Cochise and his followers, the lack of food and water in that dangerous region eventually killed them. The mules had wandered far and wide before they died.

Sometime in the 1850's, two prospectors known as Hurley and O'Connor, who were searching for Peralta's mine by backtracking the route taken by the Spaniards, found a dead burro with a full pack of gold. In the ensuing weeks several more animals and packs were discovered. Instead of going into the nearest town Hurley and O'Connor made the long trek to the U.S. Government Assay Office in San Francisco and netted for their efforts close to fifty thousand dollars. They continued this pattern of discovery and redemption of the Peralta gold for many years. Finally they quit, having already made a small fortune and because of the increasing danger posed by the Apaches, outlaws and a hoard of miscellaneous desperate treasure hunters who suspected the prospectors had found Peralta's mine. Once they announced their retirement from the Peralta burro hunt, they told everyone how they made their fortune. Hurley and O'Connor did a thorough job of finding the gold filled packs. Less than 25 burro packs

were found after their retirement and the last bit of burro gold was found, like most of Hurley and O'Connor's finds, in the region called Goldfield in 1912.

While Hurley and O'Connor were busy finding Peralta's last ill fated shipment, another man was becoming a legend for having found the lost mine. Known in the wild west as "The Old Dutchman" Jacob Walz, a German, discovered the Peralta mine with the help of his Apache girlfriend. But his story does not have a happy ending or even a cheerful middle; it is a tale of an amassed fortune admidst unfortunate circumstance.

Walz danced around Europe trying to put his degree in mine engineering to good use. He sought to find his fortune in the ground, anything would do, iron, coal, copper, any undiscovered mineral that would make him a rich man. This urge to easy wealth was not satisfied in the Old World, so he traveled to the New World and the California gold

To march with Coronado meant a chance to become rich. But Coronado missed his great hope at Superstition Mountain. His dreams linger on.

Frederic Remington

She believed in this German fellow, in the way of some women who are fiercely loyal to, and protective of, the men they chose to share their lives with. She was in her early twenties and he was in his late fifties and together they plotted to steal a little of the gold each day from the mine where Walz worked. How long they managed to skim the mine's glittering proceeds and how they actually accomplished the theft is unknown, but they were very clever. He was not the only miner who was dipping his hands into the pot of gold, but when the mine operators and the local authorities raided selected homes of miners suspected of stealing gold, only Walz was never brought to trial. The other miners went to jail, they knew that Walz was stealing also and hated him for being smart enough not to get caught. He was dismissed from his job and Walz didn't seem to care.

For the next couple of years, Walz and Ken-tee lived comfortably in a small town near Superstition Mountain. Then one day the couple packed a couple of mules and walked off into the inhospitable land where Peralta's mine was located. They returned a few months later with gold laden packs. Everyone but the Apaches believed Walz and Ken-tee found some of the burro gold. The Apaches thought Ken-tee betrayed the secret of Peralta's mine to Walz, so they raided Walz's home and kidnapped her. In the course of the townspeople's chase after the Indians, Ken-tee's throat was slashed, her tongue cut out and her body left in the badlands. It was said the Apaches did this not only to aid their getaway, knowing that the angry townspeople would stop once they found the wounded woman, but to punish her for her suspected treachery. She died with Walz at her side an hour after the townsfolk posse found her.

After Ken-tee's death Walz went to pieces. He moved to Phoenix and went on a three year binge. Now, he danced from bar to bar and became known as the man who knew the secret location of Peralta's mine. His presence in a bar would bring the greedy to his table plying him with drink to loosen his tongue. It was Walz who would stagger from the table while the gold seekers were usually found under it, dead drunk. Yet death was to become a fixture in Walz's life.

rush of 1848. Again he failed where others had succeeded, not only in California but New Mexico and Arizona as well. In the 1850's, Walz tumbled from the heights of his lifelong lofty dreams to the depths of a low salaried position as an ordinary miner in a hole in the ground called the Vulture Gold Mine.

It was this period in Walz's life that he met and cohabited with an extraordinarily beautiful Indian woman named Ken-tee.

With the arrival in Phoenix, from Germany, of Walz's cousin Jacob Weiser, The Old Dutchman snapped out of his alcoholic haze and together they went to Superstition Mountain for a few months. Gold, lots of the shiny metal is what they brought back to Phoenix when they returned. Residents of Phoenix also said that Walz admitted, in one of his subsequent drunken bouts, that he and his cousin killed two Mexicans who followed them out to the mine. Within a year the cousins were ambushed by the Apaches on one of their expeditions to the mine. Only Walz made it back alive; his cousin died with several arrow wounds in his chest. The Old Dutchman seemed to be invincible. But not so lucky were those who followed Walz, venturing to discover the secret to Peralta's mine. Nobody kept count of the luckless who never returned after setting out after The Old Dutchman, but their number is reputed to be over thirty.

In 1891, Jacob Walz, *aka* The Old Dutchman, died in the house of a friend, a black woman named Julia Thomas. People said his life was a tragedy, through no fault of his own, that he traded love for money and spent the rest of his days suffering for it. On his death bed, surrounded by his friends, he left Julia fifteen thousands dollars and to all who were there for his last moments on earth, he cryptically left the secret to the Peralta mine.

According to Walz, the mine is in a rough jagged country that all but camouflages the mine. "The mine can be found at the spot on which the shadow of the tip of Weaver's Needle rests at exactly four in the afternoon. The mine faces west. Near the mine is a hideout cave. One mile from the cave is a rock with a natural face looking east. To the south is Weaver's Needle. Follow to the right of the canyons, but not very far." Walz went on to describe the mine as an upside down funnel with ledges cut into the sides. The Spaniards also built a tunnel through the hill to remove the gold from the bottom of the shaft. The mine consisted of two 18-inch quartz gold bearing veins.

This may not seem like enough information to go and spend the rest of your life searching for the mine, but that is what Julia and the others did. Needless to say they did not find the mine. Those who came later and followed the same directions had no better luck. Just on the face of the directions there are quite a few holes. A quick computation will yield 365 places the tip of Weaver's Needle can point to, "at exactly four in the afternoon." That can be an awfully large area to cover. Since it can be safely assumed that each and every day has been noted by some treasure hunter since The Old Dutchman died, one has to wonder about the accuracy of the remaining parts of Walz's directions. If it is all a fabrication, why did Walz bother to tell a lie with his dying words?

Tim Haydock, in his book *Treasure Trove*, believes Walz made up the story about finding the Peralta mine in order to launder the gold that he and Ken-tee stole from the Vulture Gold Mine. It must be remembered, according to Haydock, that almost $200,000 in gold was recovered during the raids on the miners houses, but none was found in Walz's home. If this is true, it is possible that The Old Dutchman kept the legend of the mine alive, in order to keep the memory of his only love in his life, Ken-tee and the time they shared together, alive too. It is also possible that Walz had become so cynical and bitter in his last days that he thought his friends were still after the mine and cared not a whit for him. So he made up a set of directions knowing they might spend the rest of their lives chasing phantom gold.

Death still haunts the search for the mine. Since Walz's death close to a thousand people have officially searched for the secret of The Lost Dutchman Mine, as it is called today, to no avail. Of those who have gone into Superstition Mountain looking for that gold in this century, twenty have died under mysterious and gruesome circumstances. There is that last possibility that there was some truth in Walz's dying rants, it may all be jumbled, fact mixed with fiction, and still awaits someone to make very profitable sense out of those last words.

A FRENCH TWIST

In the San Juan Mountains, located in southwestern Colorado, there is a singular peak called Treasure Mountain. It is slightly to the north and 105 miles to the east of the town of Durango. Somewhere on or very near Treasure Mountain is $20,000,000 in gold. This was not a lost Spanish mine, but a lost French mine in territory claimed by the Spanish.

In the late 1700's, French fur trappers and traders, in the western part of the North American continent, told tales of fabulous Spanish gold mines in the southwest on their trips to the French port of New Orleans. These stories were magnified by the time they traveled across the Atlantic and reached the new French Republic. Someone in the chaotic new administration sent word

Superstition Mountain is not a place to vacation with the family. Yet each year people trek through this inhospitable terrain searching for the Lost Dutchman Mine.

back to the Louisiana Territory that a small French expedition should be mounted to explore some of the disputed areas of land with the Spanish. Knowledge and better maps was not the purpose of this venture, finding a French share of the rumored golden wealth was.

The exact number of men that left New Orleans has never been resolved, estimates range from 30 to 75. After six months of exploration the party came to the San Juan Mountains and within a few weeks of their arrival found a rich vein of gold. About half of the expedition were miners and they quickly went to work. It was a huge strike and the eager French attempted to mine their find through the winter, ignoring the advice from the Ute Indians, a tribe with which the miners had friendly relations. Bitter, biting sub zero weather and heavy snows forced the ill prepared French to hide

Another version of Jacob Walz's gold strike is told on this plaque. Perhaps the mine is only a stone's throw away?

HERE LIE THE REMAINS OF

SNOWBEARD
THE
DUTCHMAN

WHO IN THIS MOUNTAIN SHOT THREE MEN TO STEAL A RICH GOLD MINE FROM SPANISH PIONEERS, KILLED EIGHT MORE TO HOLD HIS TREASURE, THEN HIMSELF DIED IN 1892, WITHOUT REVEALING ITS LOCATION. DOZENS OF SEARCHERS HAVE MET MYSTERIOUS DEATH IN THE CANYONS THERE, YET THE ORE LIES UNREVEALED. INDIANS SAY THIS IS THE CURSE OF THE THUNDER GODS ON WHITE MAN IN WHOM THE CRAVING FOR GOLD IS STRONG. BEWARE, LEST YOU TOO SUCCUMB TO THE LURE OF THE LOST DUTCHMAN MINE IN SUPERSTITION MOUNTAIN. ERECTED BY 1938

The only proof that gold exists in the mountain are these cuff links Walz had made from the treasure of his mine.

much of the extracted gold and flee to the warmer climes of what is now Taos, New Mexico. Several members of the expedition brought a token amount of gold back to New Orleans as proof of their find. In the spring the miners returned to the San Juan Mountains and resumed their activities. In all this time, not a hint was given to the Spanish in the area of what the French party was up to.

This pattern of mining in the warm months, wintering in Taos when the weather grew cold, with small shipments of gold being sent back to France from New Orleans continued for several years. The amount of gold hoarded in the San Juan Mountains by the French, increased to an enormous sum. It was thought the miners did not want to risk losing the fortune by transporting it all at one time. They must have had a plan to bring all the wealth out at some point, but what the scheme was will never be known.

It took a certain quantity of hubris or stupidity, on the part of the French, to think no one would question their unusual activities in the San Juan Mountains after several years of "hanging out in Taos" every winter. Some said the young Spanish women of Taos finally uncovered the secret from the Frenchmen. Some have attributed the Spanish Indian allies, the Arapaho, with discovering some of the gold during one of their raids on the Utes. In either case once the Spanish knew what the French were up to in their territory they wanted them out, they wanted the gold for themselves, but the Spaniards did not want to take any overt action. So they cajoled their allies, the Arapaho, into raiding the miners. At first the raids were small nuisances, then the size and scale of the attacks grew larger, before the French could comprehend what was happening, about half their number was wiped out. It was obviously time for the miners to pack up and leave.

At this juncture in the French experience in Colorado, it is unclear whether the miners buried the gold in three separately hidden caches or in one large shaft in the side of

Treasure Mountain. The tale of the tunnel is the most widely recited, complete with all kinds of deadly traps contained within. Secret signs were cut in the nearby trees and rocks indicating either the entrance to a single treasure shaft or to the three smaller caches.

Now the Frenchmen had only one objective and that was to survive and only one Frenchman accomplished that goal. In the course of their perilous journey to friendly territory the Arapaho raids depleted the French expedition to the point where one man, Remy Ledoux was able to escape his pursuers. He arrived at a French trading post on the Missouri River babbling about the riches that were left behind.

When Ledoux recuperated from his trials and tribulations he went to New Orleans to form another expedition and recover the buried gold. He arrived only to find out France had changed during his years mining in the San Juan Mountains. There was no longer a Committee for Public Safety ruling France. Now there was one man, Napoleon, and he had his sights set on the rest of Europe, not North America. Besides, the officials in New Orleans pointed out to Ledoux, what was sent back to France was a mere pittance. They refused to believe there was a hoard of gold hidden away on a mountain. When Ledoux wanted to contact the minister who authorized the expedition, he was informed that if the man still had his head attached to his shoulders he surely didn't want to be held accountable for some failed North American gold mining scheme. Ledoux decided not to go back to France, but to stay in this new land and settle down.

Years later, in the spring of 1843 to be more precise, Remy Ledoux's grandson eagerly organized a sizable expedition to search for the family gold. He based his optimism on his grandfather's map which was handed down to him by his father, who did not believe the gold ever existed. The youngest Ledoux would have been better off if he had been as skeptical as his father.

Disappointment dogged Ledoux. His first unfortunate discovery was his grandfather's map was not drawn to scale. It was difficult to find on which specific mountain the treasure was buried. Another hindrance to finding the gold was inclusion of fictitious landmarks on the map. This was done on purpose to lead unwanted treasure hunters astray. Ledoux searched until the fall and left having only found one marker to the treasure, a fleur-de-lis etched in a boulder with an arrow underneath it. The next year

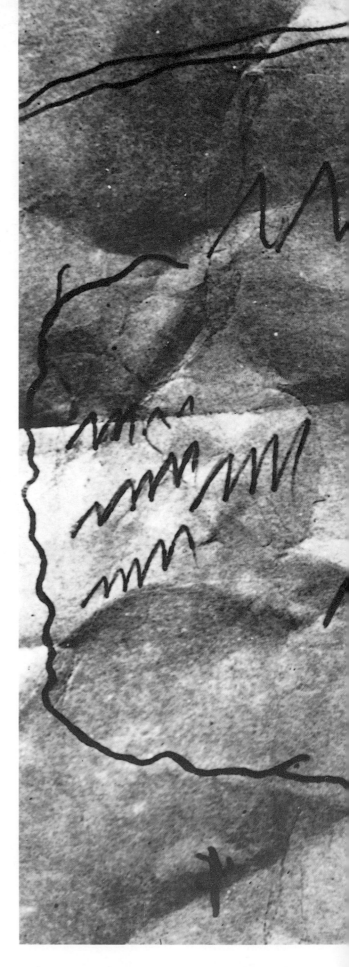

Ledoux returned to continue his search, but this time fate stepped in and prematurely ended his quest. He fell from a low cliff into a small river and drowned. A member of the expedition who carried Ledoux's body to

shore, stole the map from his pack.

The treasure map changed hands a few times before it was forever lost. Towards the end of the nineteenth century, Asa Poor was the last man known to have the map in his

This map is said to be a copy of the one made at the time of Jacob Walz's death. Julia Thomas would spend the rest of her life attempting to find the spot labelled "ore here."

KIDD AT GARDINER'S ISLAND.

Does this popular image of Captain Kidd match the reality? Some researchers answer in the negative and doubt the existence of any treasure. Still, many continue the search, ever hopeful of finding the legendary wealth.

possession. His contribution to the mystery was the deciphering of the code written on the worn edge of the map. It said "Stand on the grave at foot of mountain at six on a September morning...Where your shadow falls you will find the gold." Asa claimed to have found the grave and followed the instructions. He found for his troubles a sealed shaft of a worked mine. There was no hoard of gold, though he searched the surrounding area extensively. Asa noted the side of Treasure Mountain where the mine was located had recently been altered by snowslides and avalanches.

Treasure Mountain is not as perilous and inhospitable as Superstition Mountain, nevertheless caution should be exercised in exploring this terrain if you ever attempt to solve this mystery. But remember, others have been there before and failed.

THE TRAIL OF THE BUCCANEERS

Pirates have had a long history of losing their treasure. In North America there are many places where brigands are rumored to have left their ill gotten gains for safe keeping. In many cases nothing has been found, yet the legend lingers in the area like a heavy mist. Some places have been found to be more than a rumor, but these sites still refuse to give up the bulk of their suspected wealth.   And every so often a treasure hunter finds a hidden cache, which lends a new lease on life to the other stories of buried pirate riches. Here are some pirates and their rumored treasure.

CAPTAIN KIDD, FEROCIOUS SEA DOG OR OCEAN GOING WIMP?

Born in 1645, the son of a Calvinist minister, William Kidd spent his childhood in Greenock, Scotland. His early career is obscure, but from 1689 he sailed as a commissioned British privateer against the French and Spanish in the West Indies and off the coast of North America.

From the time Kidd received his commission until 1695 he did rather well for himself. He took up residence in New York and became known as a well liked and prosperous merchant seaman. Kidd invested his money in real estate and owned three properties in the middle of the city. It was said that the first oriental carpet in New York belonged to William Kidd and could be seen covering the floors of his country home on what is now East 79th Street.

New York City at the end of the seventeenth century was an open city. Because of the British imposed Navigation Acts, the American colonies were forbidden to trade on their own. The only legal means of trade belonged to English merchants and seamen. To counter this artificial market and distribution system, the colonists began to trade with pirates and these brigands made Boston, Newport, Salem and New York their centers of commerce.   Colonel Benjamin Fletcher, then Governor of New York, welcomed this trade to his city with open arms and ever growing wealth. His flagrant allowance of the illegal trade became too much for his corrupt friends in England and plans were set in motion to have him replaced. But while he was governor, pirate captains and their crews freely walked the streets, trading, carousing and spending their money as if it were sand on a beach.

Meanwhile Kidd was in London on a routine trading voyage. He was introduced to Governor Fletcher's replacement, Lord Bellomont. The newly appointed governor had a plan to rid the Indian Ocean and the Red Sea of pirates who were regularly attacking ships belonging to the East India Company. These brigands were the very same men who were trading with the colonists in New York and other North American ports. Lord Bellomont with the financial and political backing of four very important and influential English lords commissioned Kidd to rid the seas of pirates. To this end they were willing to finance the purchase and arming of a ship and a year's salary for the crew. As privateering deals go the contract was not the greatest. The captain and the crew were to split 25% of the spoils instead of the usual 60% and this was to be paid not at sea but after all the treasure was counted by the British Admiralty.

Kidd was given a fast and sleek three-masted frigate, armed with 34 guns and it had a supplemental power of 50 oars in case it was becalmed anywhere on the seven seas. A hand picked crew of honest former navy men came with the ship. Kidd named it the *Adventure Galley* and set sail in March 1696.

From the very beginning Captain Kidd had trouble. Whenever powerful people hatch a scheme there are always those who oppose it. As Kidd was sailing down the Thames, a Royal Navy Commander sailed alongside the Adventure Galley and boarded her. As the maritime laws were loosely written in those days, the commander was allowed to impress the crew into the Royal Navy's service, which the naval officer did with no explanation. Cries of foul were unheeded in the corridors of English political power and Kidd now had to accept newly freed prisoners and other assorted nice guys as a crew. In order to entice these men to sail with him Kidd had to offer them the going rate of 60 percent. Now the captain and crew at the same time violated the terms of his contract. Kidd sailed the seas for close to a year without having fired on one pirate ship. He did attack two small ships bearing French passes, this was allowed as part of his contract since England was at war with France at the time. Soon afterwards the captain made an unsuccessful attack on the Mocha fleet out of Yemen. Kidd had not accomplished anything of consequence, he had not taken any rich booty and the crew at the very least was becoming restless. His ship was in disrepair and he was running out of money. Captain Kidd took the only option left open to him, he became a pirate.

His first order as a pirate captain was a half hearted attack on a convoy of English and Dutch ships. When the protecting East Indian warship sailed into view, Captain Kidd sailed in the opposite direction. So much for auspicious beginnings. His next acts of piracy, on very small ships netted the fledgling pirates almost nothing in booty. But when Captain Kidd attacked a Moorish ship commanded by an Englishman he was well on the road to piracy. A few ships of little consequence followed. There were no easy pickings after that.

A turning point in the career of Captain Kidd the pirate occurred when he decided not to attack a Dutch ship, that had the look and smell of stored riches. Some say that Kidd, being the reluctant pirate that he was, suffered from guilt. His crew on the other hand had committed themselves to a life of piracy and were close to mutiny. Kidd's gunner, William Moore, became the spokesman of the crew's anger and began a violent argument with the captain. In a flash of ill temper Kidd broke Moore's head with a bucket. Moore died in a few hours as a result of the wound. People's reactions are strange at times and the crew, instead of rushing to mutiny and killing Kidd, praised the captain for his handling of the incipient mutiny. At last they may have reasoned, they had a true pirate leading them.

Kidd's biggest prize was the Armenian trading vessel *Quedagh Merchant*. Not only did Kidd take the gold, silver and gems from the ship, he took the ship itself. Since the *Adventure Galley* was beyond repair, Kidd transferred all the treasure and the crew to the slower Armenian ship and regretfully scuttled his faithful frigate. One would

think that his stock would go up in the eyes of the crew with this achievement, but when he sailed into a pirate port near the island of Madagascar looking to capture a brigand and at least fulfill part of his contract, all but fourteen of his crew abandoned him and joined one of the real pirates of the day, a blackguard named Colliford. In all fairness they did leave him half the treasure from the *Quedagh Merchant*.

While he was in the pirate port Kidd heard rumors he was being sought as a full-fledged pirate himself. Back in England he had become something of an embarrassment to his backers. Several of his crew had left his command since he first sailed with his commission in 1695. They joined pirate ships and were later captured and imprisoned by the Royal Navy. In order to plea bargain for a lighter sentence they made up some wild stories about their former captain. This coupled with Kidd's reported strange behavior on the high seas became ammunition for Lord Bellomont's political adversaries the Tories, who were attempting to have some of Kidd's financial backers removed from office.

The source of the legend of Captain Kidd's treasure was his trip back to Boston in the *Quedagh Merchant*. On the way he stopped off at various places and cached his wealth to prevent it from being seized in Boston. Kidd wanted to convince Lord Bellomont, now governor of New York, but at the moment residing in Boston, of his innocence. When he arrived in Boston he was promptly arrested. The French passes were his alibi for his choice of ships that he attacked and after several months in jail Kidd had a chance to show them to Bellomont. His former employer kindly relieved the reluctant pirate of the evidence. Kidd was quickly shipped off to England for trial, minus the French passes that he gave to Bellomont. At the trial Bellomont denied that Kidd entrusted the passes to him. His former crew members lied to save their own necks and they told tales of horror and piracy on the high seas. Due to the tense political climate there was one hope for acquittal. The Tories were willing to make a deal. If Kidd would implicate his former partners in a piracy plot, he could escape the gallows. The captain refused and added "I am the innocentest person of them all. Only I have been sworn against by perjured persons." Kidd was hanged twice, the first time the rope broke and his still breathing body had to be plucked out of the Thames River. The second time his neck broke and he died on

Did a crooked deal with Lord Bellomont start Captain Kidd on the road to unintentional piracy?

156

May 23, 1701.

Piracy was to get worse, much worse, before it was cleared from the seas. Many people refused to believe Captain Kidd was not the brigand that was portrayed at his trial. Some wanted to make the reluctant pirate the historical forerunner of all the nasties who sailed after him. Add to this a certain confusion with a pirate called Bradish, who was hanged about the same time and whose last voyage, in the same geographical area of Captain Kidd's route to Boston, had the same purpose, to hide his treasure so it would not be confiscated by the authorities. Over the years the two pirate's paths were merged together and all the possible treasure sites, for both men, were attributed to Kidd.

Gardiner's Island, located off of Long Island's north shore near East Hampton, is the only verified site of any of Kidd's treasure. Before his final stop at Boston, the captain landed at Gardiner's Island and with the help of his friend and island's owner, John Gardiner, buried a large chest and a box for safe keeping. The chest with its contents of sugar, gold and precious stones was recovered by Governor Bellomont, but many believe that the box is still somewhere on the island. If it is, there is a good chance that it contains gold and diamonds. Today the swampy section where divers used to search for the box is fenced off to prevent injury to would-be treasure hunters. The island is still owned by descendents of the original Gardiner family.

Deer Island near Penobscot Bay in Maine became noted as a Captain Kidd treasure site because of a note that Kidd left his wife before he sailed to Boston. On the bottom of the piece of paper were the boldly written numbers 44, 10, 66, 18. Years later the note disappeared but the code was remembered by treasure hunters and someone had the bright idea that the numbers represented the longitude and latitude of a particular location. Using this line of reasoning it was found the numbers neatly coincided with the map coordinates of Deer Island. No one has found any treasure on the island to date.

Once upon a time, in 1872, gold and silver coins were unearthed during an excavation at the corner of Broad and Wall Streets. It was claimed that this was the site of one of Kidd's downtown buildings and that there might be more gold buried under the street and in a neighboring basement. This caused the workers to dig in a frenzy until they fell exhausted, with no more treasure to be found.

A day at Rye Beach in 1904. No one has ever found the part of Captian Kidd's treasure supposedly buried here.

Rye Beach in Rye, New York is another possible site of Kidd's treasure. In 1699, a sailor took shelter in a farm house near the beach. To repay the kindness he left them an apron full of gold coins. Hence the legend that Captain Kidd slept there after burying some of his treasure nearby. It could be that this was the pirate Bradish and not Kidd, but in either case no gold or silver coins have been recovered from Rye Beach.

Croton-on-the-Hudson in Westchester County, New York contained the site of an odd geographical feature called the Money Hill. It was a man made mound where over the years pieces of eight were found. In the 1920's, the hill was excavated for a new highway and the Westchester County Parks Commission was so sure that there was a sizeable amount of Captain Kidd's treasure about to see the light of day, after all these years, they added a new clause in the awards contract that stipulated any treasure found belonged to the commission and not to the contractor doing the work. Nothing, not even an old button was unearthed. Yet some Croton-on-the-Hudson residents claim there are still some gold coins waiting to be found.

There are more stories and legends about the reluctant pirate William and his treasure than there is gold and silver to bury. Maybe some of the tales are about other pirates and their buried treasure, maybe some are fables and maybe there is some truth in a few of them after all.

A PIRATE'S PIRATE

Pirates bring to mind scraggly bearded seafaring rogues, led by the meanest of the bunch, who after a ship has yielded its cargo, torture, rape and murder the crew and passengers for the sheer enjoyment of watching helpless people suffer. In all fairness, not all pirates behaved in such reprehensible fashion. Yet, there was one sea captain whose legend comes awfully close. He was born Edward Teach, but history has recorded him as Blackbeard and piracy was his game.

Teach was a man who craved excitement. His origins are murky; he came to prominence during the War of Spanish Succession (1701-13), as a rather ruthless privateer commissioned by the British. The outbreak of peace meant a dreary humdrum life of merchant sailing for the former buccaneer. Exactly when he began his pirate activities is also unclear, but it is known that in the winter of 1716, he and his crew seized the large British merchant ship, *Queen Anne's Revenge*, and converted her into a warship of 40 guns.

Fear was his best weapon and Blackbeard used his talent for theatrics to instill horror in his victims. The sight that greeted his soon to be vanquished prey was of a man with a half a dozen matchlock pistols crisscrossing his chest, smoldering matches in his hair, to light the fuses on the pistols, and a long forked black beard tied up with blood red ribbons. Occasionally, on dawn or dusk raids, he would add lit candles to his beard and if the facial hair caught fire while he was boarding an unarmed merchant ship so much the better. What the merchant crew would then see is a pirate with his face on fire, charging at them with a sword in one hand and a pistol in the other. Sometimes his foes would just faint at the sight of this apparition from hell jumping into their midst. Often just a glimpse of his ship on the horizon, flying a "jolly roger" of Blackbeard's own demonic design was enough to make his victims throw down their weapons in fear.

Blackbeard's terror tactics were also used on his crew. In order to lead the group of volunteer rogues, the captain of a buccaneer ship had to command their respect. Among pirates this meant either, having the ability to make the crew more money than anyone else and/or being crazier than the rest of the bunch; Blackbeard fulfilled both qualifications. For relaxation, while at sea, Blackbeard, with a rope around his neck, would dare his crew to endure an execution style hanging longer than he could. Blackbeard never lost at this contest, but several of his crew died of strangulation trying to outlast him. If things were becoming too complacent, this pirate's pirate would shoot someone from the crew to liven up the day.

Treasure hunters have searched all along the east coast of North America for some of Blackbeard's fortune. His famous drunken quote, "Only the devil and me know where my gold is hid," has prompted many a treasure seeker to dig on some deserted beach hoping to strike it rich. There are a few locations which are still prime candidates for Blackbeard's golden hoard.

The Isles of Shoals lying off of New Hampshire's Rye Beach is a good place to start a search for Blackbeard's treasure. This was a favorite rendezvous point for pirate captains, especially those who were allies with Blackbeard. There are several stories of gold being buried on one or another of the isles. It has been said that Blackbeard met one of his confederates on White Island to split a treasure taken from a Spanish galleon. For whatever the reason, they

A man who may actually have been bigger than his legend, Blackbeard buried his treasure all along the Eastern seaboard of the United States.

buried some of the loot there and the other pirate captain left his girlfriend on the small island to stand guard for a couple of weeks. Both Blackbeard and the pirate captain never made it back to White Island. The girlfriend, tired of waiting for someone to come and take her off the island, attempted to swim for the mainland and drowned. Legend has it that her ghost can still be seen near the treasure she is guarding.

Early in this century, a man known as Captain Haley found five silver bars on Smuttynose Island, another one of the Isles of Shoals. Smuttynose Island is also rumored to have a small chest buried by Blackbeard containing pieces of eight. Add to this list Londoner Island and Star Island as possible Isles of Shoals buried treasure locations. Many of the residents on these islands have a standing offer of a 50/50 split on all treasure found on their property.

On a narrow peninsular named Plum Point, in Beaufort County, North Carolina, Blackbeard once build a small home. Around 1716, there was a lot of digging near the house by the pirate and his men. This activity was noticed by some of the pirate's neighbors and reported in the local papers. In 1928 two trappers widened a deep hole found near the site of the centuries old homestead. They discovered an empty vault built with bricks made from the early colonial period. In the middle of the hard earth floor were clear impressions made by iron straps, like those used to band treasure chests that were so popular in Blackbeard's day. No one knows who removed the chest and what the contents were. It is believed there may be more treasure nearby.

Blackbeard Island is found 10 miles off the Georgia Coast and about 50 miles south of Savannah. It was used by the pirate to watch the ships sailing near his headquarters on Ocracoke Island. In 1934 a Georgian unearthed a small wooden room buried on Blackbeard Island. A thorough search and excavation of the immediate area near the room produced no further finds, but this does not exclude the possibility of more treasure having been buried at other sites on the island.

In its heyday Ocracoke Island was the busy North Carolina headquarters for Blackbeard. It was off this island that the pirate met his end. Two Royal Navy warships under the command of Lieutenant Robert Maynard caught up with the pirate and his three ships at Ocracoke Inlet. Blackbeard sailed out to meet this threat and Maynard closed in on the pirate's ship. In a burst of belief in his own superhuman destiny, Blackbeard boarded the *HMS Pearl*, Maynard's flagship, and engaged the Royal Navy Lieutenant in hand to hand combat with swords. None too soon the pirate captain realized that he and his men were vastly outnumbered. He refused to give up and in his last dramatic stand sustained no less than 30 pistol and sword wounds before he died. Moments after Blackbeard fell dead on the deck of the *HMS Pearl* the rest of his crew surrendered. Because the pirate and his men were surprised by Maynard's untimely arrival, it is believed that a substantial pirate treasure lies waiting on Ocracoke Island to be found by some adventurous seeker.

A ROMANTIC PIRATE, BORN TOO LATE

His beginning and end will never be fully known, he seems to have sailed to this continent from out of a cloud and when luck and circumstance turned against him he vanished, sailing off into the dawn, but his part in American history is told in every classroom in the land. Jean Lafitte was born too late for the life of freebooting that he wanted to live.

What passes for information about Lafitte's early life is largely unsubstantiated by any hard documentary facts. Some believe he was born in Bordeaux, France in 1780 and ran away to sea at the age of thirteen. He is said to have been a first mate on a pirate ship in the Indian Ocean and as a result of his being captured, spent some time in an English prison. Other than he was French, the time Lafitte spent in chains at the hands of the British, is often cited as the reason for his intense hatred of the English.

It is known that he sailed for the French in the early years of the Napoleonic Wars and plundered enough English ships to make a modest fortune for himself. During this time he also managed to obtain a privateer commission from the Republic of Cartagena (today known as Columbia, South America) to raid Spanish shipping. Lafitte had finagled a legal patina to cover over what, in truth, most people would have called outright piracy. In his pursuit of wealth, he became quite a social figure for a while in the city of Charleston, South Carolina, but an unsolved murder that pointed to Lafitte as the culprit gave him a strong urge to take to the sea again.

The crucial turning point in Jean Lafitte's life came in 1807; the United States government had declared an embargo against imported goods into the country. This was meant mostly as an economic strike at the British. Relations between the two countries were deteriorating at a quick pace and this situation would eventually lead to the War of 1812. It was a chance of a lifetime for Lafitte, who saw the possibilities of trading coveted foreign made goods and recently pirated wares into America through mostly the French and Creole port of New Orleans. By 1810 he was the leader of a colony of freetraders, privateers and pirates on the Baratarian coast, south of New Orleans. So powerful was his influence that by 1812 he had corrupted most of the honest merchants of New Orleans. The Governor of the Louisiana Territory, W.C.C. Claiborne, was incensed. Illegal trading in the newly acquired land was the rule not the exception and the governor foresaw trouble for himself if he could not deal effectively with this lawless pirate.

Claiborne's first action to stem the erosion of his authority was to put a bounty on Lafitte's head of $500. Lafitte countered this move by placing a bounty of $10,000 on the governor's head and he said he would double the offer if Claiborne dared to raise his. The pirate had enormous resources and it was widely known the government funds were rather limited. Frustrated, Claiborne's next move was to send out the militia to capture Lafitte. They returned without firing a shot, each one of them wealthier than when they had left. The militia told how they were quickly ambushed and outnumbered in bayous, how the pirates instead of shooting them, welcomed them for dinner and sent them packing in the morning with pockets full of gold. After this incident became widely known in New Orleans, there was no end to the number of men willing to hunt Lafitte and be paid off by the rogue. Clai-

Jean Lafitte never intended to become an American hero. His freewheeling lifestyle made him the focal point of the Battle of New Orleans and, coincidentally, caused him to scatter his booty along the Gul;f Coast.

borne was locked in a stalemate with his foe. The crafty pirate knew the people of the Louisiana Territory better than the appointed official, they would never go against one of their own.

Men and events shape history, Lafitte was about to become, unknowingly, the focal point of these forces and a famous figure in American history. President Madison was now embroiled in an unpopular war with the British, various economic groups wanted trade on the seas to resume and political opponents were blaming the bloodshed on Madison's impetuous declaration of war in 1812. Worse yet, General Andrew Jackson was momentarily expecting a combined sea and land attack on his positions in New Orleans. What the president did not need was a pirate in the south making his appointed territorial governor look like a silly fool. So Madison decided to resolve this situ-

ation once and for all; he sent Commodore Pattison and his fleet of gunboats to New Orleans with orders to attack Lafitte's fortress at Barataria. It was an amazing attack. Pattison succeeded in sinking all of the pirate's ships and at the same time Lafitte managed to sustain hardly any casualties. Now the sea going rogue was left high and dry with no means of earning a pirate's income.

Enter the English. They had formulated a plan in which Lafitte would be given a warship and due to his knowledge of the area, help them capture New Orleans. The cunning pirate nodded in approval when he heard the British proposition and then he hastily traveled to Claiborne's headquarters. He made an offer the United States government could not refuse; in turn for supplying the English plan of attack and for aid in defense of New Orleans, President Madison would give a general pardon to Lafitte and his men. The deal was made and the pirates brought their remaining cannons to the defense of the besieged city. With the same dash and daring they showed at sea, the rogues helped to win the day for the Americans. True to his word President Madison issued a public proclamation of pardon for them.

Like many a pirate of earlier days, Lafitte, the honest citizen, now faced a lifetime of boring days of merchant trading on the high seas. In 1817 he put an end to that dreaded future and along with a thousand of his men, he occupied Galveston Island and set up an independent republic with the help of Aaron Burr. This location became the center for his raids on Spanish shipping. By 1821 he was losing the tight control over his men that he was famous for and several of his captains began raiding American shipping. Word reached Galveston Island that the United States Navy was about to attack the pirate republic. Upon hearing the news Lafitte quickly picked a crew to man his favorite ship, The Pride, and sailed away into the dawn. Some say he returned to his birthplace to live out his days in obscurity. Others claim a Spanish man of war sunk his ship in a battle and he drowned. In any event he was never heard from again, but he may have left behind more than just a legend, he may have left some legendary treasure.

Estimates of Lafitte's possible buried wealth range from the single digit millions to the tens of millions. There are also some historians who believe that there may be only a few hundred thousand dollars in undiscovered treasure. This theory is based on the usual spending habits of pirates...easy come, easy go. But in Louisiana there have been several sites which have yielded gold coins. Pecan Island, in Lake Borgne is one such site which has given up small amounts of gold and in Avoyelles Parish a pot containing almost 2,500 doubloons was unearthed. Because Lafitte had his headquarters for so many years in the bayou country around Baratarian Bay, it is a very good area to search for his treasure.

Texas, mainly the regions near Galveston and Corpus Christi are very high on the list of sites where large portions of Lafitte's hoard may still be deposited. Although there are many contradictory legends surrounding the pirate's occupation and his subsequent hasty departure from Galveston, there are at the same time good evidence in the form of discovered treasure to back up

each of them.

The first concerns Hendrick's Lake near Galveston. A popular story about Lafitte and his continuing battle to deplete the Spanish of their wealth, takes place after the pirate had successfully raided the Spanish brig *Santa Rosa*. He was leading a wagon train, loaded full of silver, to his headquarters when the Spaniards ambushed him. Surprise and numerical superiority was in favor of the Spanish, but the combat skill belonged to the pirates. Lafitte quickly realized that there was no way he would be able to escape with the treasure. In order to facilitate the pirate's getaway, he ordered all the silver, wagons and all, dumped into nearby Hendrick's Lake. At today's current price the treasure is valued at nearly $2 million. Until the 1920's it was thought to be just another legend and then a fisherman seeking to untangle his line, dove in the cool waters of Hendrick's Lake and emerged with three bars of silver in hand. As usual with such finds the following rush of treasure seekers did not yield any more of Lafitte's buccaneer gains.

Padre Island is the general location of a buried chest of gold and jewels that once belonged to Lafitte. Sometime in 1861, John Singer, brother of Issac Merrit Singer, the inventor of the sewing machine, found the chest. He withdrew some of its contents and reburied the treasure near where he discovered it. It was the beginning of the Civil War, not a very good time to be lugging such tempting baggage about the countryside. After the war Singer returned to Padre Island only to discover that several of the landmarks he used to designate where the chest was buried had been either removed or altered in such a way to make finding the chest an impossibility. It is still buried where Singer left it, in case anyone wants to look for it.

In 1940 there was considerable excitement over the discovery of a sunken ship in Galveston Bay, near the quiet town of Anahuac. Its precise location was known since 1850, but it was kept secret by the man who discovered it and later by his family. About 1910, several gold coins were found in the early morning surf on a nearby beach. The dates on the doubloons ranged from 1803-1807 giving credence to the notion that the submerged ship in the bay may have belonged to Lafitte and it was possibly loaded with gold. It wasn't until 1940 that someone obtained the necessary government permission and funds to attempt salvage of the vessel. Sadly all that was found was a handful

W.C.C. Claiborne may have smiled for this portrait, bu he found Lafitte's corrupting influence no laughing matter.

of coins.

One of the legends of Lafitte's hurried departure from Galveston Island tells of his ship, *The Pride*, running aground on a sandbar near Corpus Christi. All of his treasure was on board, some estimates put its value at $10 million. Lafitte and his men took the hoard off his beached ship and buried it on a lonely stretch of land, marking the spot with a brass rod used to support a

*President Madison made a deal with the
pirate and set the stage for a stunning
victory over the British Army.*

compass. The pirate for one reason or another never returned to claim his loot and years later the land was bought by a rancher named Hill. One of Hill's workers discovered the brass rod and took it back to show his boss this amazing find. Hill returned with the worker to the area where the rod was found, but the ranch hand could not find the exact location where he pulled the compass support from the ground. Maps allegedly showing the location of the treasure have been circulating for over a century, as of yet no one has found the spot where the brass rod was yanked from the ground and the millions of dollars in gold that was supposed to have been buried underneath. If someday you happen to have a few extra hours and a sturdy shovel, the Hills ranch is located off of Route 59, where the Lavaca River empties into Matagorda Bay.

Lafitte came to North America in search of an adventurous life that was already obsolete. The politics of the time had changed, the need for buccaneers and for the trade of embargoed goods sold by pirates had passed. Navies in the beginning of the nineteenth century were becoming larger and more powerful than any small fleet the pirates could put together. Lafitte saw the world through romantic eyes of the previous century. Had he lived a hundred years earlier he might have become the first real pirate emperor.

THE PUZZLING PIT MYSTERY

Oak Island, Nova Scotia, Canada, is a treasure location which is known to have something fastidiously buried in its dark grey clay. The big questions are, exactly what is there and who left it.

In the summer of 1795, a teenager named Daniel McGinnis took a canoe trip around Mahone Bay, which was less than a quarter of a mile away from his house in the small town of Chester. He was following the timeless urge to explore his surroundings that most boys have at the age of sixteen. Of the close to four hundred tiny islands in the bay, McGinnis was drawn to one particular isle overgrown with oaks not native to the area. After he landed his canoe he walked about the island and began to notice odd remains in one area. First, by the shore, he found a rock with a heavy ring-bolt drilled into it. There was no doubt in the boy's mind that it was used to moor large sailing ships. Inland he found a tall strong oak tree with a worn ship's block and tackle hanging from it. Below the pulley system was a wide man-made depression in the earth. Around the

site were cut trees and nearby were two roads, one ran North/South and the other ran East/West. McGinnis knew that he was onto something really important, so he paddled back to town and told his two best friends, John Smith and Anthony Vaughan.

The next day the three boys canoed to the island and investigated the matter further. With great enthusiasm, they began digging at the site of the depression. Rather soon they discovered a layer of flagstone at a depth of four feet. At 10 feet they unearthed a platform made of oak logs covering a shaft of loosely packed earth. The same kind of oak log platform was found at 20 and 30 feet. Now the hardy teenage adventurers were beyond their capabilities and needed heavy machinery to proceed any deeper. So home they went to raise money from family and friends, to continue their excavations in pursuit of the enormous treasure they believed was buried on Oak Island.

It took the trio nine years to raise the capital necessary to launch a formal expedition. In the meantime McGinnis and Smith settled on the island. Smith bought up the lots surrounding the pit and several more on the cove where McGinnis first landed. In 1804 they began their excavations on a larger scale, but the finds were much less than they expected. McGinnis and company managed to reach a depth of ninety feet. Along the way they found several layers of putty spread over a platform of logs, two layers of coconut fiber and a large flat stone with a cipher cut on one side. There was so much putty dug out of the shaft that the residents around the bay used it for decades to seal their windows.

And then the expedition met with disaster. It seems the original planners of the site had cleverly included a system of underground drainage tunnels, whose real purpose seems to be the flooding of the main shaft at high tide, thus frustrating any unknowledgeable attempt to retrieve whatever treasure is there. Unaware of the well engineered system, McGinnis, Smith, Vaughan and company tried several times, unsuccessfully, to drain the ninety foot shaft. Eventually they quit the project and left the pit with just their memories and a few trinkets.

Of passing importance is the large flat stone that the 1804 expedition discovered. It measured two feet long, 16 inches wide and a foot thick, instead of squared corners, they were rounded. The 180 pound stone was of a black granite-like substance with an olive tinge running throughout. There was an extremely faint inscription on the one smooth face of stone. In 1864, professor of languages James Liechti translated the cipher as stating...."Ten feet below two million pounds." By 1919 the inscription on the stone was worn away, it had been used as a beating stone by some of its later owners.

In 1849, a well financed syndicate was formed. It was composed of local businessmen and engineers; they were going to get at the bottom of this treasure pit in a bigger and more scientific manner. Instead of digging to the bottom of the pit, they were going to dig only to the water level of the shaft and then employ a horse driven mining drill....the pod auger, to go as deep as they wanted to go. A big advantage of the pod auger was its ability to pick up samples of whatever material it passed through. At 98 feet the drill had picked up fragments of wood and metal. The wood was as expected, oak and the metal was a dozen tiny chain links of pure gold! They sent the auger pod down twice more and discovered there were at least two chests one on top of another. Each chest was made of oak, with perhaps an iron band belted around them and each chest contained an unknown quantity of gold.

Everyone was excited. Now the big question was how to get to the treasure. Water was continuously filling the shaft from an undiscovered source. Then someone, after all these years, had the bright idea to taste the water; it was salt water, not the fresh ground water everyone assumed it was. It was then the engineers discovered the drainage system which extended to Smith Bay 500 feet away. It consisted of five tunnels dug into the hard clay at varying depths of between 110 feet to 151 feet and they all connected to a central cement chamber from which ran another conduit to the treasure shaft.

A stone floor was laid under Smith Bay beach where the tunnels ended. On top of the stones was a thick layer of coconut fiber matting. In essence the original designers of the "Money Pit," as it was called, turned the Smith Bay beach into one huge sponge; when someone opened up the money pit, the water trapped under the beach would rush into the treasure shaft due to the releasing of air pressure in the shaft. It was the air in the sealed shaft that held back the water. If you take a soda straw, put your finger over one end and put the other end in a full glass of water; you have approximated the treasure shaft as it is when the seal is left undisturbed. The air in the straw holds back the water. When you release your finger the air rushes out and the water rushes

in. This was the syndicate's dilemma, they knew the original excavators of the money pit had some plan to retrieve their gold, but the men of 1849 hadn't a clue of what it was; what method could they use to stop the water flow long enough to reach the treasure?

The Industrial Revolution was gearing up in the Western World and the time was right for a really grandiose solution from the treasure hunting engineers at the Oak Island money pit. They thought up a scheme to build a dam across Smith Bay to hold back the water from getting into the shaft. And so the dam was built. And so an unexpected storm came from the south, destroying the dam and flooding Smith Bay. The syndicate was bankrupt; thus ended another chapter in the attempt to recover the treasure in the money pit.

Determined not to make the same mistakes as the 1849 syndicate, Frederick Blair of Nova Scotia formed yet another syndicate in 1893 and this time they started the treasure retrieving process by sealing the five tunnels leading from the beach. They accomplished the goal with the use of that marvelous explosive, dynamite. Employing a new type of drill and the newer drilling techniques of the latter years of the nineteenth century, the syndicate made some startling discoveries.

The treasure chests at 98 feet were only camouflage for the real treasure which was at 151 feet. At this depth in the shaft the drill encountered a cement chamber covered with wood and iron. Clinging to the drill bit were samples of gold and parchment from the chamber. But just when Blair thought the treasure was within easy reach the shaft suddenly filled with water and created a geyser that shot 15 feet into the air, drenching everyone standing around the drilling apparatus. This should have been an impossibility, but further investigation found there was yet another series of tunnels that connected to the beach on the south side of the island, 600 feet from the money pit. Before the area around the shaft became one large mud pit, Blair made one last probe with his drill and reached a depth of 170 feet where they hit a thick steel plate, which has not been penetrated to this day. Much to Blair's dismay he ran out of money and had to quit his quest for the Oak Island treasure.

In this century there have been at least a half a dozen attempts to recover the treasure; all of them have met with failure. A notable failure occurred in 1909 when the Bowden Expedition could not even find the main shaft due to the up welling of mud

Andrew Jackson won his greatest military victory at the Battle of New Orleans. Lafitte's additional men in the right place made victory possible.

The last time British and American troops fought in North America was the Battle of New Orleans.

from the previous Blair drilling of 1893. In all this time no one has come close to answering some of the mysterious circumstances surrounding the money pit. Why was the treasure so elaborately hidden? How was this monumental feat of engineering accomplished? How was the treasure going to be retrieved? Who went to all this trouble anyway?

There have been several theories about the Oak Island treasure, ranging from a pirate treasure belonging to Captain Kidd, to the secret fortune of Marie Antoinette smuggled into North America. One of the more likely theories postulates that the French garrison in nearby Louisbourg fortress buried much of their wealth to keep the English from seizing it. This is one of the best ideas to date, since they had the time, manpower and expertise to construct such a perplexing puzzle. This treasure is not for anyone to pursue. It would take patience, time and most of all ... money; as a long shot a slow horse in the fifth race is a better gamble. But because it exists, more attempts will be made and someday, perhaps, the mystery will be solved.

AN ARMCHAIR MYSTERY

Every so often an opportunity to solve a mystery in the comfort of one's easy chair presents itself. The Beale Codes are a prime example of this type of mystery. But be warned the man who broke part of the code became tragically obsessed with this project and in turn his life ended in bitterness and remorse.

The story begins in the winter of 1820, at a hotel in Lynchburg, Virginia, owned by a man called Robert Morriss. It was the best hotel in the county and it attracted many an important guest. One of the more popular residents that winter, was a tall, dark and handsome man who epitomised the fictional Rhett Butler of a later age. His name was very Virginian, Thomas Jefferson Beale and as it would be discovered later, his sole purpose for the visit was not to impress the women of Lynchburg society, which he did, or to be known as a man among men, which he also accomplished, but rather to ascertain the honesty and character of Morriss, the owner of the hotel. At the first hint of spring, Beale left the hotel in the company of two of his friends who lived in Richmond.

In the next two years the dashing young man became a fond memory and then in the winter of 1822 he returned to Morriss's hotel, this time he left more than reminiscences; he intrusted into the care of the hotel owner a locked iron strong box. Beale said it contained very important papers. The hotel owner accepted the strong box and locked it in his safe. After a stay of less than a week, Beale asked Morriss to hold the box until such time that either himself or an agent of his could call for it. Morriss agreed to keep the box in the safe and await further instructions.

It was in late May of the same year that Morriss received a letter from Beale. Much to the hotel owner's surprise the letter requested that he keep the box for a little longer, perhaps as long as ten years. It seems that Beale expected to be gone for two years, hunting on the Great Plains, and maybe be unable to claim the box for a longer time than that. Next, the letter informed Morriss that the papers were of a financial nature. Beale listed the contents as a few letters addressed to Morriss and three encoded lists that were unintelligible without the aid of a specific key to decode them. The hotel owner was to keep the box, unopened, until May of 1832. If no one called for the box before that time Morriss should open it and read the contents. Beale ended the letter by saying a friend would send him the key to decipher the code sometime in 1832. This was a pre-

caution in case the worst should happen and Beale or his representative was unable to contact him.

The overall impression from this letter was the sincerity of the writer. Hints of danger were also woven into the letter. Phrases such as "I have been thus particular in my instructions in consequence of the somewhat perilous enterprise in which we are engaged....", caught Morriss's attention. But since he had other matters to attend to, he left the box in the safe and went about his business.

No one called for the box and when the appropriate year arrived no one sent the key to the codes. Morriss did not open the box until 1845. He claimed he wanted to give Beale or his agents every chance to retrieve the iron bound parcel. Finally the box was opened and Morriss found contained within two letters and three lists of numbers. The letters were addressed to Morriss; they helped to explain the motives of the former hotel guest as well as telling a tale of treasure found and hidden.

It all began as a big game hunt on the Great Plains. Thirty-one Virginian gentlemen went west organized as a paramilitary group with one of their own as captain, Thomas Jefferson Beale was that man. They began earnestly hunting in May of 1817. Just after Thanksgiving the group decided to spend winter in Santa Fe. They arrived before Christmas and stayed until the following March when some of the group became bored and went exploring the country north of Santa Fe. Those who were left behind waited until the middle of May before they learned the fate of their more adventurous companions. While in pursuit of one of the huge herds of buffalo that the west was once famous for, the enterprising Virginians discovered a large exposed vein of gold on the face of a cliff. The mere mention of gold changed lethargy into a frenzied action as the remainder of Virginians galloped to their new wealth.

For 18 months Beale and his companions mined the cliff. They accumulated a large hoard of gold and a smaller amount of silver. Caution, not adventure, now became their main concern, the longer the gold was left practically in open, the greater was the chance they could lose this new found wealth to the more desperate residents of the wild west. It was decided some of the men should return to Virginia and cache the treasure. Beale with ten other men transported the gold and silver back to Virginia and buried the hoard in a stone lined vault somewhere in the Blue Ridge Mountains.

There was a possibility that something unforeseen could happen to this band of Virginian adventurers. So Beale set up a system that would guarantee the treasure would be evenly divided, among the men or their heirs, no matter what disastrous circumstances might befall them in the future. Beale further explained in the letter that Morriss's reputation for honesty, made the hotel owner a prime candidate for the assignment of executor of the treasure. On his first stay at the hotel, Beale had three months to closely watch Morriss and assess his character. Beale was satisfied that Morriss was the man for the job. When he and ten other Virginians rejoined their companions at the mine site they made a pact. All the treasure was to be split thirty one ways. Each man or his heir would receive a share and it was agreed that Morriss would receive a share for keeping the strong box with the lists and for seeing to the fair distribution of the wealth should none of the adventurous Virginians survive.

It was a very good code, over the years Morriss, no longer a hotel owner, but a respected member of the Lynchburg city council, attempted to make sense of the lists to no avail. He knew the first list of numbers described where the treasure was buried, the second list was an inventory of the treasure and the third list contained the names of the adventurers' next of kin.

Enter James B. Ward. By 1862 Morriss decided that someone should benefit from the perplexing contents of the iron strong box. Ward was the son of Morriss's close friend, he was in his early twenties and possessed boundless energy. The young man listened to the story with excitement, he was eager to find the fortune. It was never recorded how or why Ward avoided military service in the only civil war this country has known, nevertheless the young man ignored the national events that were occurring around him and immersed himself in the task of decoding the lists. He was to work for 23 years with only partial success to show for his efforts.

One of the keys used in the Beale ciphers was the Declaration of Independence. Ward discovered after years of trial and error that each number in the second list represented the first letter of each corresponding word in the famous document. It works like this: the third number on the second list is 24, the 24th word of the Declaration of Independence is another, therefore the third letter is "a". The second list begins, "I have deposited in the County of Bedford about four miles from Buford in an excavation or vault

six feet below the surface of the ground....." The number 24 refers to the letter "a" in the word have. Deciphering the second list only wets ones desire to decode the first list, the one with the location of the treasure. Ward never accomplished that feat. In 1885, he gave up a bitter man, having spent his youth and a good deal of money in the elusive pursuit of Beale's treasure.

There are several theories on how to solve the remaining lists. Some have asked why would anyone want to decipher the last list? A current theory holds a partial answer. It is possible the important first list with the location of the treasure can only be decoded

after the list of heirs are known. What better way to insure the honesty of the hotel owner than reminding Morriss of his sworn duty to the heirs? Another idea postulates the remaining lists are really two number codes with the spaces added to confuse unauthorized decoding. For example: 71, 194, 38, 1701 are really 71, 19, 43, 81, 70 and 1. But above all else the proper key must be found that will decode either list number one or number three. It has been noted since the Declaration of Independence was framed by Thomas Jefferson and that the document was used as the key for the second list of numbers, the missing keys have something

Everyone knows the site of the Oak Island treasure. But how does one get to it?

in common with the name Thomas Jefferson Beale. Whatever the form the missing keys are in, they are probably something that was readily accessible to every Virginian in 1820.

Since the time Beale buried the treasure, Buford has changed its name to Montvale. The best guess as to the location of the vault is somewhere in the Blue Ridge Mountains about 4 miles east of the town of Montvale, Virginia.

The UFO Debate

No set of North America mysteries, let alone mysteries of the world, have set off such a debate in the public media as Unidentified Flying Objects, UFO's for short. Coined by Kenneth Arnold in 1947, the term "flying saucers" do not adequately describe all the shapes and sizes these unidentified flying objects have been reported as taking. What they are, who may be piloting them, where there origin may be and why, if they are conveyances of intelligent beings, are these crafts visiting our planet, are questions which have not been satisfactorily answered to date. There exists at least enough written, photographed, filmed and taped material, of a factual and fictional nature, to cover the state of Rhode Island with a layer of non-duplicated records a foot deep. Even skeptics find themselves with the irrepressible urge to add to this increasing mass of contradictory facts and opinions. As years pass the mystery of UFO's deepens and appears further from solution than before.

A PERSONAL SIGHTING

On a clear Sunday late afternoon, in early October 1973, I was driving back to New York City, from Mill River, Massachusetts, with my wife and two friends. We were driving south of route 44 between Amenia and Mabbetsville, N.Y., this stretch of the road runs parallel to a small valley. Upon casually glancing into the rear view mirror, I saw what appeared to be a bright magenta flash. Turning my head around to get a better look at what may have caused the unknown burst of light, I exclaimed, "What the hell was that!" My head did not have far to turn to learn the answer. There, outside the right side window, was a round radiant globe. So intense was the light emanating from the object that it was impossible to see any detail within the circumference of the globe. It was not a blinding blaze that we saw, but rather a soft intense luminescence as from a fluorescent bulb. Surrounding the globe was a glowing magenta haze, which was equal in size front and rear of the object and flattened on the top and bottom. If the luminous cloud was formed by particles burning off the object like the tail of a meteorite then the tail would have been much longer than the haze at the front of the object. This was not the case here, the haze

was not apparently affected by the forward motion of the object.

It's speed now matched our speed in the Volkswagon, we were both traveling south about 60 mph. For five seconds we traveled a parallel course. During this interval of time my wife kept telling me to watch the road, my friend told me "It's not what you think it is," and his wife said nothing. The object gave the impression of great power and possibly incredible speed, as it silently traveled through the air alongside of us. At the end of the five seconds the road veers slightly to the left and follows a path not readily visible from the valley, behind a small stand of trees. As I went behind the sparse stand of yellow leafed trees the magenta lit object picked up speed and vanished into the sky above.

One never quite knows what your reaction will be to an unusual event until it happens. In this case we kept driving, talked briefly about the strange object and concluded that it was a UFO in the classic sense of the word ...an Unidentified Flying Object. But none of us really became excited after the event. Our adrenalin was pumping during the incident, all the phenomena associated with such an organic chemical rush through the body and brain manifested itself. One of the reasons that this encounter was so memorable was the perception that it was happening in slow motion, of course this was due to the adrenalin charging through our physio-logical systems. Afterwards there was a fatigued calm. We all knew we had wit-nessed something extraordinary, but we were hard pressed to find an explanation to the incident.

The one question about the object's size was not resolved until years later, when I compared notes with my wife, Barbara. She was sitting next to me in the Volkswagon and could see the object in relation to the valley below. I thought it was about 10-15 feet in diameter since I had no frame of reference to compare it to on the ground and believed the object was 100 feet away. Barbara could see the object's relative position to the valley and told me it was at least a half mile away over the valley floor. This turned a small UFO into something huge, with a diameter of at least 100 feet across. If this was a meteorite it would have made quite a bang when it collided with the ground.

Whatever it was it became our personal Great Unsolved Mystery of North America.

IN THE BEGINNING

Boston was the first location in North America to record a sighting of a UFO. It was a late evening in March, 1639, as a small ferry full of passengers were crossing the Muddy River. According to James Everell, one of the passengers, a bright stationary light flashed into view above the ferry. It was about 10 feet across and somewhat rectangular in shape. The ferryman fearfully made his way back to shore and everyone on the boat hid from the specter in the night sky.

After a few minutes the object darted across the Charles River toward Charlestown. It hovered near the settlement and returned to it's former position above the ferry. For the next two and half hours it zigzagged back and forth across the river and then it would return to the ferry. In all this time no one dared to move an inch on the boat. Then as abruptly as it appeared it vanished.

Some investigators have pointed to the Bible as containing some of the earliest known references to UFO visitations. Ezekiel's account of God's appearance before him in a UFO-like chariot is just one example. Throughout the long stretch of human history similar notations of UFO sightings have been made.

In Egypt, about 1600 B.C., a papyrus recording the events of the reign of Pharaoh Thutmos III mentions an incident when a large number of fiercely bright circles held sway over the skies for a period of six days. Accompanying these strange night visitors was a peculiar odor. Sixteen centuries later Titus Livius and Julius Obsequens listed eight sightings on the west coast of Italy from 213 B.C. to 16 B.C. The Roman historian Livy referred to lights seen in the night skies during the reign of Julius Caesar as "phantom ships". During the middle ages Gregory of Tours noted fiery lights visiting the medieval countryside in 583 A.D. Monastic records from the thirteenth century mention "wyde fire" in the skies that killed people and cattle as well as poisoning grass and setting fire to barns.

Reports of UFO sightings are woven throughout the fabric of history; they are generally not perceived as major patterns or even as essential threads in that fabric, but nevertheless they are quite ubiquitous. These sightings as well as possible ancient pictorial representations of alien visitors, has led some investigators, like Erich von Daniken, to postulate the theory that superintelligent extraterrestrials have influenced the course of human history and may have even mated with early man to produce Homo sapiens.

A TURN-OF-THE-CENTURY WAVE

Often UFO's are seen in waves of sightings, in several geographical regions, lasting for several months or even years. One of the first well recorded UFO waves began on the west coast of North America and months later seemed to travel inland to Kansas City. It all started in November 1896, when cigar shaped airships were first reported from California, up the coast, to British Columbia, Canada. The largest number of people to witness this UFO wave on the west coast, was in Tulare, California. About 200 people saw a cigar-shaped craft descend from the clear night sky, hover for a minute or so, rise and then disappear into the west, all the while emitting red, white and blue lights. These phantom airships were seen on the west coast of the continent until late January of 1897, when all sightings abruptly ceased. This did not signal the end of this wave only its movement to another locale.

In February of 1897, mysterious lights were witnessed in Nebraska and in March the UFO sightings included neighboring Kansas and Michigan. The most spectacular incident in this series happened in April, when close to 10,000 residents of Kansas City, Missouri, witnessed a large dark object swiftly fall from the sky. As quickly as it descended, it abruptly came to halt and hovered sphinx-like above the city for ten minutes. After this period of inactivity, blue and white light emanated from within the craft, then it shot upward into space and vanished among the stars. This wave of strange airship sightings was reported in every state east of the Rockies until May, when all airship activity ceased as mysteriously as it began.

EARLY WAVES IN THIS CENTURY

In 1909 and 1913, there were two worldwide waves of UFO sightings. Most of the incidents were centered in Europe and the objects in the skies were believed to be some form of dirigible, probably a secret weapon being developed by Germany. Of course Germany denied these allegations and as later history proved that whatever else Germany was up to, they were not responsible for these incidents. In 1933, another wave of

UFO reports occurred over Norway and Sweden. Once again Germany was thought to be behind the "ghost fliers" as the Scandinavians called these aerial phantoms and once more history would show that this was one phenomena they were not responsible for. The Swedish airforce attempted to intercept the "ghost fliers" and lost two of their pilots in the process. During World War Two, pilots of all nations, in all theaters of the war, reported seeing intelligently controlled glowing balls of blue, orange, red or white light following their aircraft during combat missions. Needless to say these "foo-fighters", as the United States Army Airforce pilots nicknamed the UFO's, were thought to belong to enemy secret weapons. After the war there was no attempt to discover the true nature of these glowing objects, except to discount the possibility that these strange lights belonged to any of the Axis Power's secret arsenal for world conquest. Perhaps these "foo-fighters" reports would have been all but forgotten had not the post war period not been so eventful, so filled with sightings of all manner of strange aerial phenomena.

A NAME IS BORN

Kenneth Arnold was the owner of a fire-control equipment company in Boise, Idaho. He was also a very experienced civilian pilot. At 2:00 P.M., on July 24th, 1947, he took off from Chehalis, Washington airport in his own single engine plane. Arnold was taking part in the search for a missing transport plane that was presumed to have crashed somewhere in the Cascade Mountain range.

It was a perfectly clear day for flying, bright and sunny with almost unlimited visibility. Flying for about an hour near Mount Rainier, Arnold was beginning a wide turn when he was startled by a nearby flash of intense light from somewhere to his left, in the opposite direction of his maneuver. When he looked over his shoulder all he could see in the distance was a DC-4, which was also part of the search team. The other aircraft was too far away and at the wrong altitude to have been the source of the burst of light. Moments later the flash occurred again, this time Arnold was able to pinpoint its origin. The source was nine silvery disks flying in a "V" formation and traveling at what seemed to be very high speeds. He watched the UFO's as they zigzagged around the peaks of the Cascade Range. Using Mount Adams and Mount Rainier as fixed positions, Arnold was able to estimate the speed of the UFO's at 1,600 mph! This was three times faster than any aircraft at this time was capable of flying.

When Kenneth Arnold landed, he reported his encounter with the strange craft to flight personnel at the airport. In his verbal description he said they flew "like a saucer would if you skipped it across the water". Arnold's honesty and professional reputation were beyond reproach and authorities accepted his account of the incident. Soon afterwards newspapers around the country carried the story about the sighting of "flying saucers" in the state of Washington. A name was coined that would associate UFO's with science fiction, horror movies, leprechauns and any odd occurrence in the journalistic "silly seasons". But this was also the beginning of the Cold War and fears that the Soviet Union may have developed a super-aircraft, capable of incredible flight performance, prompted the US Air Force to seriously investigate UFO reports.

It seemed that "flying saucers" were everywhere and in the months following Arnold's report of the UFO's there were hundreds of sightings throughout the world. Skeptics found a rich feeding ground for debunking, with reports of little green men and seven foot giants bounding out their interplanetary craft to chat with ordinary Earthmen making the news. Perhaps the whole idea would have died the way that fads often do, had not tragedy struck a pilot chasing an unknown light in the sky.

FOLLOWING A STAR

In the early afternoon of January 7, 1948, several residents of a small town 80 miles east of Louisville, Kentucky, sighted something odd flying above them. Soon other small towns in the Louisville area were reporting a strange circular aircraft in the sky. Shortly after 1 P.M., the state police called the control tower at Godman Air Force Base inquiring if there were any unusual aircraft or missions in the area. The tower officials said all they knew of was routine training mission of F-51's. A half an hour later the tower operators saw the object for themselves.

Everyone who should have been notified, was notified, and in a matter of minutes the control tower was crowded with officers from intelligence, base operations and flight control. Someone made the fateful decision to radio the training flight and order them to fly close to the object and investigate the nature of the craft. The flight leader was a very experienced 25 year old, National Guard Captain, named Thomas Mantell. One of his three students dropped out of the formation because he was low on fuel. Mantell and his two trainees flew in the reported direction of the UFO and climbed to 10,000 feet, at which point the object was sighted. Mantell increased his speed and left his students behind as he climbed toward the UFO. They attempted to follow him, but at 15,000 feet, the students knowing they were not equipped with oxygen, dropped out of the chase. But Mantell doggedly continued to climb chasing this object. He reported back to the tower at Godman, "....The thing looks metallic and of tremendous size. It's going up and forward as fast as I am, that's 360 mph. I'm going up to 20,000 feet and if I'm no closer, I'll abandon chase." Those were Captain Mantell's last words; moments later his plane went into a fatal dive and was found splattered over a three mile area.

The official explanation has been that Mantell mistakenly chased either: an escaped weather balloon, from Project Skyhook, or the planet Venus which was low on the horizon at that time of the year; in his enthusiasm he climbed beyond the safety ceiling for his aircraft, blacked out from lack of oxygen and crashed as a result of losing consciousness at the controls.

ANOTHER PILOT, ANOTHER CHASE

Later in the same year, after quite a few other sightings, there was another airborne UFO encounter; this one would not end as grisly as Captain Mantell's chase.

It was a clear starry night over Fargo, North Dakota. The date was October 1, 1948; the time was shortly before 9:00 P.M. Lieutenant George F. Gorman was watching the rest of his National Guard squadron land after a grueling cross-country flight. Not only was he making sure that his men were safely on the ground, but by staying aloft he was also taking advantage of an excellent opportunity to log some more night flying time in the F-51. Just as he was preparing to make his own landing, the control tower waved him off, stating there was a Piper Cub below him making it's landing approach. Sure enough when Gorman looked there was the Piper Cub, but at that moment, something flashed by his plane. It looked like the taillight of another plane. The tower informed him they knew of no other aircraft in the area, so he climbed to investigate. He did not have far to go, with a short ascent of five hundred feet he spotted the mysterious object.

For its size it packed a lot of punch. Below his plane, Gorman was stunned to see a clear white globe, 8 inches in diameter, blinking on and off. When the F-51 approached the tiny UFO, it went into a sharp left turn away from Gorman and toward the control tower. At the same time the object stopped blinking and now maintained a steady white light as it began a series of complex maneuvers. Gorman went into a dive attempting to catch up to the UFO. It became a game of aerial tag, although Gorman preferred to think of the incident as a "dogfight".

With the F-51 at pushing close to it's maximum speed, the UFO kept it's speed just a shade faster. Every time Gorman attempted to outmaneuver the tiny object, it would turn, dive or climb just outside the capabilities of the F-51. Twice during the encounter the UFO came directly at Gorman. The first time this happened, Gorman chickened out and went into a dive and the object passed over his canopy; the second time this occurred, Gorman decided to see what would happen if he collided with the little light, but the UFO simply shot upwards at a tremendous velocity and disappeared into the starry sky. This incident lasted 27 minutes from the time Gorman first sighted the UFO until it vanished.

Gorman was not the only person to see the UFO. The two flight controllers watched the encounter through binoculars, as Gorman was tearing up the night skies in attempt to catch the elusive light. At the same time the pilot of the Piper Cub aborted his landing and stayed aloft, circling the field to watch the F-51 chase the UFO. All the witnesses descriptions match Gorman's account on the key points, even though they had different vantage points. Gorman told investigators, "I had the impression that its maneuvers were controlled by thought or reason".

As with the Mantell disaster, the official United States Government explanation for the "Gorman dogfight" was a weather balloon. An independent investigation found there was none released in the area. Later the U.S. Air Force claimed that Gorman was chasing the planet Jupiter. In the face of Lieutenant Gorman's considerable experience as a pilot and the other witness's statements makes the Jupiter theory seem like a rather lame effort to brush away the unknown. The final official status was then changed to "Unexplained".

Recently it has become fashionable,

Hoyt S. Vandenberg, Air Force Chief of Staff, refused to believe the findings of the Air Force's first report on UFO's.

among certain UFO skeptics, to claim that indeed it was a super-secret weather balloon project that caused the death of Captain Mantell and that was chased by Lieutenant Gorman. The claim is based on documents still in the government files. Unfortunately for this line of thought, The Freedom of Information Act allowed the release of tons of documents into the hands of trained researchers and investigators. There was no mention of such a secret balloon project, but, as will be discussed later, there is evidence of the government's cover up of its own intense interest in UFO's, despite a public posture to the contrary.

AN EARLY AIR FORCE INVESTIGATION

Shortly after Captain Mantell crashed, the United States Air Force intitiated an investigation named Project Sign. This inquiry was the first of several to be made by the Air Force and the series would conclude, two decades later, with Project Blue Book. Project Sign finished its work in late 1948 and published a report titled "Estimate of the Situation", which took the position that some of the visitations were real and their source was of an interplanetary nature. Air Force Chief of Staff, General Hoyt S. Vandenberg said he could not "buy" interplanetary vehicles and the report was was "batted down". Project Sign was quickly replaced by Project Grudge. The Grudge Report, published in December 1949, stated that of the 237 incidents investigated, 75% could be explained by natural or man made phenomena and the rest were not important enough to warrant the expenditure of further effort.

To this day the Air Force denies the existence of "Estimate of the Situation". According to Lt. Colonel George Freeman, Chief of the Civil Branch of the Office of Information's Community Relations Division, in 1967, the report lacked proof and the "Estimate" died a quick death. Some months later, it was completely declassified and relegated to the incinerator. We have no copies of this document. Another Air Force official stated the report never existed. Former chief of Project Blue Book, Captain Edward Ruppelt remembered the report; he even remembered what it looked like. It was legal sized, about 150 pages with a black cover bearing the word "Secret" stamped across the front. At least one copy, in his opinion, survived the destruct order.

In dealing with the United States Government on the issue of UFO' it must be remembered that since Project Grudge in 1949, the official position has been that these sightings are of natural or man made origins, there are no interplanetary or other such goings on in the skies over America. Unofficially the story is sometimes very different.

A LANDMARK PHOTOGRAPH

One of the most important photographs ever taken of a UFO, was taken by a McMinnville, Oregon, amateur photographer named Paul Trent.

It was 7:45 on the night of May 5, 1950. Mrs. Trent was feeding her rabbits in the back yard of the family farm, when a bright and silvery object noiselessly flew toward her home. She called her husband outside the house. He took one look at this distant UFO and ran inside to get his camera. He returned to the back yard in time to snap two pictures before the object disappeared, flying very near the house, heading northwest. They later described the UFO as "Shining like burnished silver. Like a very large dustbin with a sort of spur on the curved rim over it."Mr. Trent estimated the size of the object to be about 30 feet in diameter.

At first they would only show their close friends the two UFO photos, but word eventually reached a local reporter who convinced the Trents that they would not get in trouble with the government if they released the pictures for publication.

As UFO photographs go, this pair is perhaps the best daylight pictures ever shot. At first it was believed that they were a hoax. Analysis and common sense ruled that possibility out. First the expense and expertise was way beyond the Trent's capabilities. Second, these photos have been analyzed over the years time and time again. Even the highly closed-minded Condon Report concluded that the photographs were not the product of an elaborate hoax. More recent computer enhancement has shown that the Trents photographed an object about 60 to 90 feet in diameter, flying a considerable distance from their farm. Whatever was, it was in the sky that day, it was not something we can easily explain.

THE CASE OF THE LUBBOCK LIGHT

The incident of the Lubbock lights begins in Albuquerque, New Mexico, on the night of August 25, 1951. An employee of the Atomic Energy Commission and his wife were in their back yard having a cookout when a wing shaped UFO silently passed over the house at an altitude of approximately a thousand feet and a speed in excess of 400 mph. It was larger than a B-26, with dark bands on the wing and soft blue lights on the wing tips.

Several minutes later and several hundred miles away a woman in Lubbock, Texas, saw a giant flying wing flying over her house. It too had bluish lights glowing from the wing tips. A little less than an hour later several Lubbock college professors saw a V formation of blue lights rapidly and quietly flying in the Texas night. They saw these similar group of lights in a looser grouping about an hour later, flying in the same direction.

On August 31, Carl Hart, an amateur photographer took a series of pictures of this continuing phenomena over Lubbock skies. Only one photo had a clear image and this was the one which appeared in a local paper. The wave of sightings lasted for two weeks. Witnesses agreed that the UFO's would be first seen on the northern horizon, they would flash across the sky in three to five seconds and quickly disappear in the south. One of the observers was a physics professor who did a study with some of his colleagues, of weather conditions at the time of most of the reported sightings. They could find no known meteorological explanation for the Lubbock lights.

Of course the Air Force made its own investigation of the incident. Its conclusions left quite a bit to be desired. Alternating their explanations between reflections of mercury vapor street lamps in the sky and/or reflections of the same street lamps on the white chests of birds, the Air Force lost credibility in the eyes of those who witnessed the strange lights. There has never been a satisfactory explanation for this incident.

THE AMAZING SAUCER RAID

It was a hot humid Saturday night at National Airport, Washington, D.C., of course it was, the date was July 19th and the year was 1952. Washington is always hot and humid in the summer. The time was 11:40 P.M. and the radar screen picked up seven blips, seeming to be be flying in formation, southwest of Andrews Air Force Base. At first the speed of the UFO's was clocked at 130 mph, but when the wanted to really move they travelled in excess of 7,000 mph. No one at National Airport had ever seen any aircraft travel so fast. This is not surprising since there was no aircraft in 1952 that could even approach this dizzying speed.

Puzzled, air traffic controller Edward Nugent asked his supervisor, Henry Barns, to take a look at the odd blips. From the radar it appeared that these UFO's moved unlike propeller or jet aircraft. Their turns and erratic speeds made it impossible to track for more than 3 miles at a time. 4 notified the Air Force and they in turn scrambled several interceptors to meet this menace. At the same time a request was made to the commercial airlines in the area to report anything unusual.

The west-bound Capital Airlines Flight 807 for Pittsburgh and Detroit had just left National Airport a few minutes after midnight. Captain S.C. "Casey" Pierman was a veteran pilot who thought he had seen everything one might see in the skies of commercial flying. In response to the traffic controller's request, he was keeping a sharp eye out for unusual activity in the night sky. Pierman did not have long to wait. A few minutes after taking off he spotted seven UFO's. These were the same objects being simultaneously tracked by the National Airport radar.

Later Pierman would tell reporters he was flying at 6,000 feet and at his normal cruising speed of 200 mph as he observed the objects above him, very high in the sky. They looked like meteors without their tails. "In all my years of flying, I've seen a lot of falling or shooting stars, but these were much faster than anything I've ever seen." For Captain Pierman, on route to Pittsburgh, the whole incident lasted about twelve minutes, but for everyone in the Washington area he was leaving behind there was quite a few more hours of UFO fun still left.

Some time near 3:30 A.M. another commercial pilot radioed National Airport that he had a light trailing him. He wanted to know if they picked this object up on their radar. National Airport confirmed they had both the airliner and a "target" on their screens. The UFO stayed with the flight until it was less than four miles from landing at National. Then, for whatever its reason was, the object picked up incredible speed and rocketed out of sight.

Shortly before dawn, Andrews Air Force Base picked up a blip on their screen. Shocked, the men at Air Traffic Control called on the communication web for confirmation of what they were watching on their radar. National confirmed the presence of a UFO, they too had a blip at the same location...directly above Andrews. The tower personnel at the base was asked for a visual confirmation. Almost as one man, everyone in the tower looked up at the blue-streaked daybreak sky to see a "huge fiery-orange ball" hanging above the base. Before a scrambled F-94 jet could arrive, the UFO vanished.

One week later the blips returned. This time the Air Force interceptors arrived quickly. One pilot managed to make a visual contact with the UFO. When he tried to get closer, the object took off at an impossible speed.

Logically, the story would hear with the usual government lame excuses for what might have illogically caused the incident. And they did claim that it was a combination of radar malfunctions coupled with a double-temperature inversion that caused the excitement. Nevertheless the story really ends with the beginning.

Captain Edward J. Ruppelt, who was heading the Air Force's UFO investigation, Project Bluebook, had an advance warning of the Washington UFO sightings. It seems that several days prior to July 19th, Ruppelt was told, during a conference with a scientist from an intelligence agency, that they the unnamed agency, had been accumulating reports of UFO sightings up and down the New York-Washington corridor. These reports appeared to be reaching a peak. "Within the next few days," the scientist told Ruppelt, "they're going to blow up and you're going to have the granddaddy of all UFO sightings. The sighting will occur in Washington or New York, probably Washington."

This conversation and its implication of CIA involvement has been officially denied by the United States Government and Armed Forces.

There were quite a few reported sightings in the New York-Washington corridor a few days before the Washington D.C. incident, that somehow managed to make the local newspapers, if only to be found in some obscure corner of the page. One of these sightings was reported by a scientist from the National Advisory Committee for the Aeronautics Laboratory at Langley Air Force Base, Virginia. On the night of July 16th he and a co-worker were having drinks outside when they both saw two amber colored lights in the sky. The objects were travelling in a northerly direction when they suddenly reversed their bearing. At the same time, a third light came from the west and joined the others now travelling south. A minute later, three other objects from the west, joined the group. All the UFO's joined in formation and climbed to a point in

the south and disappeared. The event took 3 minutes and the two scientists were sure after a minute they were not watching any known aircraft.

On the evening of the Washington incident, there too preceded sightings which led up to the "Saucer Invasion of Washington."

At 10:15 two people saw several UFO's flying in formation on Staten Island, New York City. This is not as strange as it sounds. Staten Island was a vastly underpopulated borough until the mid-seventies. Mrs. Josephine Hetzel, one of the witnesses, was shocked, "I almost fainted when I looked up at the sky and saw what looked like five large dinner plates flying through the sky."

A more experienced observer was Saul Pett, a newspaperman working for the Associated Press at the time. Minutes before the first blips were seen on the National Airport radar screen, Pett noticed a large orange ball in the northwestern skies. He lived only seven miles from New York City, in the small community of River Edge, New Jersey. He watched for almost two minutes as this large fiery object silently flew to the southeast. It was too big to be an airplane and its light did not blink as domestic aircraft do. In fact, Pett had an opportunity to compare the UFO to a commercial airliner, for moments later an aircraft flew overhead, making noise and with lights blinking. He knew he saw something unusual but exactly what it was he couldn't guess. Had he not read about the Washington incident in the newspapers he would not have told anyone about the sighting. "From now on you can't convince me there is no such animal. And after 12 years as a newspaperman, I don't jump to conclusions."

Skeptics are at their worst in attempting to dismiss this sighting. Depending upon which one you read, they either claim that it was all a glitch in the old fashioned radar or in the case of the visual sightings the witness convinced themselves they should see a UFO. When the fact that Captain Pierman reported seeing a UFO at exactly the same place where the National radar was recording a blip, the reply is Pierman only saw what the tower asked him to see. When one counters with the exact request, which was to report anything unusual, the skeptics claim that the two sightings were not related. A more recent tactic taken by certain skeptics is to ignore Pierman's sighting entirely, as if it never happened. You expect this type of behavior from someone who is claiming that he just saw Bigfoot swim out to Atlantis, which is located in the Bermuda Triangle, carrying all the gold from the Lost Dutchman Mine. And not from someone who prides him/herself in being a rational person.

AN EARLY HELLO

Skeptics prefer people like George Adamski to mysterious lights in the skies and silvery disks skimming the horizon, that cannot be easily solved. They use his case to discredit the whole idea of UFO's having solutions that may include inter-planetary travel or other theories that de-mand a rethinking of the universe as we know it. As long as there are incidents like Adamski's, it would follow, in the skeptic's mind at least, that there can be the most ra-tional of explanations for all of the UFO's sighted for the last one thousand years. The fuss over Adamski involves his claimed meeting with a fellow from Venus and the cult of alien visitations that he built up as a result of his claims.

George Adamski was a Polish immigrant who, without any formal education, was called "professor" by his followers. An amateur astronomer and prolific writer, his best selling books about his contacts with ex-traterrestrials gave him a cult following which continued long after his death in 1965. He lived at the foot of the Mount Palo-mar Observatory in California. At night he would take his six inch telescope and peer at the stars alongside the 200 inch reflecting mirror much higher up on the mountain. In his years just before he made contact with the "Space Peoples" Adamski owned a part of a hamburger stand on the road to the huge telescope.

It was on November 20, 1952, when George Adamski and two of his friends saw Orthon, a man from Venus near Desert Center, California. Adamski and a party of friends were picknicking when suddenly a large object was seen hovering over a distant mountain ridge. Although everyone else was unnerved, Adamski knew there was nothing to fear... obviously these were ami-cable space travelers. A few minutes later the UFO disappeared below the mountain. He drove partway toward the mountain ridge with two of his friends. The car stopped and Adamski walked quite a ways from the road and set up his trusty tele-scope. He was ready to make out any important details, if and when the space-craft reappeared. It seems he always had the instrument handy. One never knew when occasions like this might arise.

No sooner had he sent his companions back to the car when a smaller ship flew from behind the ridge and landed behind a small hill about a mile away. There was no question in Adamski's mind that this was a "scout ship" and something very interesting was about to happen. And it did, in the form of human-like creatures appearing out of nowhere not 1,000 feet away, walking toward Adamski. He was wearing what looked to be a ski-suit and shoulder length sandy hair. Around his waist he wore a broad belt made of some metallic-like fabric.

Adamski learned a lot from his visitor. They engaged in a couple of hours of con-versation consisting of sign language and telepathy. The visitor's name was Orthon, his home was the planet Venus. Orthon was a member of a community of Space Peoples who only had the friendliest of intentions toward Earth; although they were becoming concerned about the "radiations from our nuclear tests." After their chat Orthon took Adamski behind the small hill and showed him the scout saucer. Adamski declined to take a ride in this wonderful fly-ing machine and Orthon entered his craft and flew silently away.

According to Adamski this was not his first encounter with extraterrestrials. He had seen his first "spaceship" in 1946, as it glided over his home in Palomar Gardens. A second sighting took place in August 1947, several months after Kenneth Arnold had his historic incident.

The two friends who were watching by the car later stated that they saw Adamski talking to a short man in a strange brown suit. They even retraced Adamski's and Orthon's footprints in the sand. Orthon's footprints went behind the hill and just dis-appeared, or so they claimed.

Several weeks later Orthon's saucer vis-ited Adamski near his home in Palomar Gardens. It was then that Adamski took his famous saucer photos. These photographs, although never duplicated, have been thought to be of an old fashioned surgical light or a tobacco humidor with ping pong balls, among other possibilities. In his later books, Adamski did take a ride with some of the "Space Peoples." He visited the moon and met a Martian and a fellow from the ringed planet Saturn. By Adamski's ac-count the moon had rivers and towns on the dark side. Apollo flights have revealed the "Space Peoples" removed the idyllic settings and replaced them with barren rock.

It is too bad that this kind of encounter receives as much publicity that it does. After his books gained a large cult following, Adamski became a favorite guest on radio and television talk shows as well as being interviewed for countless magazines and newspapers. His message was heard by millions and the skeptics found an easy target to use in their quest for discrediting all unexplained UFO sightings.

A BRIEF ENCOUNTER

Not all contacts with UFO inhabitants are as fanciful as Adamski's. Many times these encounters are filled with dread, dread of the unknown or of the enigmatic. Their occurrences are devoid of the friendliness and good cheer of Orthon and the rest of Adamski's "Space Peoples." Often people who have been contacted by UFO aliens are left with deep psychological wounds, although this result may not be intentional. Betty and Barney Hill are one such example.

It was September 15, 1961, and the slogan "See the USA in your Chevrolet" was the current example of the rewards for participating in the American Dream. Since the Hills indeed did own such a car, even if it was vintage 1957, it seemed a great idea to do on the spur of the moment. So they began their minivacation, travelling from their home in Portsmith, New Hampshire to one of the great American sights of the northeast, Niagara Falls.

The vacation was a success and on the night of September 19th or the morning of the 20th, the Hills found themselves on a lonely stretch of Route 3. It was a sparkling clear night, the moon was growing into a full silvery circle. Betty Hill was watching a light moving in the sky near the moon and above the planet Jupiter, which was visible as a very bright star. As she watched the object she felt herself becoming excited. Barney stopped the car several times so Betty could view the light better with a pair of binoculars. He thought that Betty would see that it was just another commercial flight on its way to Montreal. Finally they stopped and Barney took their pet dachschund for a walk, while Betty again peered at the light. This time the light made a sharp turn and headed lazily in their direction.

The Hills felt uneasy about the object's maneuvering and decided to keep driving. One of the reasons for their unexplained discomfort was the fact that at this hour of the evening, they were the only car on this stretch of Route 3. At each bend and turn in the road the approaching light was matching their every change in direction. As it drew closer Betty was able to see a much

lighter band of light in the middle of the craft. Betty again used the binoculars to view the UFO and this time she saw that the parts of the object was spinning, but the band of light was not. It looked like a fat frisbee, with the top and bottom in motion, and the middle band lit and stationary. The UFO was now on the right side of the car and 100 feet above the ground. For some unexplained reason, Barney felt compelled to stop the automobile on the highway and leave the car to get a better look at the craft, but he left the lights on and the engine running.

Through the binoculars Barney peered at the object which had now taken up position, in front of, but about 100 yards away from the car. It seemed to move with a soundless and effortless grace. The band of light now appeared to be a series of windows and inside there were about 8 human-like creatures staring at Barney. Betty would later describe them as being dressed in shiny black uniforms, wearing baseball like caps on their heads. Suddenly there was a burst of activity. All but one of the creatures turned their backs on the couple and began to pull at lever-like devices. At that point two fins extended from the UFO; on the end of each fin was a ruby red light. The whole craft began to slowly, very slowly, tilt toward the couple and in the same motion descend in a diagonal line which would bring the object within a few feet of the Hill's automobile. Barney was astonished. He began to mutter to himself, "I don't believe it, I don't believe it." Then Barney had a revelation. He was watching the remaining humanoid in the window, when he began to sense the creature's intense concentration on a specific task. Like a dam breaking, all of Barney's rational concepts crumbled; he realized what these creatures wanted to do. "They're going to capture us," he said to his wife in a hysterical tone of voice. At that moment the humanoid looked at both of them with a totally alien smile. Barney jumped into his car and sped away.

It seemed like they made a successful escape from the UFO. They drove for a short while in silence. Betty finally turned and asked her husband if he "...believed in flying saucers now." Barney answered: "Don't be ridiculous. That wasn't a flying saucer." It was at that very moment they heard a series of beeps and a cloud of drowsiness enveloped them. It seemed to the Hills that they abruptly awoke from a deep trance after hearing a second series of beeps and found themselves driving on Route 3 approaching

a sign which read: Concord--17 miles. It was two hours later and they had no memory of anything after their quick flight from the UFO.

Shortly after the incident the nightmares began. Each night Betty would relive unremembered bits and pieces of the encounter in the form of a rcoccurring dream. The plot was always the same. They would be driving away from the UFO when they encountered a roadblock of ten black unformed creatures. Barney would stop the car and the leader of the group would reassure them they would not be harmed. The humanoids would gently escort the Hills from the car. Somehow they found themselves inside the UFO without knowing exactly how they got there. Both Betty and Barney would be examined by the aliens. This part of the dream always terrified her. Lastly they would be returned to the car and the UFO would take off. She did not remember dreaming the whole story each night, just parts of the event every so often. But the results were always the same, sheer terror upon awakening and apprehension stalking her waking hours.

Travelling home along a lonely road in the late summer of 1961, Betty and Barney Hill had no way of knowing that their encounter with a UFO would become both famous and controversial.

Barney Hill points to his drawing of the UFO containing a series of windows conatining humanoid creatures.

The Hills suffered from the encounter with the UFO. Barney had an ulcer as well as insomnia. Betty would have reoccurring nightmares, sometimes for a whole week. Both of them were anxious and irritable almost all of the time. They sought help from their family doctor who could do nothing to help relieve their distress. He recommended another doctor who could not help the couple either. Dr. Benjamin Simon was the third specialist the Hills consulted and he was able to unravel the mystery of Betty's nightmares through hypnosis.

All the details and the trauma of being examined by creatures not of this Earth, unfolded from the minds of Betty and Barney Hill under Dr. Simon's hypnosis based therapy. The process started in January of 1964,

and continued for 6 months. Their stories were essentially similar in all respects and followed the basic pattern of Betty's nightmares. Recalling the physical examination made the Hills anxious. Betty remembered under hypnosis the scraping of her skin and the needle that was inserted into her navel. Barney recounted being examined near his groin by a machine which had tiny needles arrayed in a circular pattern. Several months later the area became infected with warts. It was clear that whatever happened had a profound psychological effect on the Hills.

Dr. Simon later stated that he believed the abduction portion of their story was a shared fantasy. He further stated that Barney absorbed most of the matching details from listening to his wife's retelling of her night-mares. Many UFO investigators believe that had the Hills recounted a story that Dr. Simon could believe as a conventional and common place event he would not have said it was part of a shared fantasy, rather, he might have concluded their anxiety was the result of a real traumatic experience.

There was one other interesting item uncovered by the hypnosis. Betty said the leader of the aliens had shown her a map of his home star system. Under posthypnotic suggestion Betty reproduced the map. There was nothing known at the time which even remotely matched her drawing, but several years later a new cluster of stars were discovered near Zeta Reticuli and this system very closely matched the map drawn by Betty Hill. Skeptics have said, in essence, "so what" claiming this is a mere coincidence. Believers point to the map as independent verification of the Hill's abduction story. If the Hill's experience was unique in the annals of UFO lore it would be easy to believe as Dr. Simon did that it was just another form of fantasy. They were not the only people to report abductions.

OTHER AND RECENT ABDUCTIONS

Since 1961, there have been quite a few tales of abductions by creatures in UFO's. Admittedly some of the stories abound with sexual encounters as well as knowledge given to the abductee as to a greater plan of guidance given to the human race. Perhaps there is some truth to these reports and perhaps they are highly imaginative fantasies of over wishful minds. The supermarket tabloids abound with many of these tales and these stories add static to some very substantial reports.

Recently a new light has been cast on the UFO abduction question by a novelist who claims to have been kidnapped by aliens from a UFO. Whitney Strieber has written horror novels such as "The Wolfen", "The Hunger" and coauthored "Warday", a novel about World War III. On the evening of December 26, 1985, he awoke to find a humanoid standing in his bedroom in his Northern New York cabin. He lost consciousness and awoke in a small grey room crowded with more of the same creatures that first appeared in his bedroom. He tells a tale of terror, in his book "Communion", as his brain was probed with a needle-like device and various other pokings and scrapings were done upon his body. When he was transported home, he found his wife still asleep in their bed, unaware of her husband's incredible encounter.

Like Betty and Barney Hill, Strieber found his emotional life in shambles after this incident. And like the Hills, hypnosis unlocked memories of the encounter. As Strieber recalls the experience of discovery in his book, "...the confused swirl resolved into a specific series of recollections, I just about exploded with terror and disbelief." In writing "Communion" which later became a best seller, Strieber states that one of his motives was the easing of the traumatic burden suffered by abductees.

Since it's publication in February 1987, Whitney Strieber has received a great deal of mail by people who claim to have had similar abduction experiences. Most of the contactees do not wish to be in the glare of public media, for their stories have been as equally painful as Strieber's and they do not have the stamina to hold up emotionally to the harsh interrogation of the skeptical press. Yet another author of the UFO abduction phenomena has been conducting a support group to help victims of these encounters.

Budd Hopkins is a successful sculptor and painter. His interest in UFO's began in 1964, when he first saw an elliptical shaped object hovering over Cape Cod. For the last 12 years he has conducted 135 interviews with sighting witnesses and contactees. In his two books "Intruders; The Incredible Visitations at Copley Woods" and "Missing Time", Hopkins describes some of the encounters with UFO aliens.

Not only did these people describe probings with needle-like instruments and the taking of flakes of skin, but more advanced procedures that included skin grafts, the taking of sperm and ova and hybrid beings that certain female abductees somehow knew they had an unwilling part in their making. This is strong stuff and if it is true, quite frightening in its implications.

In order to help these people, Hopkins has been conducting an informal abductee support group in his Manhattan townhouse. "The abductees are victims of trauma, a severe, nightmarish thing that none of them wanted to happen;" Hopkins said in an 1987 interview in the New York Times. Some of the attendees at the meetings describe them as group therapy to ease much of the anxiety associated with these UFO encounters. There was nothing like this available to the Hills when they had their encounter in 1961.

Strieber visited the Hopkins home in early 1986. Up until that point, Strieber was unwilling to face the facts that pointed to this incredible experience with beings that travelled in UFO's. Although his was just not a group meeting, listening to Hopkins confirming that Strieber was not alone in his experience brought him out of his fearful apathy. Soon afterward the idea for "Communion" was born.

THE OFFICIAL ATTEMPTS TO EXPLAIN THE UNEXPLAINABLE

Too many proponents of the extraterrestrial origins of UFO's, the two famous United States Air Force sponsored reports, Project Blue Book and the Condon Report, have flawed conclusions. In the words of one of the Project Blue Book's consultants and one time UFO skeptic, Dr. J. Allen Hynek, the reports were nothing more than "....public relations effort directed to debunk the whole thing." And yet the reports mark the best efforts of a United States Government Agency to deal with the question of UFO's.

After the highly negative Project Grudge's attempt to erase the bitter battles over validity and origins UFO's reflected in the previous Project Sign, the Air Force decided to show its presence in an area which frequently surfaced in the press with a revitalized investigation, code named Project Blue Book. Project Blue Book's first director was Captain Edward J. Ruppelt. He was the most energetic and, perhaps, the most controversial man to head the investigation.

A World War II veteran, Ruppelt was assigned to Air Technical Intelligence Center (ATIC) at the Wright-Patterson Air Force Base, Dayton, Ohio, to analyze the performance of the Soviet MIG-15 fighter during the Korean War. ATIC was the agency responsible for creating both Project Sign and Project Grudge. In September 1950, the Air Force brass ordered ATIC to undertake another study of UFO's. Ruppelt was one of the authors of the report delivered to the director of the ATIC and on the basis of the report he was ordered to reactivate the investigations. Shortly before Christmas 1951, Project Blue Book was born.

It was to investigate over 12,618 cases spanning twenty-two years. Out of these cases there was 701 which remained unidentified, the rest were explained as mistaken natural phenomena or as known aircraft in the vicinity of the sighting. Much was to be made of these findings including: the addition of easily explained sightings to weight the final result, the inability of the staff to handle unusual cases which fit no known pattern, the arbitrary labeling of cases, the lack of staff scientists, and that

the whole project was merely a front for a secret, more serious investigation conducted by the Air Force. When it was finally terminated in 1969, Project Blue Book's conclusions were exactly what the Air Force was saying throughout the 50's, "...there has been no evidence submitted to or discovered by the Air Force that sightings categorized as 'unidentified' represent technological developments beyond the range of present scientific knowledge." Controversial to the end, the Air Force needed an independent study to close Project Blue Book down.

In the middle of the 60's, Project Blue Book, and by implication the Air Force, found itself embroiled in a series of confrontations with the press and many private UFO organizations over sightings which seemed to be beyond the capabilities of the group to study, let alone provide explanations for. In 1966, the Air Force, busy with a war in Vietnam, did not need any rounds fired at it over something as elusive as UFO's. To this end it commissioned a team of scientists from the University of Colorado under the direction of a prominent physicist and former head of the American Association for the Advancement of Science, Dr. Edward U. Condon, to study and report on the UFO phenomena. From the very beginning the Condon Report, as it became known, was in trouble.

Condon proceeded by closing his mind from the start. He was not interested in drawing a conclusion from the facts found in the investigation; he already knew what the report should say. In the first few months of study, Condon issued a press release which stated that the subject of UFO's was nonsense and when the investigation was finished that would be its final statement. On January 9, 1969; the Air Force released the Condon Report and sure enough it stated that after 21 years of UFO study had added nothing to the advancement of science and that further study was unwarranted. Condon also added that "it is safe to assume that there is no 'intelligent life elsewhere' out of our solar system has any possibility of visiting Earth in the next 10,000 years." This conclusion was really quite contrary to the direction the project's case by case analysis pointed to.

Of the 59 cases studied by scientists taking part in the Condon Report, 23 of them were classified as unexplained. Surprisingly, Condon did participate in the analysis of any of the cases. He did however fire psychologist Dr. David Saunders, a co-principal project investigator and electrical engineer, Dr. Norman Levine, a research associate, for disagreing with his negative approach. One of the unexplained cases was the McMinnville, Oregon sighting and subsequent UFO photograph taken to Paul Trent. The Air Force used the Condon Report's recommendation to phase out Project Blue Book and thereby, at least publicly, get out of the UFO investigation business.

GONE BUT STILL ACTIVE

Several people found their lives changed in the course of doing investigations and analysis for the Project Blue Book and Condon Report. The subject of UFO's would become their avocation if not vocation and their work would follow them for the rest of their lives.

When Ruppelt retired from the Air Force he did not leave the subject of UFO's behind. In 1956, his book "The Report on Unidentified Flying Objects" took a much more positive approach than the one Project Blue Book was espousing. Reading this edition one is left with the impression that Ruppelt thought there was validity to the notion of extraterrestrial UFO origins.

A few years later he updated his book with the addition of three new chapters. Now the book took a turn in the direction of the Air Force's public statements. Some UFO investigators believe Ruppelt was coerced into adding the chapters by virtue of his employment as an engineer with Northrop Corporation. a large Air Force contractor. The Air Force, like most governmental bodies, do not like to be embarrassed by former employees. To this end they applied pressure on Northrop, who in turn turned the screws on Ruppelt. No evidence for this theory of Ruppelt's change of heart has ever been found. Other investigators believe Ruppelt could not accept the abductee reports, like Adamski's accounts of Orthon, that were surfacing in the mid-fifties and this in turn made him not want to contribute to the growing fanciful fad. Ruppelt's reason for changing his mind went to the grave with his death in 1960.

Another man who changed his mind on the issue of UFO's was Dr. J. Allen Hynek. His impressive credentials as a consultant grew as he worked on Projects Sign and Blue Book. Hynek went from an astronomer at Ohio State University, to a position as associate director of the Smithsonian Astrophysical Observatory and finally became chairman of the astronomy department at Northwestern University. During his association with Project Blue Book he gained notoriety among UFO proponents as the skeptic's skeptic. In 1966, he claimed the wave of UFO's sighted over Michigan, that year, were nothing more than mirages arising from swamp gas. But the one constant in nature is change and people are not immune to this immutable law.

Sometime in the late 60's Hynek began to change his mind. There were too many plausible cases left unexplained. If one took the easy and obvious cases out of the lists of reported sightings you were left with 20 percent of the cases labeled unexplained; to Hynek this represented a real phenomenon warranting serious investigation. To this end he started the Center for UFO studies in 1973.

The movie "Close Encounters of the Third Kind" owes it title to Hynek's UFO identification system. In his structure all UFO's reported at more than 500 feet are divided into three subcategories: nocturnal lights, daylight disks and radar visuals. These divisions are self explanatory. For sightings at less than 500 feet were originally three classes of cataloging, a fourth was added later. These are as follows: Close Encounters of the First Kind, which are those cases where there is no interaction between the environment and the UFO; Close Encounters of the Second Kind, in which there is some interaction with the environment such as burn marks on the ground or electromagnetic disturbance such as interference with car electrical systems; Close Encounters of the Third Kind, in which actual UFO aliens are seen. The last classification is the recent addition and it is Close Encounters of the Fourth Kind, in which there is contact of some kind. This would include all UFO abductions such as Whitney Strieber's account.

There was also a change in Hynek's thinking of what UFO's are. This is best shown in a 1976 interview. "The conclusion I've come to after all these years is that first of all, the subject is much more complex than any of us imagined. It has some paranormal aspects but certainly it has very real physical aspects too. We will push the physical approach as far as we can. If we are finally forced by the evidence itself to go into the paranormal then we will."

A FAMOUS INCIDENT

It should have been just another routine evening for Exeter, New Hampshire, police patrolman, Eugene Bertrand cruising on Route 101. It was half past midnight on September 9, 1966, when he came upon a

Dr. J. Allen Hynek announced that the wave of UFO's sighted over Michigan in 1966 were nothing more than luminous swamp gas and became known as a skeptic's skeptic. Ten years later he reversed his position and stated his belief in the existence of UFO's.

woman parked by the side of the road. Upon inquiring if there was any trouble the lone driver told Bertrand she had been chased by a red glowing object flying only a few feet behind her. It was clear the woman was distraught and the patrolman asked her where this object was now. The driver pointed to the dark horizon; Bertrand searched the night sky for a minute, horizon to horizon and saw nothing but stars and a few clouds. To reassure the woman he escorted her car through town and promptly forgot about the incident, chalking it up to one of those nights.

About the time Bertrand was listening to the upset woman's story, 18 year old Norman Muscarello was hitchhiking on Route 150, to his home in Exeter from Amesbury, Massachusetts. He was walking along the road, two miles from town, when he saw a UFO with five bright red lights emerge from a nearby woods and silently glide across a meadow and hover above a farm house. The object was ninety feet in diameter and dwarfed the house under it. After less than a minute elapsed the UFO gracefully flew back to the woods and disappeared. Muscarello ran to the house and attempted to rouse the farmer and his wife. He did, but Clyde Russell and his wife ignored him thinking he was another rowdy town drunk. Muscarello managed to get a lift into Exeter, where he went straight away to the police station and reported his sighting in an extreme state of nervousness.

Sometime after 2:00 A.M. Bertrand listened to his second UFO story of the night. The officer in charge decided that Bertrand should go with the young man and investigate his story. Up until Bertrand walked into the Russell field adjacent to the farm house he must have believed this was an amusing but fruitless waste of his time. He was examining the dewy ground when Muscarello started yelling it was coming! When Bertrand looked up he saw the UFO rising like an apparition, from behind the trees. By instinct the police officer started to draw his revolver on this dark elliptical object with a row of intense red lights spanning its middle section. But a very wise voice inside of Bertrand told him to forget the heroics. The two men ran back to the police car and Bertrand called headquarters to report his confirmation of the sighting. Another officer arrived in time to see the UFO sail over the trees and disappear.

According to Hynek this case which is now a classic in UFO investigation, was a "...showcase illustration of Blue Book negligence, put-down of witnesses, attempts with a parade of official explanations to explain away testimony of responsible witnesses." Many months later the Air Force would admit it was not a weather balloon, as they had claimed, and the case was labeled "unexplained."

A NEW YORK WAVE

Some have called the Hudson Valley, New York, sightings the largest ever recorded in North America. The wave of reports began in March 1983, when a meteorologist, who worked for the National Weather Corporation at Westchester Airport, was driving home on the Taconic Parkway. He saw a bright object a hundred or so feet above and in front of his car pacing him. "I've been around aircraft all my life and I can honestly say I've never seen anything like this." The meteorologist also said he felt as if he was being observed by an intelligence inside the UFO and was by some unknown criteria, rejected. His basis for this surmise was purely emotional but he also thought under the circumstances accurate. In a split second the object zoomed out of sight, leaving the witness shaken.

Early in the morning of October 28, 1983, bio-engineer Jim Cooke was coming from New Rochelle, New York. His route took him over the Crotin Reservoir Causeway. No sooner had he entered the causeway when his attention was distracted by a group of bright lights high in the sky. Their motion fluid but rapid as the objects flew toward the reservoir and descended. It took Cooke less than a minute to reach the other side of the causeway, but by that time the objects had reached tree top level and slipped over the reservoir and out of sight.

Cooke pulled his car to the side of the road and watched for any further appearances by the UFO's. About two minutes later a lone triangular shaped craft appeared 50 feet away from the far shore. It was about 100 feet in diameter with a dark body and three or four glaring red lights belting its middle. For 45 minutes Cooke watched this craft hover 25 feet over the reservoir, intake water through a tube, zip to another spot along the shore and repeat the procedure. The UFO never, at any time, acknowledged his presence. When it was finished, it quickly vanished.

This was not a known aircraft. There have been attempts by ultralight aircraft pilots to create a hoax in the Hudson Valley area and Cooke was familiar with these crafts.

For the next year men and women from all walks of life observed UFO's in the area. Members of the New Castle Police Department saw a series of UFO's fly over the station house while the town council was in session 150 feet away. One officer, Andi Sadoff, had a UFO buzz her car. It was less than 20 feet off the ground and she was able to get a good look at the underside of the craft. It was not like any helicopter or aircraft she had ever seen. Commanding Officer, Detective Division of Ossining, New York, Ray Stevens watched four lights from the deck of his home one night in July, 1983. Moving silently, they were flying north, away from Indian Point. The lights stopped and changed direction, as they were attached to a wheel and vanished in the western skies.

One of the startling events in this wave of UFO sightings occurred at the Indian Point Nuclear Plant. Twice in late 1984, a large, very large UFO hovered over the water outlet pool of the nuclear plant. It size was estimated at 900 feet in diameter. Over 14 New York State security guards witnessed the UFO extend a tube and probe the water. The last sighting lasted over 15 minutes. The skeptics call this sighting a mass hallucination.

Dr. Hynek investigated reports of UFO's very carefully. It was the weight of the unexplainable cases which turned him into a proponent.

The whole controversy over the Hudson Valley sightings is compounded by pilots who were flying at this time attempting to create a hoax. An official of the Federal Aeronautical Administration claimed to have talked to the pilots and told them that it was ultralights and dangerous to fly in tight formation from twilight on. He did this to protect the agency from criticisms should there be an accident while these aircraft were in formation. They complied and the sightings ceases. The sightings continued but the current skeptical wisdom disclaims any sightings past late 1984 as sheer imagination.

UFO'S, WHO KNOWS?

The subjects of UFO's as observed in North America, let alone any place else in the world, is very complex. They are reported in all shapes and sizes, in all locations, in all types of weather, by all kinds of people. Granted there are those who claim to have sighted a UFO for purposes of self aggrandisement, but by the same token there are many more who never gave the subject much thought until they were confronted with their own sighting. Some day the mystery of UFO's may be solved and I suspect the answer will be quite startling to proponent and skeptic alike.

Index

Numbers in italics indicate illustrations.

Adamski, George, 181-182,187
Alkalie Lake creature, 5-6
Anastasia, Albert, 105-109, *110-111*
Arnold, Kenneth, 173, 175, 181
Avenger airplane, 34, 35, *40, 41*
Bahmer, Pearl, 89, 90-91
basilosaurus, 12
Beale Codes mystery, 169-171
Beale, Thomas Jefferson, 169-171
Bellomont, Lord, 153-154, *155*
Berlitz, Charles, 16, 37
Bermuda Triangle, *14-15*
    disappeared ships in, 20-29, 37-38
    naming of, 13-16
    unexplained power losses in, 38-40
Bierce, Ambrose, 132, 134
Bigfoot, *46-47, 56-57, 60-61, 66*
    abduction of Osterman by, 45, 48, 65
    early sightings of, 43-44
    film of, 67-70
    Michigan sighting of, 70
    New Jersey sighting of, 70-72
    sighting by Roosevelt of, 44-45
    sighting in Bluff Creek Valley, 65-70
    theories about, 72
Blackbeard, *See* Teach, Edward
Black Dahlia unsolved murder, 100-105
Borden, Lizzie, 83-88
    trial of, 87-88
Braddock, General Edward, 139, *140-141*
Braddock Heights Treasure, 139
Buchalter, Lepke, 105
Burr, Aaron, 20-21, *22,* 162
Burr, Theodosia, *19,* 20-21
Carpender, Henry de la Bruyere, 90-92
Carroll A. Deering, abandonment of, 29-34, *41*
Champ (lake creature), 10-12
Champlain, Samuel de, 10, *11*
Claiborne, W.C.C., 160, *163*
Cochise (Indian chief), 143
Colvocoresses, Captain George M., 79-80
Columbus, Christopher, 16-20
Condon, Dr. Edward U., 186-187
Condon Report, 186-187
Coronado, Vasquez de, 142, *144-145*
Costello, Frank, 106, *108*
Cox, Lieutenant Robert F., 35-37
Crater, Judge Joseph, 134, 136-137
Crater Lake, WA, *60-61, 62-63*
Crew, Jerry, 65
Croton-on-Hudson, NY, 158
Cyclops, disappearance of, 27-29
Deer Island, ME, 156

Diamond Shoals, NC, 29, 31, 32, *33, 36*
Dillinger, John, 141
Drew, Daniel, 79, *85*
Fall River, MA, *88*
Fink, Isidore, 80-81
Five Points, NY City, 75-79
Flight 19, disappearance of, 35-37
Fort Lauderdale Naval Air Station, 34-37
Gaddis, Vincent, 13
Gambino, Carlo, 106
gangs, 75, *79*
Gardiners Island, NY, 156
Genovese, Vito, 106
Gisbon, Jane, 92
Gigantopithecus, 72
Gimlin, Bob, 67-70
Good News, power loss of, 38
Group, David, 16
Hall, Rev. Edward Wheeler, 89-93
Hall-Mills unsolved murder, 88-93
Hansen, Detective Harry, 100-105
Harrison, Ethel May, 96, *98*
Haydock, Tim, 146
Hayes, Clifford, 90
Hayward, Victor, 37
Henry, Captain Don, 38
Hill, Betty and Barney, 182-185
Hillary, Sir Edmund, 65, *68-69,* 72
Hoffa, Jimmy, *135*
Hopkins, Budd, 185-186
Hynek, Dr. J. Allen, 186, 187, *188,* 189, *190*
Ice Age, 5
Jackson, Andrew, 161, *167*
Jeffery, Adi-Kent Thomas, 16
Jones, Bob, *71*
Kidd, Captain, *64,* 140, *152,* 153-158, 168
    buried treasure of, 156, 158
Kirkpatrick, Sidney, 99
Kusche, Lawrence, 16, 28, 35
Lafitte, Jean, 140, 160-165
    buried treasure of, 162, 164
Lake Champlain, NY, *9,* 10-12
Lake Champlain creature, 10-12, *52-53*
lake creatures, 5-12, *52-53*
Lake Manitoba creature, 10
Lake Manitou creature, 6
Lake Utopia creature, 6, 7, 12
Lang, David, 130, 132
Lansky, Meyer, 106
Ledoux, Remy, 150-151
Loch Ness, 5, 12, *52*
Lost Dutchman mine, 144-146, *151*
Luciano, Lucky, 105

Mackal, Dr. Roy P., 6-7, 11-12
Madison, James, 161-162, *164*
manatees, *51-52*
Mangiacopra, Gary, 10
Manipogo (lake creature), 10
Manley, Robert "Red", 102, *104*, 105
Mansi, Sandra, 11-12
Martin Mariner airplane, 35
Mary Celeste, abandonment of, 23-27, 29
mermaids, 51
Meshejian, Dr. Wayne, 40
Mills, Eleanor, 89-93
Mills, James, 90-91
Minter, Mary Miles, 95-99
Mount Rainier, WA, *52-53*
Murder, Inc., 105-109
Neanderthal man, *56-57*, 72
Normand, Mable, 93-99
Oak Island, NS, buried treasure, 165-168
Ogopogo (lake creature), 7-10, 11
Okanagan Lake, BC, 7-10, 12
Old Brewery, 75, 78-79, *80-81*, *82-83*
Osterman, Albert, 45, 48, 65
Patriot, disappearance of, 20-21
Patterson, Roger, 67-70
Payne, John Howard, 21, *26*
Peralta, Miguel, 143
Pickford, Mary, 96
pirates, 20-21, 140, 152
plesiosaur, 12
Powers, Captain Edward Joseph Jr., 35-37
Project Blue Book, 178, 180, 186, 187, 189
Project Grudge, 178, 186
Project Sign, 178, 187
Raleigh, Sir Walter, 129, *131*
Roanoke colony disappearance, 129-130, *133*
Roosevelt, Theodore, 44-45, *73*
Rosalie, disappearance of, 21-23
Rouse, George, 16
Ruppelt, Captain Edward, 178, 180, 186-187
Rye Beach, NH, *64*
Rye Beach, NY, 156, *157*
Sanderson, Ivan T., 13-16
Sands, Edward, 93, 99
San Juan Mountains, 146-147
Sargasso Sea, 16, 18
Sasquatch. *See* Bigfoot

Schneider, Raymond, 89, 90-92
Schuster, Arnold, 106, *107*
Sennett, Mack, 93, 99
Shelby, Charlotte, 99, 100
Shipton, Eric, 65
Short, Elizabeth, 100, 102, *103*, 105
Sites family, 70-72
Society for the Investigation of the Unexplained, 72
Southern Cities, disappearance of, 37-38
Stevens, Frances, 89-93
Stevens, Henry, 89-93
Stevens, Willie, 89-93
Strieber, Whitley, 185, 187
Stump Pond creature, 7
Super Sabre jet, 37
Superstition Mountain, 139, 142-146, *147*
Taylor, Lieutenant Charles, 34-37
Taylor, William Desmond, 93, *94-95*
    unsolved murder or, 93-100
Teach, Edward, 140, 158-160
Trafficante, Sam, 106
treasure hunting, 139, 140, 141-142
Treasure Mountain, 146, 149-151, 153
UFOs, *54-55*, *114-128*, 123
    abductions by, 182-186
    early reports of, 174-175
    Exeter sighting, 188-189
    Hill abduction, 182-185
    Hudson Valley sightings, 173-174, 189-190
    investigations of, 176, 178, 186-187
    Lubbock Lights sighting, *116*, 178-179
    McMinnville sighting, *122-123*, 178, 187
    sightings by pilots of, 175-178
    Washington, D.C. sightings, 179-181
Valachi, Joe, 106
Vandenberg, General Hoyt, *177*, 178
Vidor, King, 99, *101*
Walz, Jacob, 144-146, *148*, *149*, *151*
Ward, Michael, 65
War of 1812, 161-162, *171*
waterspouts, 25, *30-31*
Worley, Lieutenant Commander George W., 27-29
Wormell, Captain Willis B., 29-31
Yeti, 65, *68-69*, 72. *See also* Bigfoot
Zarzynski, Joseph, 10-12
Zodiac Killer unsolved murders, 109-110
Zukor, Adolph, 93, 95, 96